Crossing the River Kabul

Crossing *the* River Kabul

An Afghan Family Odyssey

KEVIN MCLEAN

Potomac Books

An imprint of the University of Nebraska Press

Unless otherwise stated, photographs originally appeared
in *Afghanistan: Ancient Land with Modern Ways*, published
in 1960 by the Ministry of Planning of the
Royal Government of Afghanistan.

∞

Library of Congress Cataloging-in-Publication Data
Names: McLean, Kevin, author.
Title: Crossing the River Kabul: an Afghan family odyssey /
Kevin McLean.
Description: Lincoln: Potomac Books, an imprint of the
University of Nebraska Press, 2017.
| Includes bibliographical references.
Identifiers: LCCN 2016034822 (print)
LCCN 2016056610 (ebook)
ISBN 9781612348971 (cloth: alk. paper)
ISBN 9781612349213 (epub)
ISBN 9781612349220 (mobi)
ISBN 9781612349237 (pdf)
Subjects: LCSH: Popal, Baryalai, 1952– | Afghanistan—Politics
and government—20th century. | Afghanistan—History—
Soviet occupation, 1979–1989. | Communism—Afghanistan—
History. | Afghans—Biography.
Classification: LCC DS361 .M36 2017 (print) | LCC DS361
(ebook) | DDC 958.104/5092 [B]—dc23
LC record available at https://lccn.loc.gov/2016034822

Set in Minion Pro by Rachel Gould.

For Naomi, the love of my life

By blood, we are immersed in love of you.
The youth lose their heads for your sake.
I come to you and my heart finds rest.
Away from you, grief clings to my heart like a snake.
I forget the throne of Delhi
When I remember the mountaintops of my Afghan land,
If I must choose between the world and you,
I shall not hesitate to claim your barren deserts as my own.

—AHMAD SHAH DURRANI

Contents

Illustrations

Author's Note

Baryalai Popal fled Afghanistan in 1980 after the Russian invasion. When U.S. and Afghan forces ousted the Taliban in 2002, Bar returned to Kabul for the first time in twenty years. That summer Bar told me the story of his return. "That is the most amazing story I've ever heard," I said.

"I have many such stories," he replied.

Bar's stories became the threads from which I would weave the history of his family and, with it, the history of Afghanistan.

I have chosen to tell Bar's story in his voice. At his request some family names have been changed.

Acknowledgments

This book represents two journeys, Baryalai's incredible journey from Kabul to America and the ten-year journey we took together in writing this book. I am in Baryalai's debt for taking the time and effort to relate his many stories to me, for his diligence in ensuring my telling of them was accurate, and for his amazing memory. Baryalai's wife, Afsana, contributed stories of her own and helped flesh out others while sharing her extraordinary Afghan dishes. I am grateful to Pamela Feinsilber, who provided invaluable editorial help teasing out more from every story and finding an organizational approach to a sprawling saga. My thanks to Tim Foxley and Nabi Misdaq, who reviewed the manuscript and provided useful input based on their vast knowledge and experience in Afghanistan, and to Dr. John B. Alexander, former U.S. Army colonel, for his advice and support. I also owe a great deal of thanks to Ronald E. Neumann, former ambassador to Afghanistan, whose positive response and faith in my book shepherded it to publication.

And I owe my undying thanks to my wife, Naomi, without whose constant support, suggestions, editing, and encouragement this journey would not have seen an end.

Prologue

My story is entwined with that of my country. As in any relationship, you will find love, hate, battles, resolution, despair, hope—
all greatly magnified because my country, the country of my birth
and that of my grandparents and parents, my uncles, aunts, and
cousins, my wife and my children, the country that I hold most
close to my heart in my thoughts and memories, is Afghanistan.
When an Afghan tells a story, he knows not to begin by boasting
of how powerful his family is. For the storyteller to make himself
appear more important than his listener is disrespectful, and the
most important thing you can offer others is respect. But I must
tell you that I am a Popalzai from one of Afghanistan's two royal
families. Legend has it that one day, many centuries ago, when the
aging King Zirak asked his eldest son, Barak, for help getting onto
his horse, Barak mocked his father's weakness. Popal, the youngest son, took pity on his father and helped him into the saddle.
When King Zirak named Popal to succeed him, Barak refused
to recognize his younger brother as king. From that time on the
Popalzai and the Barakzai have fought for control of Afghanistan.

In 1747 King Nadir Shah, who had created a great empire that
stretched from Persia to Delhi, died. Ahmad Khan, a Popalzai,
declared himself the new king—but of course, the Barakzai refused
to accept him. Rather than go to war, Ahmad Khan called a *loya
jirga*, a decision-making council of tribal elders that is still used
in Afghanistan today.

The loya jirga elected Ahmad Khan king and proclaimed him
Durr-i-Durrani, the "Pearl of Pearls." His kingdom became known
as the Durrani Empire. Under Ahmad Shah Durrani the nation of
Afghanistan began to take shape. Until the Communist coup in
1978, Afghanistan was governed by either a Popalzai or a Barakzai.

All members of the Popalzai tribe once had Popalzai as their
family name. It is said that my grandfather Mukarram, a Pashtun
and a khan of Kandahar, shortened our last name to Popal over
a disagreement with his fellow Popalzai. My grandfather's cousin

Khair Mohammad, another local khan (and the grandfather of former Afghan president Hamid Karzai), changed his family name from Popalzai to Karzai, for the village of Karz near Kandahar where the Karzai family has its roots.

In 1952, the year I was born, the United States allied itself with Pakistan to counter Russia's influence with Afghanistan and India. Like two mighty storm fronts on a collision course, the Cold War clash between the United States and Russia would bring death and devastation to Afghanistan and my family and force me on an odyssey that would keep me from my country for over twenty years.

Crossing the River Kabul

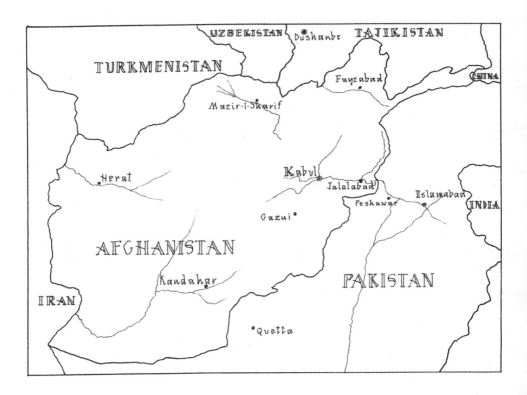

MAP 1. Afghanistan and surrounding countries. Map by Kevin McLean.

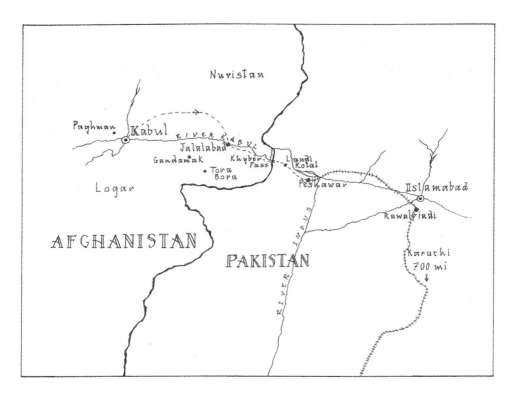

MAP 2. Baryalai's route of escape, October 1980. Map by Kevin McLean.

1

Kabul Airport, Afghanistan, October 1980

Flight

Our driver, Saed, sat behind the wheel of our old black Mercedes, shivering in the predawn October darkness. My cousin Abbas and I slid quickly inside. We headed for the airport on the far side of Mount Asmayi, the mountain that separates my neighborhood, Karta-i-Char, from downtown Kabul. Behind the walls of our family compound, the weight of my absence rested heavily on my father and mother and on my wife, Afsana. The whole of the life I had known was behind me now. What lay ahead was completely unknown.

I had no plan of escape beyond flying to Jalalabad. I could make no plan because I could trust no one. The division and mistrust that had overtaken Afghanistan had infected friends, neighbors, families, cousins, brothers, fathers, sons. Even relatives might turn you in because they had been threatened or because they felt the ruling Communists were here to stay or because they were tempted by the rewards offered to those who would identify "Enemies of the People." Although you suffered greatly if you did not cast your lot with the Communists, many refused to do so. The problem was one could never tell who had sold out and who had not.

It was deathly silent in the car as we made our way through a maze of streets, all deserted at this time of morning. We knew National Security had set up checkpoints, which the guards changed nightly—often putting them on one-way streets so there was no escape. We prayed we would not encounter them.

We drove past the Kabul Zoo, which I had visited with my class when it first opened in 1967. We were all excitement and noise because none of us had ever been to a zoo. I held a rabbit for the first time, petting its soft fur, feeling its warmth in my hands, the beating of its heart as it nestled against me, little knowing that during the civil war to come, the rabbits would be food for starving families. As we passed near the tomb of Babur Shah, a descendant of Genghis Khan who had created the Mughal Empire, which stretched from Afghanistan to India, I thought of the words there: "If there is a paradise on Earth, it is this, it is this, it is this!" What had been my own paradise was gone—perhaps forever. Suddenly Saed pulled over to the side of the road and stopped. My heart stopped as well. "You must walk from here. It's too dangerous to get any closer," Saed announced. "May God protect you."

We carried no luggage—that would arouse suspicion—only documents in small plastic bags. The mountains surrounding Kabul appeared as jagged teeth against a rose-colored sky. Afraid to be seen in the growing light, we followed the large, old panja chinar trees that lined the road to the airport. Afghan rebels fighting the Russians—the mujahideen—would later use these trees as shields to shoot at the Russians. The Russians would solve this problem like they did so many others—they destroyed the trees.

The airport terminal was a long, low, cement block structure from which the control tower jutted skyward. The small plane for the short flight to Jalalabad sat on the tarmac, the stairway in place awaiting its passengers. Dozens were already at the entrance gate, pushing to get on board. This part of the airport was also used by Russian military planes and helicopters. Security was tight. Guards scrutinized each passenger. Abbas and I quickened our pace, making our way into the middle of the crowd, which carried us past the guards. "We made it," I said to Abbas, feeling relieved.

But my relief soon turned to terror—a Russian soldier and his Tajik translator, both armed, stood at the bottom of the stairway, checking passengers' papers. They wore the gray wool uniforms of the Russian military, the Russian's trimmed in the black of the Russian Special Forces. The Russian's eyes narrowed as he studied each passenger's papers. The Tajik waved them on with his Russian-made Kalashnikov. I had to fight the urge to turn and run as I tried to think of a way to explain why I had no papers.

Suddenly I found myself staring into the cold black eyes of the Russian Special Forces soldier as the Tajik gripped the trigger of his AK-47.

"How many more passengers?" a voice boomed from the top

of the stairway. "We're almost full." The guards turned their attention from me to the bear of a man in a pilot's uniform towering above them. I looked up. Sorosh! His father had worked with my father in the Foreign Ministry. Before the Russian invasion, he had piloted international flights. Now the Russians used him to fly short domestic flights. With his bushy black eyebrows and black goatee, his large head and body and huge hands, he was an unmistakable presence. He was not a man to disagree with. As he surveyed the passengers, he caught sight of us and pounded down the stairs.

"They're okay. They're with me," he said. The guards eyed Sorosh with contempt but said nothing.

"What the hell are you doing here?" Sorosh asked us as soon as we were aboard the plane. "Where are you going in days like these?"

"We have some things to do on our houses in Jalalabad," I said.

"Ah," he smiled, "it seems everyone has a problem with his house in Jalalabad now. I wish I were free to check on my house in Jalalabad." Lowering his voice, he added, "You know, the Russians transport their troops in planes like this. The mujahideen will shoot down anything, especially this kind of plane. I never know if I'll live from day to day. You're lucky—you fly only today."

I had not thought of myself as lucky, but even in war, everything is relative.

Our route took us high over the snow-covered mountains to the east of Kabul. Suddenly several passengers began shouting and pointing out the windows. The rest of us jumped out of our seats to see what was happening. National Security guards ordered us to sit down, but everyone ignored them. Russian helicopters were firing rockets into the sides of the mountains below, sending great plumes of dust and smoke skyward. I felt sick. The mujahideen would be firing back and could easily hit an aircraft like ours.

But soon we were crossing high above the sixteen thousand–foot Safid Koh, the "White Mountains," which are perpetually covered in snow. I sat back and stared at a photograph of my family, the only one I had brought with me. It had been taken in the spring in Uncle Ali's front yard, the day my Uncle Gholam and his German wife, Lilo, left Afghanistan. Because Afghans assumed any foreigner was Russian and should be killed, Gholam and Lilo were returning to Germany for Lilo's sake. There I am, towering over everyone. Uncle Gholam is to my right, then Uncle Ali and Uncle Sultan. To my left, hands on hips, is my son, Walid, only five years old. Beside him stands my mother, Babu, so kind and patient. She loved to spoil me—which my father disliked because he thought she distracted me from my schoolwork.

My wife, Afsana, is at the far end because she is not a blood relative. She is not even a Pashtun but a Turk. My father could never forgive her for not being a Popal. But I could not resist her intelligence, her compelling eyes, and her wonderful sense of fun—something that my mother and father lacked and that I, as an only child, had longed for. Baba is missing from the photograph. His amputated leg made it difficult for him to leave the house—and he never liked having his picture taken.

As we descended into Jalalabad, flames flickered through heavy layers of smoke. The terminal, its walls pockmarked with craters and bullet holes, was ringed by Russian military vehicles and tanks occupying the parking lots and nearby streets.

Abbas and I let the other passengers exit ahead of us, planning to leave with Sorosh. One of the guards shouted at us, "Get up! Go!" We didn't move. He approached us, brandishing his Kalashnikov and a fierce look, and stuck his face in mine, his bushy mustache shaved in the form of the Persian symbols for the numbers 2 and 6—the date Daoud, backed by the Communists, overthrew the king. Such mustaches were worn only by the most fanatical and brutal Party security men.

Abbas and I slowly made our way to the front of the plane, where Sorosh sat in the cockpit writing in his log. He looked up as we stood outside the cockpit door. "Wait for me," he said. The security guard immediately barked, "You must wait outside."

We stood still as if we hadn't heard him or didn't understand.

"Why are you not moving?" he demanded. "Show me your papers."

"Leave them alone," Sorosh said, ducking his head low as he exited the cabin. The guard turned his weapon on Sorosh and glared. "They work for me," Sorosh said more firmly. The guard hesitated before lowering his weapon. He turned to the other guard, spoke to him in Russian, then they left the plane. Outside dozens of Russian military personnel and Party members guarded the entrance to the main terminal. Not even Sorosh could get us past all that security.

2

Jalalabad, Afghanistan, October 1980

Behsood Bridge

To our surprise Sorosh did not go into the main terminal but led us to the pilots' lounge, where we slipped in through a side door. Pilots sat in a haze of pipe and cigarette smoke, reading magazines and newspapers and drinking tea. Abbas said to Sorosh, "That was very brave of you. You could have been arrested."

"True. But the Russians need pilots like me. If they had arrested me," he smiled, "*they* would have been the ones in trouble."

"*Tashakor*, Sorosh," I said, thanking him.

"If you survive, that will be thanks enough for me," he said. "May God protect you."

Abbas and I plunged through the door out into the airport parking lot. Twilight was descending quickly, the cold October air a thick gray mist that smelled of rubber burning. Men cradled AK-47s as they surveyed the parking lot. Others clustered around Russian tanks, trucks, and personnel carriers that had arrived on the "Sky Bridge"—a convoy of Russian planes so vast it was said you could have walked across them all the way to Russia.

"Walk slowly—as if you belong here," Abbas muttered under his breath, "and pretend we're having a normal conversation."

The guards eyed us as we made our way across the parking lot, fingering their weapons. With every step I feared hearing a voice shout "Stop!"—or worse, the sound of gunfire. My heart pounded wildly until we reached the highway, the only major route between Jalalabad and Torkham now used by Russian military vehicles. The two of us dressed in the dark suits and leather shoes of Kabul would look very suspicious walking along this highway. But the road to Jalalabad was deserted at this hour.

We crossed quickly and found ourselves in a small park, where we collapsed onto a wooden bench. I sat drained. I looked at Abbas, who sat hunched over, exhausted, his breathing labored. The son of Uncle Gholam, he had served in the military and with the Kabul police. At thirty-nine—ten years older than me—Abbas was like a second father to me. But unlike my father, who was large, heavy, and imposing, with penetrating brown eyes and a love of talking, Abbas was short, wiry, muscular, and quiet. When I was in elementary school, he often drove me to school or sports. Abbas taught me how to shoot a gun—something Baba never would have done. The military had not been Abbas's choice. He had dreamed of becoming a medical doctor like his brother in Italy. But my Uncle Ali was a member of the prime minister's cabinet, and everyone in the cabinet had to have a family member in the Afghan military. Uncle Ali's son Shabir was too young, so it was Abbas who was sent off to Germany for military training.

When I told my father I could not let Abbas risk his life for me, Baba said, "I asked him to do this for me." And then I understood. I was his only child. If anyone could get me safely to Pakistan, it was Abbas.

Suddenly I felt as if the life I had known was flying away from me faster and faster—as if it were a kite whose string had been cut and a strong wind was pushing it farther and farther away until it was just a dot in the vast blue expanse of sky.

"What is the plan now?" Abbas asked. I was silent. "What do we do now?" he repeated.

"I don't know. My only plan was to escape to Jalalabad, which we have done."

Abbas stared at me. "I can't believe you have no plan beyond this."

"How could I? You can't trust anyone in Kabul."

Abbas sat without speaking for some time until the silence became painful. I wanted to say something but could think of nothing to say. I had let him down.

"We'll make our way into Jalalabad," I finally said, "and find a way across the border."

"Nay," Abbas said, taking charge. "We'll go to Abdien—to Nasir's."

Abdien was a village not far from Jalalabad where Abbas and I had visited Nasir and his wife and child many times. Nasir worked as a tailor in Abdien. He grew oranges and vegetables in a little garden. It would only be an hour walk to his house. But there was one problem—we would have to cross the Behsood Bridge, and we could not risk being seen.

We waited until dark. Soon we found ourselves walking through farmland, where houses were few and far between, past orange groves, sugarcane fields, and rice paddies bordered by the silhouettes of tall, slim trees. Mud brick walls surrounded each farmhouse. The only entrance, a wooden door large enough to accommodate the comings and goings of the farmer's sheep, goats, and cows, was kept closed at night. The walls, built to protect the women from the eyes of strangers, protected us from being seen as well.

We hugged the riverbank as we neared the Behsood Bridge, which spanned the Kabul River. Moonlight glinted off the water as it coursed through a shallow gorge. Lines of people, cars, and trucks waited to cross, while National Security guards and Russian soldiers examined papers and searched vehicles. Russian tanks aimed their turrets toward the mountains across the river. The rebels' small arms and rockets were no match for the Russians, but the mujahideen took great pleasure in harassing their Russian enemy. At night they launched rockets and unleashed their automatic weapons at the Russians. Russian tanks fired in response, and after an hour or so of this "battle," the mujahideen would run out of ammunition and fade back into the mountains. The night would be silent again.

I thought of the time my father took me to see the king at his Winter Palace, passing through its many flower and vegetable gardens. In Afghanistan we have a saying: "Wherever an Afghan ruler settles, there springs a garden." Baba and I sat with the king in the shade of an ancient panja chinar tree amid the sweet fragrance of orange and lemon blossoms. When the king spoke, his words were drowned out by the music of a hundred songbirds.

Now the Palace's gardens were untended, the flowers dead, the songbirds gone.

The road along the river was used by trucks excavating sand for cement. We huddled in a hollow in the riverbank not far from the bridge. Suddenly the earth shook with the explosion of rockets launched by the mujahideen, followed immediately by the deafening blasts of Russian tank fire. Automatic gunfire pierced the air. Stray bullets ricocheted off rocks outside our shelter, sending sparks flying like tiny shooting stars.

"The bridge is too dangerous," I yelled to Abbas. "We'll have to cross the river."

In the spring the Kabul River, fed by snowmelt from the mountains, becomes a rushing torrent hundreds of feet wide. Now in October, after months of summer sun, the once broad river was broken into deep-channeled fingers of slowly flowing water separated by sandbars. We walked along the riverbank until we were far from the bridge.

"We can cross here," I said.

Staring at the broad stretch of water, Abbas did not look so certain. "I hope you're a strong swimmer," he said.

"Don't worry about me," I replied. "Worry about yourself. I know this river."

We stepped from the moist, sandy riverbank into shallow icy water that bubbled and gurgled over submerged rocks as we made our way to a rocky sandbar, beyond which the river widened. We waded in. The churning river grew suddenly deep and grabbed us as if it wanted to take us with it, and we began paddling with one arm, the other holding aloft our plastic bags of documents.

At the bridge the fighting began again—guns firing, rockets exploding—as we fought our own battle, struggling to swim across the bone-chilling river. Finally, our feet found the river bottom. As we staggered up the steep riverbank, the wind hit us like a thousand knives slashing through our wet clothing. We followed dirt paths through fields of tall sugarcane and rice paddies bordered by stands of trees, the white peaks of the Safid Koh glowing faintly in the distance beneath a bone-colored moon.

Suddenly a dog blocked our path, growling and baring its inch-long, hook-like fangs. It was a Kuchi, a vicious fighting dog bred by the nomadic Kuchi tribe to protect their camels, sheep, and goats. A dog that could scare a mountain lion or take a hunk of flesh out of a thief. Near Kabul before the war, over a thousand men would gather to bet on Kuchi dogfights. We stared at the snarling dog, its ears cropped almost to its head to prevent an opponent from latching on during a fight. Its tail was cropped for the same reason and jutted out from its body at a slight angle. It was not a large dog, but its wedge-shaped head and broad, muscular shoulders exuded power. As I stood paralyzed with fear, Abbas gave it a sharp kick in the nose, and the dog ran off into the darkness.

After another hour, the glow of lights in the distance told us we were approaching Abdien. The paths grew wider, the trees thicker, the farmhouses closer together. Like all the villages in Afghanistan, Abdien had a mosque, a tiny one, with a single minaret and room for twenty men. When we reached Nasir's house, which sat just behind the mosque, I thought of how people no longer lived in their own homes because National Security had confiscated them—or they were dead. "Are you sure Nasir still lives here?" I asked, gripped by a sudden fear. "We don't know who lives here now, Abbas. It could be dangerous."

Abbas gave me a withering look, grabbed the tarnished brass door knocker, and banged it three times into the depression in the old wooden door.

3

Abdien, Afghanistan, October 1980

Nasir

The door opened just wide enough to reveal a pair of dark, searching eyes. Then it flew open, and there stood Nasir, thin as a wheat stalk, his weathered face circled with a stubble of salt-and-pepper beard. Though only fifty years old, Nasir's hands were rivulets of veins, his fingers worn from years of tailoring. You could see that he and Abbas were cousins. They had the same long oval faces with high foreheads, the same prominent ears and full noses, the same eyebrows that drooped at the ends. Nasir's face, haggard from years of war and deprivation, lit up at the sight of us. "Abbas! Bar! I did not expect to see your faces, but it is a joy to see you."

We followed Nasir across a small yard, past orange trees and a vegetable garden, to a modest house brightened by window frames painted a vivid blue. Inside, the floor was littered with sleeping men, all relatives of Nasir visiting from Jalalabad or escaping the war in Kabul. Nasir's wife and young daughter were asleep in a separate part of the house out of sight of male guests.

Nasir went outside to the cooking fire and filled a metal bucket with glowing coals. He returned and set the bucket at our feet, still blue from the icy river water. We welcomed the warmth.

Abbas changed out of his wet city clothes into a *gebi*—loose, pajama-like trousers and a shirt that hung just past his knees that was worn by men in the countryside. Abbas kept his own gebi at Nasir's house, where he often visited. As I struggled to squeeze into the gebi Nasir brought me, he looked at me and smiled. "I'll make you a new one."

We sat and ate beans and spinach that Nasir had dried for cooking in the winter months. Nasir sewed me a blue gebi to wear and gave me a gray, many-pocketed *waskat* (a very long vest), and a *patoo* (a long, heavy scarf made from the wool of his goats). When Baba gave me my first patoo, he said, "This may look like just a piece of cloth, Bari, but it will keep your head warm and protect your face from sandstorms and serve you as a washcloth, a towel, or a pillow cover. I have even known men to use it as a prayer rug. Sometimes the simplest thing can be much more than it appears."

I put on my new gebi and waskat. I had left Kabul behind.

We were exhausted and ready for sleep, but there was no room on the floor. Nasir had created an extra bedroom on the rooftop of an extension he had built. He led us outside and placed a ladder against the wall. Abbas and I climbed up to find two bamboo cots with mattresses and pillows.

A couple of miles distant the lights of the Behsood Bridge and Jalalabad glowed softly. It was well after midnight, and all was quiet. I wrapped my patoo around the worn pillow and fell asleep staring up at the brushstroke of the Milky Way.

Suddenly explosions pierced the night air, drawing closer and closer until a huge blast sent debris raining down upon us. "Help! Nasir!" we shouted. He raised the ladder, and we almost tumbled down in our haste. We spent the rest of the night propped against a wall, not even trying to sleep.

After breakfast Abbas told me he had sent word to his cousin Malem that we were at Nasir's. Malem's father was the khan in the Behsood region. Malem had joined the Communists when they came to power. His family was originally from Nuristan, an isolated province in the high mountains of the Northeast, where the Nuristanis once worshipped humanlike deities. Then Islam came to Afghanistan, and the region became known as Kafiristan—the "Land of Nonbelievers." The "Iron Amir," Abdur Rahman, forced the people to convert to Islam, then named the province Nuristan, the "Land of Light," because the Kafirs had seen the light of Islam.

"How is it you trust a Party member?" I asked Abbas.

"He's my cousin," Abbas replied. "We need his help to get across the border."

"What if he turns us in to win favor with the Party?"

"Don't worry. I did Malem and his father many favors when I was in the military. Now it's his turn to do me a favor. That's why I have the tongue to ask him."

"Abbas!" called a loud voice, cracking the morning air. "It's good to see you."

Nuristanis are thought to be descended from the army of Alexander the Great, which passed through Afghanistan on their quest to conquer the world. Looking at Malem's blond curly hair and blue eyes, it was easy to believe this. The influence of the Party was evident in his clean-shaven face and his dress—even though Malem lived in the conservative countryside, he wore a suit and tie. "I have a favor to ask of you, cousin," Abbas said. "We need a ride to the border tomorrow."

The question stole the smile from Malem's face. "Are you *diwana*? You ask me to do something I cannot do, something I would never do. Because if I did, you would not see the face of Afghanistan again, and I would not see your face again, cousin. Nay, ask me anything but not this."

"I have done your family many favors over the years," Abbas said. "This is all I ask in return."

"You know I'm still a Party member," Malem said. "Do you know why? Because the Russians are not leaving. To help you would put me and my family at great risk. Why would I risk my position and my family? Tell me, Abbas, why would I do that? Nay, I'll help you any way I can. But not to leave Afghanistan. This I cannot do."

"Malem!" Nasir called from the doorway. "Come, I need you."

When Malem was gone, I whispered to Abbas. "We don't know who Malem is speaking for. We must leave as quickly as possible."

Malem's large figure suddenly appeared in the doorway. "I must go now. Can I give you a ride anywhere? Except Pakistan, of course." He smiled.

"Nay, we're exhausted," Abbas replied. "We'll see you tomorrow."

When Malem was gone, Nasir approached us. "I don't trust him," he said. "I'll have someone drive you to Jalalabad at first light."

Morning was quiet, even at the Behsood Bridge. The war was carried out under cover of night, and both the Russians and the mujahideen needed to let people carry on with their lives in the daylight. The guards paid us no attention as Nasir's friend drove us over the bridge into Jalalabad. We traveled through the streets and markets hoping to recognize someone we knew. "Let's try the radio repair shops," I said. "I had friends who worked there." But I recognized no one. Then I remembered Mohammad, a landscaper who had become good friends with Baba when we had spent our winters here. I had been to his house a few times. Surely he would remember Rahman Popal and be willing to help his son. I directed the driver to the house, praying Mohammad still lived there.

Like all the houses near Jalalabad's downtown district, Mohammad's was hidden behind a wall on a lane just wide enough for one car. We asked our driver to wait until we were inside. I knocked and held my breath. A man opened the door.

"Bar Popal?" he said, surprised. "Come in, come in."

Mohammad looked far older than I remembered. His black mustache contrasted with the scrubby gray beard on his cheeks and chin. He led us to a small brick house with peeling whitewashed walls. Only a few sad orange trees remained in the yard. I introduced Abbas to him.

"How are you doing? How is your father?" Mohammad asked me.

"Things are very bad in Kabul now," I replied. "My life was in danger. I had to leave. Baba is still doing as well as can be expected."

Mohammad's look of pleasure at seeing me was replaced with disappointment. "I never thought I would live to see the day you would leave your father," he sighed. "You're his only child. . . . But now you are here, and there's nothing to be done. I would do anything for your father. Do you need a place to stay? . . . money?"

"Nay, tashakor, but we need help getting to Pakistan."

"Ah, so you are leaving Afghanistan," he said, shaking his head sadly. He thought for a moment. "The Russians and the mujahideen are fighting to control the main highway, and there are thieves as well. Nay, you cannot take the highway. You must drive the backroads, then take the long walk to the border. It's difficult to know who you can trust. It will take me some time to find someone. Many guides don't know what they are doing, and they get lost or desert the people they are supposed to be helping. Stay with me here tonight. Tomorrow I'll find you a guide."

I had not considered walking to the border, and it unsettled me.

There were so many dangers: landmines, bandits, Russian soldiers. But everything was a risk now.

We ate a simple meal of tea and naan together and spoke little.

That night Abbas and I lay on rugs in the entry room, trying to sleep.

"Are you awake?" I called to Abbas.

"Of course. Who sleeps in Afghanistan anymore?"

"I'm worried about the guide."

"Why?"

"He might be a Communist, or he might work for the Communists. Maybe the Communists have threatened him. You don't know."

"You worry too much."

"But if he finds out I'm a Popal from Kabul, I could be killed."

"True."

"So, it's not foolish to be afraid."

"*Baleh*, it is because there's nothing you can do about it. Whatever happens is your fate."

"Then why weren't you asleep?"

"Because only a fool isn't afraid."

4

Somewhere Near the Afghanistan-Pakistan Border, October 1980

Minefield

Is your life written in a book before you are born? Is everything that happens to you preordained? Baba would have smiled at this thought. He believed that you write your own book. He wrote his, or at least it seemed that way. Maybe in all the hard work he did he thought he was making decisions, but he was only making choices that had already been made for him. I know he would have laughed at me for thinking this. He would have pressed his hand against his cheek, leaned his head slightly to the side, and shaken it slowly. Then he would have reminded me that I am young and that it's all right to have such thoughts, but I must never forget that there are theories and there is reality. The theory is that we have no choice, but the reality is we do make choices. His philosophy was grounded in the real—what we can see, feel, taste, touch, and smell—while I believe there are worlds beyond this world. But it was difficult to argue with Baba. He was always so convincing—and he was usually right.

I slept little that night and awoke with memories of dreams that were like kites soaring off in all directions, some sailing upward, others plummeting like birds shot from the sky.

After we ate a breakfast of naan, black tea, and oranges from Mohammad's trees, Mohammad left to find a guide. We stayed inside, afraid to venture out.

Mohammad returned a few hours later. "What you are undertaking is very risky," he said. "The only way to guarantee your safety is to drive halfway to the border and walk the rest of the way."

We regarded him anxiously while he paused as if to let his words sink in before continuing. "I found a guide. You are to meet him tomorrow at the tobacco shop."

"How will we recognize him?" I asked.

"You won't. He will recognize you."

It was a long wait to the following day. The tobacco shop was only a ten-minute walk from Mohammad's but, for us, a dangerous one. The streets were crowded with shoppers buying bread, tea, rice, sugar, greens, and soap. Only a few were women, some covered in burkas, others in shawls. We concealed ourselves in the throng of people until we reached the sidewalk across from the tobacco shop, then stopped in our tracks—a National Security guard was standing near the entrance. "If we hesitate, we'll look suspicious," Abbas said. "Let's go."

I followed him, but with every step I took, I could see my leather shoes jutting out from under my gebi. The shoes of Kabul were not the sandals of Jalalabad, something the guard was sure to notice. I shuffled along to conceal them, worried about my odd gait, but realized it was no different than that of thousands of Afghans maimed by the war.

The National Security guard took no notice.

The tobacco shop was very small. A forest of red, yellow, and blue cartons of cigarettes rose from the floor; green tins of pipe and chewing tobacco were stacked so high, I was afraid I might knock them over. There were only a few customers, but it seemed crowded. As I pretended to look for a pack of cigarettes, a voice whispered in my ear. "Tomorrow before daybreak a blue Toyota will appear at Mohammad's. Be prepared to pay me."

I turned my head slightly and found myself looking into the eyes of a thin young man about my age. He had a delicate face with only the wisp of a beard. His wool *pakol* was pulled down on his forehead almost to his eyes, making his large ears stand out even more. I nodded and whispered, "I have money. Don't worry, we will pay you."

He bought a pack of cigarettes and left.

The next day, just before dawn, an old blue Toyota pulled up outside Mohammad's. It was the kind of rusty, battered car that is kept running forever in Afghanistan. I hoped it would make it halfway to the border. Mohammad was up to see us off.

As soon as the man from the tobacco shop walked in, I said, "I have your money."

"Don't worry, Mohammad has taken care of it," he replied.

I looked to Mohammad. "Tashakor," I said. "How can I repay you?"

"I do this out of respect for your father. I don't need to be repaid. I ask only one thing and it is that you give my best wishes to your father when you see him."

"Baleh, I will," I said. As I spoke these words, I suddenly felt a great fear that I might never see Baba again.

The back door of the Toyota popped open, and we slid inside. The guide sat in front, next to the driver.

"My name is Afzel," he said as the car pulled away. "I will be your guide across the border." I looked at him, concerned. "Don't worry . . . I have done this many times, and as you can see, I am still here."

We were soon heading east on the two-lane Jalalabad-Torkham highway, past the same park across from the Kabul Airport where Abbas and I had begun our escape—all that effort to arrive back at our starting point.

An hour later the driver turned off the highway onto a dirt road muddy in spots from irrigation runoff. After another hour driving past farmland and orchards, we pulled off the road beside several small buildings where local farmers dropped off their produce to be stored before transport to Jalalabad and Kabul. But there were no farmers now, only piles of blankets the farmers used to warm themselves while waiting for the trucks. Bins overflowed with oranges, lemons, melons, and nuts.

"Get out," Afzel said, opening the door. Soon the three of us were standing by the side of the road next to the blankets and fruit bins. The Toyota turned around in the direction of Jalalabad and sped off in a spray of dirt and gravel. Abbas and I stood in the still, silent morning air wondering what was next.

"The Toyota would look suspicious here," Afzel said, breaking the silence. "We will take the van like local farmers."

A half-hour later a large white van pulled up. Six men were already crowded inside. To my relief no one greeted us or asked where we were going. I feared that they would recognize my Kabul accent. We drove along rutted, dusty roads, trailing a small sandstorm behind us, fields of grain and sugarcane on either side. Every now and then a lone line of trees in a field revealed the presence of a farmhouse. We passed a few men, a dog, some cows walking along the road, but never any women. We stopped at several small villages, each indistinguishable from the last: mud brick buildings amid a few trees planted for shade against the harsh summer heat.

We were the only passengers left when we got out. The van made a U-turn and headed back down the road. Afzel led us away from the village into the countryside. The farms grew fewer and fewer until we found ourselves in a barren landscape of dry, sandy soil. In the distance appeared poplar trees, the tall, thin trees that marked a source of water and a farm. "Not much farther," Afzel said, pointing in the direction of the poplars.

Before we reached them, we came to a farmhouse, a vision of poverty and disrepair. Only one wall remained, jagged from decay. The others had collapsed into a heap of rubble from age and neglect. No one had the money, or the will, to fix them. Time and the elements had returned them to the soil. From dust to dust. We walked a bit farther and came to another farmhouse, this one decrepit but with walls more or less intact. The walls were not very high because few ventured out this far. Afzel knocked loudly and waited. He knocked again, louder this time. The door opened to reveal a tall, rail-thin man wearing a gebi the same tan color as the soil, his white turban frayed with age. He looked us up and down until he recognized Afzel, and I breathed a sigh of relief. The farmer did not introduce himself but led us through his sad garden of withered plants and thirsty fruit trees to his tiny farmhouse. The only furniture in the entrance room were two mattresses on the rug-covered dirt floor. The walls had once been whitewashed, but the paint had yellowed and fallen off in places, revealing the mud beneath. As Afzel counted out several bills and placed them in the farmer's hand, the farmer looked at us with contempt, as if he despised us for leaving Afghanistan. But he had no right to judge us—he was taking money to help us.

"It's a six-hour walk to the border," Afzel said, "but the real danger is behind us. Wait for me here. I'll be back at midnight."

As soon as Afzel left, we lay down on the mattresses but could not sleep. Children's voices coming from the back rooms reminded me of my own children. I said to Abbas, "We don't know this farmer. He could make a lot of money turning us over to the Russians. Who knows? Maybe even Afzel would do the same."

Abbas was awake but did not answer.

Just as I fell asleep, the creak of a door opening startled me awake. We followed Afzel outside. Two men in gray gebis stood waiting, one older, with the long beard of the countryside and a white turban like the farmer. The other, much younger, wore a dark brown turban the color of his beard. They said nothing, and Afzel did not introduce us.

"Before we start, there are a few things I need to tell you," Afzel said. "If you see anyone or hear anything, hide quickly—there are thieves on this route. There are also Russian helicopters. You'll hear them long before you see them. If you hear one, dive for shelter. There are landmines everywhere—especially along the escape routes—so walk in a line directly behind me. And no talking." He began walking along a narrow path, and I fell in line behind him, staring at his back, Abbas behind me, then the younger stranger, and the old man at the rear. We walked at a steady pace on narrow dirt paths beneath the moon and stars. I came to hate the irrigation ditches that crisscrossed the land, forcing us constantly to leap across them. Each time I saw Afzel make the short hop, I followed his lead. At first I feared spraining an ankle, but it soon became routine.

As we neared the Kabul River, there were more farmhouses, all taking advantage of its precious water. We steered far clear of them. Afzel's voice broke the silence. "Everything okay? Stay with me," he said. I stumbled and bumped into his back. "Not so close!" he hissed.

The farmland gave way to a hard, sandy, rock-strewn landscape. We had left the irrigation ditches behind, and Afzel quickened his pace. I stayed with him, keeping my distance. Ahead of us mountains loomed like sleeping giants. To reach Pakistan, we would have to climb the steep ascent to the Khyber Pass.

"Anyone need a rest?" Afzel called back to us.

"Nay," we all lied. We were cold and tired but afraid to stop.

"Good. Let's keep going." Afzel increased his pace, then quickly changed directions across an open field. Beyond the field I could make out the landscape rising steeply toward the mountains: the trail to the Khyber Pass. I had fallen behind and hurried to catch up, excited that each step was bringing me closer to Pakistan and safety. For the first time since we'd left Kabul, I felt at ease.

A flash of light, bright as a signal flare; a deafening blast; a sudden feeling of warmth covering my body in the bitter cold of the night; the stench of something burning, like meat left too long on the fire; Abbas's voice coming to me as a distant, muffled sound, as if he were speaking underwater: "No one move!" My heart felt as if it were trying to escape my chest, and I gasped for breath. I swiped at my face over and over, trying to wipe the thick warm liquid from my eyes, but my hands were dripping wet. A wave of nausea overcame me as I realized what had happened. "Afzel stepped on a landmine," Abbas said now in the measured tones of the experienced military man he was. "Everyone sit down where you are."

Afghanistan had me in its grip, and it wouldn't let me go.

5

Afghanistan

Afghanistan is shaped like a compressed tree, with a wide, short trunk and a tall, broad, ragged canopy that looks as if a strong wind is blowing it to the east. One elongated branch of that northeastern canopy touches China. To the north the top arc brushes against Tajikistan, Uzbekistan, and Turkmenistan. To the west is Iran; to the east Pakistan wraps beneath Afghanistan as if gripping it in its hand.

Afghanistan is the product of great clashes, both geological and cultural. Eons ago all of Earth's continents were joined together in one great landmass called Pangea, which floated on one great ocean called Panthalassa. But deep inside, the planet's molten core churned with a violent energy that broke Pangea apart. On one of these landmasses, millions of years of rain created the Tethys Sea, where mollusks flourished. Now fossils of these ancient Tethys Sea mollusks lie in the mountains surrounding Kabul.

A great clash of tectonic plates forced the land upward, creating the Himalayas, the highest mountains in the world. In the northeastern corner rose the Hindu Kush. Geologic forces created not only mountains but also the Wakhan Corridor, a broad 30-mile-wide by 140-mile-long passage that connects China to Afghanistan. In this remote corner of the world, the Siberian ibex and famed snow leopard have found refuge along with the Marco Polo sheep, named for the great explorer who crossed the Wakhan Corridor to reach the China of Kublai Khan in the thirteenth century. The great geological forces created beauty as well—the mystical lapis lazuli, gemstone of Egypt's pharaohs.

I was born in Kabul, the capital and largest city of Afghanistan, which sits in a mile-high mountain valley in the northeastern part of the country, only 125 miles from Pakistan. Three hundred miles to the south of Kabul in a parched desert valley, where the summer's dust storms and 120-degree heat can make life unbearable, lies Kandahar, the great Pashtun stronghold and center of Afghanistan's history. Jalalabad, another major Pashtun city located only 50 miles from the Pakistan border, is the gateway to Pakistan. Far to the west, Herat looks to Iran and the Middle East.

In Mazar-i-Sharif, two hundred miles to the north, live the Hazaras, Tajiks, and Uzbeks, whose long history of rivalry with the Pashtuns—and each other—predates Islam. The Hazaras are descendants of the great Mongol tribes that swept into Afghanistan centuries ago. When Islam arrived in Afghanistan in the seventh century, the Pashtuns became Sunnis. The Hazaras adopted Shia Islam in the sixteenth century.

Why this split? The Prophet Muhammad died in 632 without naming a successor. Some believed in worshipping God only through the Prophet's writings and teachings—his "sunna." They became known as "Sunnis," who saw Muhammad's father-in-law, Abu Bakr, as the rightful heir. But Abu Bakr was not related to Muhammad by blood. Others believed Muhammad's blood relative, his cousin Ali, was the rightful heir, and these "followers of Ali" (*shiaat Ali* in Arabic) became known as "Shia." Both believe Allah is the only God and that Muhammad is his messenger, and both follow the Five Pillars of Islam. But Sunnis worship God through the Prophet's writings, while Shias worship God through their spiritual leaders—their ayatollahs—whom they view as reflections of God on earth. Sunnis consider Shias as worshipping men in place of God—heretics who do not follow true Islam. The split gave the Pashtuns and Hazaras another reason to fight.

The British defined Afghanistan's eastern and southern borders in 1893, when they created the Durand Line to define the border between Afghanistan and their Indian colony. When India gained its independence and Pakistan was created, Britain's Durand Line became the border between Afghanistan and Pakistan. More than half of all Pashtuns live in Pakistan, in the cities of Quetta and Peshawar, close to the Afghan border. The Durand Line cut off the majority of Pashtuns from their fellow Pashtuns in Jalalabad, Kabul, and Kandahar. This artificial border sowed the seeds of war and destruction.

Afghanistan's geography brought it both the greatest of fortunes and the greatest of misfortunes. Traders on the major trade route from China to Persia known as the Silk Road traveled through Kabul and Jalalabad to get to India. Not just silk, jade, and lapis traveled the Silk Road, but paper, books, culture, and religion. Afghanistan's strategic location beckoned all the great conquerors: the Persians; Alexander the Great; the White Huns; the Turkish Arabs, who in 642 CE replaced Buddhism, Judaism, and Zoroastrianism with Islam; and Mahmoud of Ghazni, who created Ghazni, a walled city south of Kabul from which he ruled an empire that lasted until Genghis Khan and his Mongol horde arrived from China in 1219. Genghis Khan was one of Afghanistan's most brutal invaders. His Mongol horde devastated the countryside, burned cities to the ground, and massacred the Afghan people. Genghis Khan created the Mongol Empire, only to have it collapse after his death. During the sixteenth and seventeenth centuries Afghanistan's empire stretched from Kabul across northern India to Iran.

In the eighteenth century Ahmad Shah Durrani, the great warrior leader who succeeded Nadir Shah, came to power in possession of Nadir Shah's treasure of conquest, including Persia's Peacock Throne and India's Koh-i-Noor diamond. Durrani was a Pashtun and a leader of the Abdali tribes in Kandahar, one of which, the Popalzai, is the tribe of my family. With the wealth he inherited from Nadir Shah, Durrani formed a great army that conquered the Mughal territory in northern India, part of Persia, and the territory from the Amu River in the North to the Arabian Sea in the South. He created an empire that would become modern Afghanistan. When he died, in 1772, Ahmad Shah Durrani's body was placed in a mausoleum in Kandahar. Afghans call him "Ahmad Shah Baba"—"the Father of Afghanistan."

The Afghan kings who followed Durrani ruled only a few cities: Kabul, Jalalabad, and Kandahar. The people in Herat and Mazar-i-Sharif ignored the king. The farmers and animal herders in desert oases and mountain valleys hardly knew he existed. Afghanistan was not so much a nation as a collection of tribes operating under tribal law, coming together only when necessary to defend Afghanistan from outside invaders.

When Britain extended its empire into India, Russia countered by pushing its empire south into Tajikistan, Turkmenistan, and Uzbekistan. This powerful fight over Afghanistan became known as the "Great Game." While Russia constantly interfered in Afghan politics, the British invaded Afghanistan not once but three times. In the Second Anglo-Afghan War in 1878, Britain conquered Kabul and replaced the king. The Afghans of the countryside revolted. After two years of war British troops headed back to India, pursued by Afghan sharpshooters. Twenty years later Rudyard Kipling warned:

> When you're wounded and left on Afghanistan's plains,
> And the women come out to cut up what remains,
> Jest roll to your rifle and blow out your brains
> An' go to your God like a soldier.

6

Kabul, Afghanistan, 1919

General Nadir

When the British departed Afghanistan in 1880, they left Abdur Rahman on the throne because he was loyal to Britain and would keep Russia out. His brutality earned him the name the "Iron Amir." Because he was a Barakzai, the Popalzai khans of Kandahar refused to recognize his authority. Abdur Rahman attacked Kandahar and defeated the khans, including my grandfather Mukarram. Because of *Pashtunwali* (the way of the Pashtuns), even the Iron Amir could not kill my grandfather but exiled him instead.

Pashtunwali is the Pashtun tribes' ancient unwritten code of honor, handed down from father to son. It guides Pashtuns from birth to death. Pashtunwali embodies many traditions: kinship, friendship, hospitality, disputes, war, and morality. When there is a conflict between Pashtunwali and Islam, Pashtunwali governs. In a Pashtun's home it is Pashtunwali that rules. Afghans would never gamble in a mosque because the Koran forbids gambling. But outside the mosque Afghans gamble on everything. They are Afghans first and Muslims second.

When a dispute arises, tribal elders, following Pashtunwali, convene a jirga to settle the matter. All Afghans, no matter their status, obey the jirga's decision. This is still the way in Afghanistan. Under its code of hospitality, a host must offer anyone protection without expectation of favor. Under its code of revenge, an Afghan is honor bound to avenge a death, an injury, or an insult, particularly if it involves one of the three z's: *zan, zar,* and *zamin* (women, wealth, and land).

If the Iron Amir had killed my grandfather, he would have had to fight the Popalzai of Kandahar until they were avenged. That is why, instead of executing my grandfather, Abdur Rahman confiscated all his lands and belongings and exiled him and his family to Gandamak, a mile-high valley of farms and mulberry trees near Jalalabad. And that is why, in 1902, my father was born in Gandamak and not in Kandahar. My grandfather named him Abdul Rahman Popal, but my father never liked the name Abdul because it was an Arab name. He called himself "Rahman," a traditional Afghan name that reflected his love of Afghanistan.

The Iron Amir died in 1901, the year before my father was born. His son Habibullah succeeded him. Perhaps wanting to restore relations with the Kandahar Popalzai, King Habibullah pardoned my grandfather. But the king did not want him to return to Kandahar—or any other city. The pardon was conditional: Mukarram had to stay at least twenty-five miles away from any city. That suited Mukarram because he was content to stay in Gandamak. But when his wife (he was the rare khan who had only one wife) insisted on moving out of the cold mountain valley and closer to Kabul, he relented and moved the family to the pleasant, fertile Logar Valley, twenty-five miles to the south of Kabul.

When my father turned seven, he was sent to the local religious school, the madrassa, to study the Koran. Although he spoke Dari and Pashto, he sat for hours, head bent over the Holy Book, memorizing every word in Arabic. The mullah placed a pinch of sand in the hollow of each student's bent neck, warning, "Do not let a grain of sand touch the floor." My father did not.

When my father turned sixteen, Mukarram tried to arrange his marriage to the daughter of a wealthy local farmer. Although once rich and powerful, our family had little money after the exile. The farmer demanded land, which my grandfather did not have, and the proposal was rejected. When my father heard this, he was so ashamed, he ran away, hitching a ride with a farmer to his sister Abiba's house in Kabul. Baba expected Abiba would greet him warmly, but instead, she scolded him. "How could you, the eldest son, leave Aga?" But Baba was defiant. "I will never go back until I've made something of myself."

Soon after he arrived, Baba followed Abiba's husband to the Foreign Ministry, where Abiba's husband worked as a guard. Baba was surprised to find hundreds of illiterate men waiting outside the ministry to have letters read or documents prepared by the ministry's clerks. Baba began reading and writing letters for them as they waited outside. A few weeks later Baba was writing a letter when it was snatched from his hand by the head clerk at the Foreign Ministry. The clerk read the letter and, to my father's great surprise, offered him a job. At eighteen Baba began work as a scribe, his first position in the Foreign Ministry.

At the beginning of 1919, as the biting winds of January blew snow through Kabul's narrow lanes, the deputy foreign minister called my father into his office. The head clerk was absent that day, and the deputy foreign minister needed a document prepared. My father worked quickly and handed the document to the deputy foreign minister. The deputy read with widening eyes, then went to a cabinet and pulled out a folder. He removed one of the many documents the folder contained and compared it to Baba's. "Did you write this?" he asked as he handed Baba the document for him to see.

"Baleh," Baba replied.

"I had been led to believe these documents were the work of someone else," he said, almost to himself.

The next day, when Baba arrived at his desk, he found the head clerk sitting there. "You are head clerk now," he told my father.

That year King Habibullah was assassinated while on a hunting trip. His twenty-seven-year-old son, Amanullah, only third in line for the throne, was governor of Kabul and controlled the army as well as the Treasury. His position won him the support of the tribal leaders over the stronger claims of his brothers, and Amanullah took the throne. During World War I Amanullah's father had kept Afghanistan neutral, though he could have attacked British interests in India. But Amanullah was part of the young activists who wanted to attack Britain, which still controlled Afghanistan's foreign policy, keeping it from being an independent nation.

As the new king, Amanullah told the British envoy: "Afghanistan is as independent a state as the other states and powers of the world. No foreign power will be allowed to have a hair's breadth of right to interfere internally or externally with the affairs of Afghanistan, and if any ever does, I am ready to cut its throat with my sword."

When the British still refused to recognize Afghanistan's independence, King Amanullah ordered General Nadir to attack the

British in western India. Not only did the Pashtuns in the British force refuse to fight against the Pashtuns in General Nadir's force; they joined them in staging guerrilla attacks on the remaining British force. The British commander in India received a rare bit of wise advice from London: "You will not have forgotten the lessons of history that we have not so much to fear from the Afghan regular army as from the irregular tribesmen and their constant attacks on our isolated camps and lines of communications." It was advice the Russians would fail to heed sixty years later.

The Third Anglo-Afghan War was soon over. On August 19, 1919, the Treaty of Rawalpindi was signed between Afghanistan and Britain, recognizing Afghanistan as an independent nation—but the hated Durand Line remained. Russia, of course, wanted to take advantage of Britain's loss and began providing money and military equipment to Afghanistan.

Amanullah was the first Afghan ruler to be captivated by the liberal views of the West. Among the political exiles he allowed to return to Afghanistan was Mahmoud Tarzi, who had been banished by the Iron Amir. Tarzi was opposed to religious extremism and supported freedom of the press. King Amanullah was so taken with Tarzi's views that he married Tarzi's daughter Soraya. Together King Amanullah and Queen Soraya shared a passion to modernize Afghanistan. In a break with Afghan tradition, Soraya would be the king's only wife.

After making a tour of Turkey and Europe, King Amanullah and Queen Soraya returned to Afghanistan intent on expanding women's rights, building schools for girls, allowing a free press, requiring the wearing of Western dress, and creating a new constitution. King Amanullah's sister shared these views as well and spoke about the need for educating women: "Old women discourage young women from learning by saying their mothers never starved to death because they could not read or write. But knowledge is not man's monopoly. Women also deserve to be knowledgeable. We must on the one hand bring up children and on the other hand help men in their work. We must read about famous women of this world to know that women can achieve exactly what men can achieve."

Amanullah was king, but as has always been the case with Afghanistan, the tribal leaders were really in control, and they opposed his reforms. The Afghan government paid tribal leaders to provide fighters for the Afghan military. But the soldier's loyalty was always to his tribe and tribal leader. When General Nadir opposed Amanullah's attempt to weaken tribal influence, urging him to respect tribal tradition, Amanullah appointed him ambassador to France—the Afghan way of exile. The general needed a personal secretary to record meetings and prepare documents in the embassy in Paris. He asked his brother in the Foreign Ministry for a recommendation, someone who had not gotten his position through family connections, someone who came from poverty and was hungry for work, a man of good character who was honest and could be trusted.

That man was my father.

7

Paris, France, 1920

Hélène

In the Afghan tradition my father, as the eldest of ten children, was responsible for his brothers and sisters. When Baba told his father, Mukarram, that he was leaving for Paris, my grandfather's face darkened. "If you go to Paris, you will marry a foreigner and I will be forced to sell everything to support her extravagant Western ways. It will be the ruin of the family." Mukarram reminded my father of his obligations and asked him what he intended to do.

"Give me your Koran," my father replied. He opened the Holy Book, then wrote on the inside cover:

First: I will never use your property in Logar for anyone but family.

Second: I will not marry until I have finished my education.

Third: I will never let you or my brothers or sisters suffer.

My father placed the Koran back in his father's hands. With every line he read, Mukarram grew angrier and angrier, until he looked up and hissed, "You start a war with me."

"Nay, Aga," my father replied respectfully. "It is not a war. It is an honest promise from a son to his father to give you peace of mind."

"Go if you must," Mukarram told him, "but serve Afghanistan well—and never forget your family or your promise. That's all I have to say."

As my father walked to the door, Mukarram called after him. "If you leave, you will never see me again."

The Paris of 1924 in which Baba found himself was a revelation. It was as if he had landed in another world. Everything was different: the politics, about which people talked openly and constantly; the fashions; the music; the respect men and women showed for each other. Paris was not just the center of France—it was the cultural center of the world, and all the world's great writers and artists flocked to it. Baba was open to it all. He found it difficult to keep to the old ways. He dressed in the latest fashions while watching women walk about freely in dresses and skirts. And he learned French.

The general enrolled my father in the Sorbonne because he wanted Baba to be well educated so he could serve Afghanistan. When Baba wasn't working, attending classes, or studying, he tutored Zahir, the general's ten-year-old son, and Daoud, Zahir's fifteen-year-old cousin and the son of General Nadir's brother Aziz. Baba was their "Ustad," a title Afghan students use for their teachers as a sign of respect, a title that lasts a lifetime. Baba was more than a teacher; he was like an older brother to Zahir and Daoud.

The first time General Nadir met with Henri Jacquieux, the president of France's national bank, he took my father with him. General Nadir asked Jacquieux for funding to build an Afghan railroad. He told Jacquieux that Afghanistan was suffering from interference by Russia and Britain and wanted to develop closer ties with France. The king wanted to bring French professors to Afghanistan to teach. General Nadir introduced my father: "Rahman is my personal assistant, but I consider him a son. He has my complete confidence and will be handling all the bank accounts."

It was the beginning of a close relationship between Jacquieux and General Nadir. Jacquieux invited General Nadir to join him at his palatial residence in Paris, where he entertained heads of state, government officials and foreign ambassadors to cultivate favor and expand the bank's interests abroad. Jacquieux, his wife, and their twenty-two-year-old daughter, Hélène, were there to greet them. Hélène was the most beautiful woman my father had ever seen, and he and Hélène wandered off alone together—something that would never have happened in Afghanistan. Hélène was intelligent and sophisticated, and she made my father laugh. After dinner, while many of the men stood together talking politics and finance, my father and Hélène listened to a piano and violin performance. He was captivated.

Over the next few months several more invitations arrived from Jacquieux. The general welcomed the chance to meet with the very powerful guests who attended. When my father had the private ear of the general, he said, "I am in love with Hélène and want to marry her."

"Does Jacquieux approve?"

"Jacquieux does not trust the rich men who are after her, but he has come to know me, and I think he knows I'm interested in Hélène, not her money. What do you think?"

"I've invested much in you so that you would serve Afghanistan. If you marry Hélène, you will remain in Paris."

My father always said that making choices in life was like playing a game of chess. You need to think of all the options before you make your move. When you move, there are consequences. That is why you must study and learn as much as you can. You must call on all of your knowledge and make the best choice. Then if it goes badly, don't worry, destiny has taken over. But chess is a game of the head, and this was a game of the heart. My father loved Hélène. If he asked her to marry him, he knew she would accept. But every time he wanted to, he thought of the promises he'd made to his father on the Koran and his obligations to his brothers and sisters. And General Nadir had done so much for him— how could he betray his trust as well? Baba did not ask Hélène to marry him, but they remained close for many years. Perhaps that was why he insisted on returning to Paris to finish his education, why he stayed as long as he could, and perhaps, too, why he married so late in life.

8

Kabul, Afghanistan, 1929

Nadir Shah

General Nadir could not tolerate the reforms King Amanullah was imposing in Afghanistan and resigned as ambassador in protest. He and his brothers Hashim and Wali moved to the South of France, far from Paris. Baba remained in Paris, where he continued to work at the embassy and study at the Sorbonne.

In much of the world there is a division between intellectuals of the city and social and religious conservatives in the countryside. Afghanistan was and is no different. The people of the countryside agreed with General Nadir and saw Amanullah's reforms as a threat to their religion and way of life. In 1929 they found a hero in Habibullah Kalikani. When Kalikani and his followers marched on Kabul to overthrow Amanullah, Amanullah's tribal army deserted him, forcing the king and queen to flee in their Rolls-Royce. Kalikani's horsemen gave chase. Only the greater horsepower of the Rolls saved the king and queen from certain death.

For the first time Islamic fundamentalists had demonstrated their violent opposition to Western influence. It would not be the last.

By the fall of 1929 Kalikani's harsh rule under Sharia law had plunged Afghanistan into chaos. When Kalikani turned to Russia for support, Britain decided to oust him. General Nadir had been born and raised in India. He was more sympathetic to British interests, more moderate than Kalikani, and did not like Russia. Britain needed a strong and respected Afghan leader to replace Kalikani.

Baba traveled from Paris to the South of France to visit the general. A few days after he arrived, a delegation of British military officers and Afghan tribal leaders appeared to meet with the general. My father offered to take notes at the meeting for the general, as he had at the embassy, but to his surprise the general told him he would not be needed.

Baba stood outside the meeting room, ear pressed against the door. All he could hear were muffled voices. The voices grew louder and louder. Suddenly the room went silent. The door flew open, and Baba barely managed to leap aside as a grim faced General Nadir strode quickly past him.

A few days later General Nadir and his brothers left for Waziristan in what is now western Pakistan. After gathering a force of tribal Pashtuns with the help of the British, the general attacked Kalikani, forcing him to flee Kabul.

After General Nadir assumed the throne as Nadir Shah, he sent Kalikani a Koran inscribed with an invitation to the Palace—a gesture that ensured Kalikani's safety. Kalikani was suspicious of Nadir Shah's intentions but wanted good relations with the new king and accepted.

As soon as Kalikani arrived at the Palace, Nadir Shah had him executed.

Nadir Shah appointed his brothers Hashim and Wali as co–prime ministers. King Amanullah's many supporters had assumed Nadir Shah would restore Amanullah to the throne. But Nadir Shah, having taken the throne from Kalikani, was not about to give it up. He replaced Kalikani's Sharia law with a modest version of Amanullah's reforms and a new constitution. Nadir Shah, a strong believer in the importance of education for Afghans, founded a College of Medicine, which would eventually merge with other colleges to become Kabul University. He established Afghanistan's first bank, Bank-i-Meli, to finance new businesses in soap, seed oils, leather, and cotton. When faced with the fact that Islam forbids charging interest on loans, the bank sold special stamps that had to be attached to each payment. Borrowers were not paying interest—they were only buying stamps.

Nadir Shah called my father back to Kabul. When Baba arrived there, his younger brothers, Ali and Sultan, greeted him with the terrible news that his father had died while he was away. Baba recalled his father's last words to him: "If you leave, you will not see me again."

The king offered my father a position as advisor in the Foreign Ministry, which Baba reluctantly accepted. My father loved Afghanistan, but at that moment in time he loved Hélène and Paris even more. He lived a simple life in the oldest part of Kabul with his mother, Abo, five sisters, and three brothers: Gholam, seventeen; Sultan, thirteen; and Ali, eleven. In Paris, Baba had been like an older brother to Zahir and Daoud. At thirty years old he was like a father to his much younger brothers. Every day Abo would make bread dough for the evening meal, and every day Gholam and Sultan would fight over who would take it to the communal oven. One evening my father came home to find Abo upset at their arguing.

"You take it!" Gholam yelled.

"Nay! You take it!" Sultan shouted back.

"What is all this about?" Baba steamed.

"It's embarrassing to be seen carrying the bread dough through town," the brothers complained.

"Fine. You don't have to do it anymore. I will take it." With that Baba grabbed the woven reed basket holding the dough and, still dressed in his suit and tie, strode out the door. Gholam and Sultan, humiliated, ran after him.

"We're sorry, Baba. We will do it in the future. We won't fight again."

"We cannot pay someone to carry our bread to the public oven for us," Baba said. "It is something we must do ourselves. From now on you will do it without complaint. Never be ashamed of who you are."

My father, his heart still in Paris, went to see Nadir Shah and told him he wanted to return.

"It's not good if the young here think like this," the king said.

"I'm not leaving Afghanistan for good, Your Excellency. I only wish to finish my studies so I can return to serve my country."

"Then I will send you," the king said. "But you are too young to be ambassador." Nadir Shah thought for a moment. "Here is what I will do. I will make you second in charge at the embassy—but I won't appoint an ambassador. You'll be ambassador in fact but not in name. What do you think of that?"

"I think you are a good and wise king."

9

Kabul, Afghanistan, 1933

Zahir Shah

Ruling Afghanistan had always been a perilous undertaking. Rulers were dethroned either by a relative or by the British or assassinated. Nadir Shah was in charge in Kabul, but he had made enemies of the Charkhi brothers, including Ghulam Nabi, who despised him for stealing Amanullah's throne. In the tradition of Afghan rulers, Nadir Shah got rid of Nabi by appointing him ambassador to Turkey. After Nabi returned to Kabul in the fall of 1932, Nadir Shah discovered that Nabi was plotting to overthrow him. Nadir Shah summoned Nabi to the Palace and had him executed.

Nadir Shah's brother Aziz was ambassador to Berlin, in Germany, where he lived with his son Daoud (whom Baba had tutored in Paris). Adolf Hitler was giving rousing speeches advocating a return to greatness for Germany after its defeat in the First World War. Years later Daoud, inspired by this message, would become obsessed with reuniting the land of the Pashtuns in western Pakistan with Afghanistan.

When Aziz was assassinated in Berlin by an Amanullah supporter, his brother Hashim took charge of Daoud—the son he had never had. An intense man who devoted all of his hours to the Afghan government, Hashim was a perfect match for Daoud. They were both headstrong and hungry for power.

In November 1933, a year after he executed Nabi, Nadir Shah, with his son Zahir at his side, attended a high school graduation ceremony. As the king handed out an award to one of the students, the son of one of Nabi's servants pulled a gun and assassinated Nadir Shah. The supporters of Amanullah and Charki's family had their revenge.

Although Nadir Shah was a ruthless leader, my father knew another side of him: a man of intelligence and humor; a man with a good heart; a man who could shape a person's character and bring enemies together; a man who taught my father the arts of negotiation and diplomacy.

Zahir Shah was only nineteen when he ascended the throne. His uncle Hashim, the prime minister, took control. The young Zahir Shah knew he was no match for Hashim. He needed someone to advise him, someone honest, someone he could trust like a brother.

Zahir Shah called my father back from Paris.

"You know I don't want to be king, Ustad," Zahir Shah said to my father. "I have no interest in power. I would prefer to remain a student my whole life."

"As would I, Your Excellency, but you must rule as king, and I must serve you however I can."

10

Kabul, Afghanistan, 1934

Tajwar

My father always said politics is not a science, it is an art, and just as you need to understand how to draw to be an artist, you need to understand people to be a good leader. It pained him to see Hashim ruling the country like a despot, filling the provincial assemblies and national Parliament with loyal friends and suppressing all opposition.

It also pained Baba to see Hashim promoting the rash Daoud, who, although he cared passionately about Afghanistan, was too blinded by his dictatorial nature to see what was good for the people. When my father tutored the young Daoud in Paris, he had tried to teach him that to gain respect, you must give respect, but Daoud never listened. Behind his back people called Daoud the "Crazy Prince."

When Hashim appointed the twenty-six-year-old Daoud governor of Kandahar, Daoud ruled so harshly that the people of Kandahar revolted and Zahir Shah was forced to travel to Kandahar himself to bring the city under control. Hashim tried to dissuade the king from going. "You will be risking your life if you go to Kandahar," he said. When Zahir Shah arrived at the airport in Kandahar, Hashim's men tried to direct him away from the terminal, where hundreds of protestors had gathered, and lead him to a tent where Hashim's handpicked tribal leaders awaited. Zahir Shah waved Hashim's men away. He entered the terminal and made his way to the center of the excited crowd. "I have come to listen," he said. "I have come to hear about any misunderstanding between you and the governor." The crowd began shouting, "Zahir Shah! Zahir Shah!" Men in gebis dusted gray from miles of traveling on horseback and camel hugged the king, turning his dark blue suit the color of the desert. The king sat down with the elders, who wanted Daoud replaced, and told them, "Don't worry, I will take care of this and get you the result you want."

After the king returned to Kabul, Daoud was replaced as governor. Daoud left Kandahar in disgrace. But Daoud was young—and Hashim was a patient man.

At one of the many government social functions Baba attended, he was speaking to Mohammad, one of the king's advisors and a powerful leader of the Seloman tribe, Pashtuns from south of Kabul who historically protected the Palace and the king. "Why does a man in a position such as yours not have a wife?' Mohammad asked.

"I'm too busy," my father replied. "I have no time for a wife."

A very powerful and well-connected khan overheard and said to Baba, "I have a daughter, Tajwar, who would make you the perfect wife. She is both beautiful and intelligent."

"I'll send my mother to consider your offer," Baba said out of respect.

Abo was responsible for making sure the girl was an appropriate match and went to visit the family. Tajwar was only twenty-three years old—ten years younger than Baba. She was every bit as beautiful and intelligent as her father had said. My father married her and stayed happily married to her until the day he died. Tajwar, or Babu, as I always called her, had grown up in one of the many mountain villages that dot the valleys from Jalalabad to the Hindu Kush. Although she had never gone to school, her mind was sharp. Baba gave her many books to read, and she learned quickly.

As a new wife, Tajwar needed a house of her own. Her father urged Baba to buy land in Karta-i-Char on the other side of Mount Asmayi to the west of Kabul. Baba was reluctant to leave his old house in downtown Kabul, but he bought six acres—enough land to build a new house for himself and Tajwar as well as houses for Gholam, Sultan, and Ali. That is how family lives in Afghanistan.

Baba's brothers all attended Nedjat High School, a German language school staffed by Germans that the Germans had built in 1924 to counter the influence of Great Britain. After the brothers graduated, each studied at a German university. Germany also built arms manufacturing plants in Afghanistan. There are two things a ruler of Afghanistan cannot say "nay" to: arms and money. Over the years the German government supplied arms and ammunition to the Afghan government and taught Afghan students and soldiers in Germany. My cousin Abbas was one of them.

At the outbreak of World War II, Zahir Shah was placed in a difficult position. Germany had long been Afghanistan's main source for aid and development because the king could not accept aid from either Britain or Russia without antagonizing one or the other. Afghanistan also had close relations with Turkey. When Turkey entered the war on the side of Germany, many Afghan military personnel and civilians were living there. Although Afghanistan had been close with Germany and Turkey, the king knew it would be foolish to have the United States, Russia, and Great Britain as enemies. Zahir Shah kept Afghanistan neutral, and ordered his military officers to leave Turkey for Iraq. Many Afghan civilians left as well. The king appointed my father ambassador to Iraq to supervise the distribution of food, shelter, and medical care.

Baba was well suited for the job because he spoke not only French, English, Dari, and Pashto but also Arabic. Babu went with him to help with the refugees and learned to speak English and Arabic.

After the war Hashim resigned, citing poor health. His successor, Mahmud Khan, tried to impose modern economic and social reforms, especially with regard to women, but as usual, all such efforts ended badly. Once again, the government needed foreign support to survive. Because of Afghanistan's strategic location, both the United States and Russia tried to win Afghanistan's favor, and Khan played them off against each other.

While Uncle Gholam was living and working in Germany, he married a German woman named Lilo, which upset Baba very much. Like my father, Gholam worked for the Foreign Ministry, and Baba felt Gholam had an obligation to Afghanistan to work there. But once Gholam married Lilo, a non-Afghan, he was forced to leave the Foreign Ministry and accept work as a cultural attaché assisting Afghan students living in Germany. My father believed strongly in the tradition that Afghan men should marry Afghan women, which generally meant relatives, unless it was a political union. Baba never truly forgave Uncle Gholam for marrying Lilo.

In 1953 Shah Mahmud resigned as prime minister. Zahir Shah appointed his cousin Daoud to replace him. Daoud appointed his brother Naim as foreign minister. Naim preferred the social life of embassy functions to the difficult work of the Foreign Ministry, so Daoud appointed my father to be Naim's deputy. Baba not only took care of the ministry's business; he recorded each meeting of the ministry in a thick, leather-bound journal, preserving not just the workings of the Foreign Ministry but the history of Afghanistan itself.

Although every ruler before him had failed, Daoud attempted to modernize Afghanistan in the style of the West and improve the lives of Afghan women. He insisted his ministers wear suits and ties. The religious conservatives of the countryside might have tolerated this if Daoud hadn't also banned women from wearing veils in public. When Islamic leaders protested, Daoud responded:

"Show me a single verse in the Koran requiring that women be veiled."

When the religious leaders continued to complain, Daoud had them imprisoned.

11

Kabul, Afghanistan, 1953

Pashtunistan

When Britain carved Pakistan out of its former colony of India in 1947, it imposed the Durand Line as the border with Afghanistan. The Pashtuns of western India who found themselves in Pakistan had never really been part of Britain's India. When it suited their purposes, they would fight on the side of the British, but the British never controlled them. The Pashtuns in Pakistan were socially, economically, religiously, and through family connections part of Afghanistan, and the area in which they lived, once part of the Afghan Empire, was naturally part of Afghanistan.

Pakistan's new provinces were named for their major ethnic groups—Sindh for the Sindhis; Balochistan for the Balochs; and Punjab for the Punjabis. For the province that was majority Pashtun, Pakistan kept the British name the "Federally Administered Tribal Areas."

After Daoud became prime minister, he proposed that these Pashtuns should decide for themselves whether they wanted to be part of Afghanistan, Pakistan, or an independent state—the same right of self-determination that many other ethnic groups were being given, including the Muslims, who had demanded the creation of Pakistan itself. When Pakistan refused, Daoud was outraged. To him this area would always be Pashtunistan and rightfully part of Afghanistan. Daoud's attempt to reunite Pashtunistan with Afghanistan would cost him his life.

When the United Nations voted to accept Pakistan as a new member, Afghanistan was the only country to vote no.

Pakistan was the United States' newest ally only because India, having been harshly ruled by Britain for over a century, became close to the Soviet Union. When U.S. vice president Richard Nixon met with Daoud in Kabul before his visit to Pakistan in December 1953, my father sat next to Daoud. Nixon announced that as a condition for resuming U.S. assistance (which had been stopped because of Daoud's ties with Russia), Afghanistan must sign the Baghdad Pact, a mutual defense agreement among Great Britain, Pakistan, Turkey, Iran, and Iraq. Daoud said he would do so only if the United States would support self-determination for the Pashtuns in Pakistan. Nixon refused, but his next words had my father stirring in his seat. "If Afghanistan will sign the Baghdad Pact, the United States is willing to use its influence with Pakistan to give Afghanistan access to the Arabian Sea."

Daoud was unmoved. "Afghanistan will never recognize Pakistan's right to Pashtunistan," he said. "I will not sign the Baghdad Pact until the Pashtunistan issue is resolved."

"Then there is nothing more to discuss," Nixon said, and the meeting was over. My father was devastated. Nixon had opened the door to Russia.

In the days following the meeting, my father tried to convince Daoud to accept Nixon's offer. "Our country needs access to the sea," he told Daoud. "You can deal with the Pashtuns in Pakistan another time." But Daoud gave my father a look that Baba knew only too well—the look of the stubborn child he had known in Paris. In a speech to the Pakistan Parliament the following day, Nixon ridiculed Daoud's position on Pashtunistan. Seething with anger, Daoud called a meeting of his ministers.

That night Uncle Ali came to our house. "I know you'll be meeting with Daoud tomorrow," he said to my father. "And I know that Daoud has been approached by Russia. I don't agree with this, and I know you don't either. But for your own sake as well as that of your brothers, when Daoud mentions this, you must hold your tongue, or it could cost us our positions."

"I don't know who is more difficult to argue with, you or Daoud," Baba said impatiently. "I have listened to you, but there are things about which you cannot compromise, and one of them is the future of our country."

"If you don't keep quiet, you'll destroy our family," Ali warned.

"And if I don't speak out, I will have to watch the destruction of our country, knowing I kept silent." He paused briefly before he spoke again. "If anyone suffers, it will be me."

At the meeting the next day, Daoud said, "Russia has offered me twenty thousand military advisors and its support on Pashtunistan. I intend to accept."

The room was silent.

Daoud looked at my father. "Mr. Popal, why are you so quiet? This isn't like you."

"Don't misunderstand me, Mr. Prime Minister," Baba replied. "I believe Pashtunistan should be part of Afghanistan as much as you do. Send the Pashtuns arms if you want and let them fight for their freedom. Nixon offered us the strength of the Baghdad Pact and access to the Arabian Sea. I think it would be foolish to lose this opportunity. The Russians have sought to control us for a long time. If we invite them in, it will be like the lamb inviting in the wolf."

"You of all people should know I will never give up Pashtunistan."

"I understand, Mr. Prime Minister. I am a Pashtun like you and share your passion. But we are a country of fourteen million. Pakistan has seventy million and the support of the United States. We cannot fight Pakistan; we cannot fight the United States; we cannot fight Russia. If we cannot solve the problem with Pakistan ourselves, how is Russia going to help? Solving this problem with war will never work. And the Russians are dangerous. Once they are here, they will never leave. If we try to use them to reclaim Pashtunistan, we will only destroy ourselves."

"What do you suggest we do then?"

"Pashtunistan must seek independence through self-determination. It is naturally a part of Afghanistan. If we remain patient, this division will not stand. Provide the Pashtuns with money and arms, and when they've won their freedom, the world will accept it. I tell you as a servant of this country I love very much that the policy you propose is foolhardy. You should not let your disdain for Nixon cause you to destroy our country. As your deputy foreign minister, I advise you to sign the Baghdad Pact and negotiate access to the Arabian Sea."

Daoud erupted. "You sound like you are talking for Pakistan!"

"If you don't realize whose country I'm speaking for now," Baba replied, "you never will."

Daoud sat unmoved.

My father rose from the table. "You are making a grave mistake, Mr. Prime Minister, and I will not be part of this decision. Since you refuse to listen, you leave me no choice but to resign."

Baba stood up and left the meeting. He walked to the Foreign Ministry and made his way down into the basement, where he opened the large leather-bound journal filled with his handwriting in which over the years he had recorded all the ministry's important meetings. After making one last entry, Baba returned to his office and cleaned out his desk.

12

Faizabad, Afghanistan, 1955

Badakhshan

After he resigned from the Foreign Ministry, Baba abandoned government service completely. He stayed at home and devoted his time to entertaining relatives and people of influence who often came to see him. But when Daoud began imprisoning those who disagreed with him, Baba decided it was time to move to Kandahar and buy a farm. Not wanting to make any enemies, he first spoke with the elders and farmers. Although Baba was now far from Kabul, Daoud did not like that Baba, who possessed so much inside knowledge about the government and who disagreed with him so passionately, was living in Kandahar, where Baba's family had powerful roots. When word of Daoud's concerns reached Zahir Shah's ears, the king became concerned and called my father to Kabul.

"I don't trust my cousin, Ustad," Zahir Shah told my father. "He's doing many rash things now, and I fear your life might be in danger."

"With due respect, Your Excellency," Baba replied, "if there were a way to smooth things over between the prime minister and myself, I would, for your sake as well as mine. I respect his love for our country and know he wants only what is best for it. I know he is honest and has done many good things. But I cannot be a party to my country being destroyed by his stubbornness and recklessness. He is like a bus driver who must get his passengers to Jalalabad, and though the highway is full of thieves, and gunmen, and bad stretches of road on which the bus can break down, he just drives off without taking into account their safety, and when the bus arrives, all the passengers are dead. If he continues with his Pashtunistan policy, Daoud will drive Afghanistan into the Russian ditch."

"They say, Your Excellency," Baba continued, "that it is better to have a smart enemy than an irresponsible friend. You can learn from a smart enemy and use the knowledge to your advantage. But an irresponsible friend is dangerous, and we are allowing our country to be driven to destruction by a reckless friend."

"Of course, you are right, Ustad. I know my cousin all too well. Someone who has the wrong side of Daoud as much as you do is not safe here. For your own sake, I'm appointing you governor of Badakhshan."

Faizabad, the capital of Badakhshan Province, sits deep in Afghanistan's northeastern corner, where Afghanistan and China meet in the long, narrow valley of the Wakhan Corridor. It is surrounded on three sides by Tajikistan, whose capital, Dushanbe, is closer than the nearest Afghan city, Mazar-i-Sharif. Faizabad is as remote and different from Kandahar as possible. Kandahar sits in the middle of a hot desert in a land of sandstorms; Faizabad sits in the high Hindu Kush in a land of earthquakes, flash floods, and landslides—a land so cold that farmers harvest just one crop a year.

Faizabad nestles in the bow of the Kokcha River. The river flows around the city in a rock-peppered gorge, the surging waters crashing into boulders with explosions of spray before the river continues its sinuous journey southward. The Kokcha brings life to the valleys but also destruction when it floods. The land fights back, often breaking the river into braided ribbons that flow around islands and shallow sandbars. On the mountain slopes above the river, bushes take root several feet from each other, as if not to encroach on one another's water. The few trees that do manage to survive—the poplar and willow—gather in clumps where the water runs slowly and where they are protected from the rushing torrent of snowmelt in the spring. Farmers' mud brick houses dot the hillsides above a patchwork quilt of wheat, rice, mulberries, and the most profitable crop of all—opium poppies.

The earth gave Faizabad one great gift: lapis lazuli, the blue stone of heaven veined with golden pyrite. The sarcophagus of the boy pharaoh Tutankhamen was encased in lapis to protect his body and soul. The Romans used it as an aphrodisiac. Afghans use it as a medicine to prevent miscarriages and cure epilepsy and dementia.

The mujahideen would use captured Russian landmines to mine lapis, then sell the precious mineral to buy weapons.

Baba, Babu, and I lived in the governor's residence in Faizabad surrounded by several acres of walled orchards and gardens. Baba's office door was always open to anyone who wanted to see him. Shortly after we arrived, Baba told his aides to spread the word that after prayers on Friday he would hold a meeting to find out what the people needed. The aides were surprised because no governor had ever done such a thing. Governors did only what profited themselves.

On the appointed Friday thousands of men arrived on foot and on horseback. Baba asked the crowd to choose a few from among them to speak for all of them. After a time several elders came forward. "What do your people need?" Baba asked.

"Water for our crops," one of the elders replied.

Another said, "There is plenty of water in the river, but our farms are on the other side of the mountain."

Baba considered the problem for a moment. "I will build a tunnel through the mountain and bring the river's water to your farms."

The villagers had heard governors make promises in the past, but nothing ever came of them. And this project was far beyond anything they had ever imagined. It would require building a tunnel through one of the highest mountains in the world. The men departed believing Baba could not do any such thing—but they did not know Baba.

The next day Baba called the minister of planning and the minister of public works, requesting equipment and engineers. They ignored him. He called the minister of the interior. The minister of the interior ignored him. Baba called the ministers again and again and told them that if he did not get engineers and dynamite by the end of the month, he would call the king.

The minister of the interior went to see Daoud. "Mr. Prime Minister," he said, "you must do something. There's a governor who is driving all of us crazy with his demands. Now he wants dynamite! When I don't respond, he complains to everyone. He has threatened to complain to the king."

"Who is this governor?"

"Rahman Popal, the governor of Badakhshan."

"Ah!" Daoud said. "Now I understand. Give him anything he wants. Just keep him away from Kabul."

Engineers and supplies poured into Faizabad. So many workers were needed that Baba hired all the inmates in the prison. He would build a tunnel.

One evening at dinner a few months after our arrival, an old man calling himself the "One Who Knows the Stars" appeared at our door. He told Baba there would be an earthquake soon and we must sleep outside for the next three days. Baba listened intently. As he was leaving, the One Who Knows the Stars turned to Baba. "Do not go near the river," he warned. "Something bad awaits you there." When the One Who Knows the Stars was gone, Babu asked my father what he meant by this.

"I have no idea," Baba replied. "They are just the mutterings of an old man."

Babu didn't like that. She told Baba he should listen to the elders here and that we should sleep in a tent in the garden for the next three nights. "If we do that," Baba said, "people will think I am a weak governor who will do whatever anyone says. We are not going to sleep outside. On this I am very firm."

That night we slept outside in a big tent in the garden. Babu held me as Baba told me a story.

"Once upon a time a great leader, Sultan Mahmoud of Ghazni, ruled over many people and had vast lands and gold. But even sultans do not know everything, so Sultan Mahmoud had a wise man as his advisor. Because the wise man was always right, Sultan Mahmoud began to worry that the people might think the wise man should be sultan, so Sultan Mahmoud came up with a plan to make the wise man look foolish. He told the wise man to meet him in the morning outside the Palace walls. The next day hundreds of men gathered outside the Palace to hear what Sultan Mahmoud was going to say to the wise man.

"'Several gates lead into the Palace,' the sultan said.

"'Four,' the wise man said. 'North, south, east and west.'

"'Precisely,' Sultan Mahmoud said. 'I am going to ride into the Palace. You are to write down how I will enter. If you are right, you will remain my advisor; if you are wrong, you must leave me.'

"The crowd murmured loudly. They had not expected such a challenge to the wise man, who they thought was Sultan Mahmoud's right hand. They all looked to see the wise man's reaction and were surprised to see him so calm. They were even more surprised when the wise man spoke.

"'You are unhappy with me because I am your mirror,' he said. 'I reflect the truth, which may be good or bad, and that sometimes displeases you. But I will do as you command and abide by the outcome.'

"The wise man wrote his answer on a piece of paper, which Sultan Mahmoud folded and placed in his pocket. Then Sultan Mahmoud mounted his horse and rode toward the Palace. All eyes followed him. When he reached a solid section of wall, Sultan Mahmoud stopped his horse, looked back at the wise man, and smiled. Suddenly many men with sledgehammers appeared and with great effort smashed a huge opening in the wall. Sultan Mahmoud proudly rode through it into the Palace grounds. When the sultan rode back to the wise man, all the men smiled at Sultan Mahmoud's cleverness.

"Sultan Mahmoud took the paper with the wise man's answer out of his pocket, unfolded it, and with a grand gesture read it to the crowd: 'Your Excellency will not enter the Palace through any gate but create your own way through.'

"Everyone gasped, including Sultan Mahmoud, and forever after, Sultan Mahmoud listened to the advice of the wise man."

After the first two nights in the tent, Baba wanted to go inside and sleep in his own bed, but Babu was adamant. "It's only for one more night."

On the third night we were awakened by the ground shaking beneath us so violently that we feared our tent would collapse on us. Daylight revealed our house was still standing, but many things inside had been tossed to the floor, some broken. Babu seemed quite pleased with herself.

Badakhshan sits in the path of the greatest horsemen in history—the Mongols from the Asian Steppe. The people there are great horsemen who live on their horses. When I turned six, I learned to ride a horse. A small horse, it is true, but a horse nonetheless. It was the beginning of my love affair with horses.

When my father's tunnel through the mountain was almost finished and the time came for the last section of mountain to be cleared, the engineers called him to discuss the final detonations. He took me with him.

When we arrived at the river across from the mountain where the tunnel would appear, several engineers were already down by the riverbank. Baba walked the short distance to the riverbank to talk to them, leaving me behind in the car.

As Baba talked with the engineers, a man ran up to them frantically waving his arms, "You must leave immediately," he shouted. "The last section of the mountain is about to be dynamited." Before anyone could react, the entire side of the mountain exploded in a huge cloud of dust and debris, shaking our car violently, raining rocks down on its roof and coating it in dust. Frightened and confused, I rolled down the window to see what had happened. Several men were making their way from the riverbank to the car, struggling to carry a limp bundle. One of the men opened my door, took me into his arms, and held me against his chest as I struggled to see what was lying on the ground.

It was Baba.

His left leg was bloody and mangled, and he was moaning terribly. "Baba! Baba!" I cried, tears staining my dust-covered face. The sounds of my crying filled the car as we all drove away from the river.

The doctor at the local clinic could do nothing, so we drove Baba to the governor's house and laid him in bed. Babu was beside herself, not knowing what to do.

Soon several tribal elders appeared at our house.

"Are you doctors?" Baba asked with much difficulty.

"Nay, but we have much experience fixing the broken arms and legs of *buzkashi* players."

"If you are good enough for buzkashi players, you are good enough for me," Baba said.

The elders cleaned and wrapped Baba's leg, then elevated it with a rope attached to the ceiling. "Don't let anyone move your leg until we tell you," one of the elders said. "You are not a young buzkashi player, and the break is very bad. It will take a long time to heal."

A month later the king heard of my father's accident. Two doctors from Kabul arrived in a helicopter. The elders told the doctors not to touch Baba's leg, but the doctors insisted on taking over. "The bone hasn't been set straight," one of the doctors said. "If it heals like this, one leg will be shorter than the other. We are going to have to break it and reset it."

"Nay!" one of the elders protested. "We will make him a shoe with a higher heel. If you break the bone, it won't heal properly."

The doctors ignored him and began lowering the leg. There was a loud snap. Baba screamed.

I have always been terrified of heights and hated loud noises. The helicopter that flew Baba, Babu, and me back to Kabul soared upward in a deafening roar. Even now, the whup-whup-whup of a helicopter sickens me. After arriving in Kabul, Baba, Babu, and I flew to Germany, where Baba could get special treatment. Baba endured sixteen operations.

I hated Germany. I was seven years old and a foreigner in a land of light-skinned, light-haired people who despised me and let me know it. Every day was a misery of taunts and loneliness. Every day I prayed we could leave. When I visited Baba in the hospital, he was always in pain. The nurses regarded us with disdain, as if we were taking advantage of medical treatment we did not deserve—even though the king was paying for it.

Baba's leg became infected and developed gangrene. The doctors amputated it.

The next day Uncle Gholam took me to see Baba. When Baba saw me, he asked, "How was school today, Bari?"

"It was okay," I lied. "How are you feeling, Baba?"

"My leg feels good for a change. It feels light. Come, help me sit up."

As we raised him up, a puzzled look crossed his face. He leaned forward. "My leg—it's gone. . . . Who decided this?"

"The doctors said they had to amputate it or you would die," Gholam replied.

"I see," Baba said. "Well, at least I'm no longer in pain."

But that was only the effect of the drugs. Once that wore off, Baba suffered great pain for the rest of his life.

13

Kabul, Afghanistan, 1959

Baba Naeem

Baba now wore a prosthetic on his stump of a leg, allowing him to walk—though with great discomfort. Zahir Shah welcomed him home and asked him to work for him as an advisor. With Daoud still prime minister, Baba was reluctant to accept, but in the end he obeyed the king's wishes.

Baba was driven back and forth to the Palace by Baba Naeem, a bullheaded Turkoman my father had hired away from the Foreign Ministry. Baba Naeem had worked his way up from washing official cars to bringing them to the drivers to being a driver himself. He always called my father "Mr. Ambassador" because of Baba's ambassadorship in Iraq during the war. I think it made Baba Naeem feel important to be the driver of "Mr. Ambassador." He lived in a small cement block room at the back of our garage. As far as I knew, we were the only family he had. When Baba Naeem wasn't driving us somewhere, he sat in a chair in front of the garage keeping a watchful eye on my comings and goings. When he saw me doing things I shouldn't (which was often), Baba Naeem would tell my father. No one—not my uncles, not even Babu, who was generally kind to everyone—liked Baba Naeem. He was mean to everyone and complained loudly about everything, even his meals. "This food is bad!" Baba Naeem would shout, and my father would sigh, "What's he complaining about now? It's the same food everyone eats. He should be happy he has food to eat."

I was constantly trying to jump into the driver's seat of our car and play with the steering wheel. Baba Naeem was constantly trying to stop me because, even though it was our car, Baba Naeem thought of it as his child. Each week Baba Naeem drove my father and me to the marketplace. My father liked to take me on trips because he considered them opportunities to instruct me. He sat in the front seat because he needed room to extend his prosthetic leg. On one such trip Baba Naeem and a bicycle entered an intersection at the same time. The bicyclist loudly rang his bell, and Naeem slammed on the brakes.

"What are you doing?" my father shouted, acting like a kind of backseat driver in the front seat. "Why did you stop for a bicycle? You must be getting old. You stop at anything. Drive like this and you're going to cause an accident."

Baba Naeem squeezed the steering wheel as if he wanted to crush it. Then he turned off the engine, got out, slammed the car door, and strode off.

"Go get him, Bari," my father said.

I ran off after him, calling as loudly as I could," Come back, Baba Naeem!"

When I reached him, he said, "Nay!" and kept on walking.

"You must return to the car!" I shouted.

"Nay!"

"The car is blocking traffic! You must come back and move it!"

Baba Naeem stopped and turned to me. "I'll only do so on one condition," he said.

"Nay, do as I say," I told him.

By now a crowd had gathered to watch in amusement as this young boy and his driver argued in the middle of the street, traffic backing up farther and farther. It was a stalemate. I returned to the back seat, my father gazing out the side window, fuming.

Suddenly Baba Naeem appeared in my father's face.

"Have I ever involved myself in your work in the government, Mr. Ambassador? Nay! Then I don't want you involving yourself in my driving!"

"You're diwana! Get in the car and drive," my father ordered. Then he turned to me. "And you, Bari, I don't want you to speak like that to our driver ever again."

I scowled but held my tongue.

Baba Naeem said, "Then you understand what I'm saying, Mr. Ambassador."

My father just stared straight ahead, not saying a word.

"Good!" Baba Naeem said. "Then I'll continue doing my job."

He climbed into the driver's seat and drove on.

Each autumn Baba Naeem and my father made the four-hour drive over the Hindu Kush Mountains north of Kabul to our farm in the Baghlan River Valley, where the farmers grew cotton and sugar beets. When I was nine, Baba took me with him for the first time.

It was a frightening journey. Baba Naeem had to negotiate narrow, unpaved roads cut into the mountainside. If he missed a turn, we would plummet down the face of the mountain to the valley a thousand feet below. And there were bandits—which is why an armed guard was sitting next to me in the back seat. As we ascended the mountain, the steep road turned white with snow. Suddenly the road curved sharply, but the car did not, and we found ourselves sliding toward the edge of the cliff. In my stomach I could feel us plunging to our deaths, the car exploding on impact. Right before we reached the edge of the cliff, the car stopped.

Baba Naeem tried to back up, but the wheels just spun in place. Our guard got out and wedged a large rock under each front tire. I was convinced we were going to freeze to death.

A truck appeared from around the bend and stopped. "What are you doing driving in the mountains without chains?" the truck driver asked my father.

Baba glared at Baba Naeem, "I asked him the same thing."

Baba Naeem shrugged. "I didn't know there would be snow so early," he said, "so you cannot put the blame on me."

"You should've known there would be snow in the mountains!" I burst out. "There's always snow in the mountains!"

"This is your first time driving to the farm, little one," Baba Naeem said, "and now you're an expert on snow, and you think you can tell me how to drive? I should leave you here and go on with this truck driver!" He got out of the car and stood next to the truck, pouting and flapping his arms to keep warm.

Who is he calling little one? I thought.

While Baba Naeem sulked, the truck driver installed chains on our tires. I was sure the driver did this because he didn't want to be stuck with Baba Naeem. The truck driver continued on his way down the mountain. Baba Naeem got back in the car. Scowling and gripping the steering wheel hard, he drove off.

At every curve of the road I worried he might drive us off the face of the mountain.

We descended into the valley floor and arrived alive, if a bit shaken. We spent the night at a local farmhouse. The next morning we rose to find the farmers who worked for my father waiting outside with horses. "Choose one," a farmer said to me. I could hardly contain my excitement—like the very first time I had grabbed a horse's reins in Faizabad. I looked the horses over very carefully and stopped before a pure black one who seemed eager to run. "I'll take this one," I said, grabbing the reins. The horse snorted loudly and reared back wildly on its haunches.

"Nay," said the farmer." Not that one. That one is a crazy horse."

That only made me want to ride it more. "I want this horse," I said.

"You don't know these horses," Baba said. "Listen to him!"

"Nay. I will have this horse!"

"Fine!" Baba said. "Give it to him. Let him break his neck!"

As soon as I jumped on, the horse took off running as if stung by a bee.

"This is good, Bari!" Baba shouted after me. "You will learn something today!"

I pulled hard on the reins, but it was a clever horse and had taken the bit into its mouth in such a way that I couldn't control it. The harder I pulled, the faster it ran. I dropped the reins and grabbed the horn of the saddle, holding on for my life. The farmers gave chase, but the black horse only ran faster until one of the farmers pulled alongside my horse, took hold of its reins, and gradually brought it to a halt. I dismounted, shaken—but elated. Then I was hoisted—rather roughly, I thought—onto a different horse.

"See what happens when you don't listen!" Baba called to me.

"I did listen," I shouted back, "but I liked that horse!"

Over the next few hours we rode through vast fields of sugar beets and cotton, up and down hills covered with rows of grapevines and through stands of pistachio and pomegranate trees. All the while on grassy hillsides Karakul sheep grazed like living cotton balls. My bottom became sore from riding. "When will we reach our farm?" I asked.

"Bari," Baba replied with the trace of smile, "we have been on our farm the whole time."

14

Kabul, Afghanistan, 1961

Kite Flying

When we returned to Kabul from our winter break in Jalalabad, the first thing I always did was go see my grandmother Abo. She was seventy and mostly confined to her bed because she could no longer walk. Her face was small and narrow with a long thin nose and thin lips, which made her mouth look severe. Her eyes were dark and deep, shining with a sharp intelligence that measured you from behind metal-framed glasses. Although strong in mind and spirit, she was frail as a bird, just as thin, and ate like one. But this tiny frame held as much power as my father. She controlled the family finances—not only the money my grandfather Mukarram had left her and the profits from Baba and Uncle Ali's farms but the money my father and uncles earned from their government positions as well.

Our home was divided in two. Abo lived in the back. Although she was housebound, she had many visitors and was never bored. Most Afghans, especially those in the countryside, do not work from nine in the morning until five at night, five days a week. They are farmers and herders and work to the rhythm of crops and animals. They often have free time to travel and visit, which they can do without asking anyone's permission. Abo was the mother of four sons who held powerful positions in the government. There was a constant flow of guests to see her: people from Kandahar and Gandamak, Logar and Badakhshan. Some came to visit, some to ask favors, some to ask advice. Her part of the house had many bedrooms because many visitors needed a place to stay after their long journeys. She had her own kitchen and cook. And she was never alone with two granddaughters who were always somewhere about. I was often there as well. "How is school going, Bari?" she would ask, and "How are you getting along with your uncles?" She was well aware that I was a very strong-willed child who was constantly in trouble. "Does Baba still love you?" she would joke.

60

Her bedroom windows were covered because the light bothered her eyes. The dimly lit room held an almost mystical atmosphere for me. She looked at me eyes to eyes one day. "If you ever have a problem, Bari," she said, "you come straight to see me, baleh?"

"Baleh," I answered. "I will."

"If there are things you feel you cannot tell anyone else, you come to me and tell me, baleh?"

"Baleh."

Abo was my protector.

During the fall months, when the winds rose, I was on the flat rooftop of our house as often as possible—much to the dismay of my father. It was the best place in all of Karta-i-Char to watch battle kites dance their deadly tango in the sky, each maneuvering to cut another kite's string. "Kite flying is a waste of time!" Baba would lecture me. "You should be studying!"

Ignoring Baba's words once again, I was on our rooftop with my cousin Shabir, flying my favorite red kite, which I had purchased from an old kite seller in the bazaar. The spars were of Indian bamboo, strong and flexible; the paper so light, it was translucent. I had prepared the string for battle myself, first boiling rice to make a sticky paste, then crushing glass into a powder—cutting myself in the process, so that when I mixed the rice paste and crushed glass together, I added my own blood. I formed the sharp paste into a sticky pink ball and pulled the string through it. When the paste dried, my kite's string had the teeth to sever the string of any opponent. I launched my crimson kite into Kabul's blue dome of a battlefield and flicked my wrist at just the right moment. My opponent's kite seemed to hesitate, as if startled, then it spiraled downward, crashing to earth.

"You never let me have a turn," Shabir whined. "You've cut five kites already!"

Suddenly, over Shabir's complaining, I heard Baba's car door slam shut as Shabir reached out to grab the *charka* from my hands. For once I let him take it. I slipped quietly downstairs to hide in my room while his eyes were on the sky.

"Shabir! You know what I think of kite flying during school!" I heard Baba's loud voice on the roof.

"Please don't tell my father," Shabir begged.

"I have every intention of telling your father," Baba said.

My father and Shabir's father, Uncle Ali, both hated kite flying. They both shared a strong sense of duty and great respect for authority, learning, and family. Baba was big as a bear, with a large, round head and a serious demeanor, but this seriousness was tempered by a dry sense of humor. Uncle Ali was short, thin, impatient, and ill-tempered. He had no sense of humor.

Getting Shabir into trouble and myself out of it at the same time was almost too good to be true. That evening Uncle Ali exploded. "Shabir!" he yelled. "How do you think it will look if the son of the minister of education does poorly at school? I will not tolerate it. I will hear no more of kite flying." He gave Shabir a note to give to his teacher the next day.

The teacher read the note, picked up a wooden pointer, and ordered Shabir to the front of the class. Shabir couldn't stand any pain and always swore when he was hurt. He held out his hands. The teacher smacked them hard as Shabir howled and cursed.

After school, when I saw Shabir and he told me what had happened, I said, "Thank God I left the rooftop when I did. It must have been fate."

The following week Uncle Ali caught me flying my kite on the roof. He brought me downstairs, wrote out a note, and handed it to me. I threw the note to the floor and took off running. To my great surprise, Uncle Ali ran after me.

I ran to my grandmother's bedroom and leaped beside her on the bed. Uncle Ali was tough, but he was no match for Abo. He rushed into her bedroom, then stopped in his tracks, seething with anger and frustration. He wanted to throttle me but couldn't—not while Abo had her arm around me. He stared at me, and I stared back, neither of us blinking.

I felt very powerful.

"Why do you keep staring at us like that, Ali?" Abo asked, annoyed. "Sit down!"

Uncle Ali immediately took a seat in an armchair at the foot of the bed. We all sat there in silence, Abo waiting for Uncle Ali to say something, Uncle Ali remaining silent. After a while he got up and left.

Uncle Ali couldn't punish me himself, but he would not be denied. The next day at school, I got the worst caning of my life.

15

Kabul, Afghanistan, 1962

The New Great Game

The following summer Pakistan accused Afghanistan of aiding the Pashtun revolt in its western territory—Daoud's Pashtunistan. Daoud, in turn, accused Pakistan of imprisoning hundreds of Pashtun tribal leaders and sending troops into Afghanistan. When Daoud demanded self-determination for the Pakistan Pashtuns, Pakistan closed the Khyber Pass, shutting off the main route for supplies to Jalalabad and Kabul. U.S. president John F. Kennedy offered to help resolve the crisis. Russia agreed to provide Afghanistan military aid, including Russian jets, tanks, and artillery. Afghanistan severed all diplomatic ties with Pakistan.

With no food supplies crossing the border, the people of Afghanistan began starving. The United States forced Pakistan to allow the United States to deliver humanitarian aid to Afghanistan. That summer, again at the urging of the United States, the Shah of Iran mediated the dispute between Afghanistan and Pakistan, and diplomatic ties were restored. Once again trucks rolled through the Khyber Pass, and the new Great Game between the United States and Russia (rather than Great Britain and Russia) continued as the United States and Russia competed for influence by building power stations, irrigation channels, highways, airports, and schools—including Nangarhar University, only the second university in all Afghanistan.

Baba, no longer able to tolerate Daoud's continued obsession with Pashtunistan and his dangerous alliance with Russia, told Zahir Shah he would no longer serve as an advisor. Zahir Shah reluctantly accepted Baba's decision. That night Uncle Ali marched into our house at dinner, demanding to know why my father was no longer advising the king.

"What's the use?" Baba said. "My greatest desire is to see Afghanistan become peaceful, modern, prosperous, and truly independent. But I see only foreign dependence, ancient tribal ways, and religious fanaticism. The country is falling apart. Daoud's desire to wrest Pashtunistan from Pakistan will be the end of us. I told the king this, but he can do nothing against his hardheaded cousin. Nay, I will no longer be a part of this."

"If you keep on this course," Ali said, "you will get us all in trouble."

"The only way to avoid making enemies in Afghanistan is to say nothing: 'see no evil, hear no evil, speak no evil'—that is a monkey law, and I will not follow a monkey law. I will speak the truth when it needs to be spoken, even to Daoud and even if he doesn't want to hear it."

Uncle Ali, who always looked very tough, now looked broken.

"If good people like you refuse to work in the government, that is a very bad sign," he said.

Baba shrugged. "These are bad times, and I'm afraid things will only get worse."

16

Kabul, Afghanistan, 1963

The King Acts

Zahir Shah, unhappy with how his cousin was governing the country, which was falling into chaos, drafted a new constitution that barred members of the royal family from holding positions in the government. Daoud was forced to resign. The new prime minister, Dr. Mohammad Yusuf, had been a classmate of Uncle Ali at Nedjat High School. Dr. Yusuf named Uncle Ali his deputy prime minister and minister of education. At the same time, Zahir Shah appointed my father to the Senate.

The new constitution created a two-house Parliament: a one hundred–seat Wolesi Jirga (House of the People), elected by the people; and a twenty-eight-seat Meshrano Jirga (House of the Elders, known as the Senate), appointed by the king. But it had a fundamental flaw—it did not really give any power to the people. The king appointed the prime minister, the king appointed the senators, the king appointed the Cabinet members, and as commander in chief, the king controlled the military.

Afghanistan had a new constitution, but the rivalry between the United States and Russia had not changed. They continued to compete to win Afghanistan's favor. A U.S. airline, Pan Am, provided new planes for Ariana Afghan Airlines. Russia not only provided weapons and military equipment but also agreed to build a nuclear reactor to counter the nuclear capabilities of America's ally Pakistan.

But the greatest weapon Russia was given in its battle to control Afghanistan was contained in the king's new constitution: the right to form political parties.

We were in Jalalabad on our winter break when the king invited Baba to lunch at the Winter Palace. Baba took me along with him, of course, so I would not miss this opportunity to learn. I was surprised to see dozens of other guests. "Why so many people?" I asked my father.

"When the king is in Jalalabad, he invites all of the tribal chiefs and many elders for miles around to meet with him for lunch. A wise king listens to his people."

A servant appeared in a bright white shirt and white-gloved hands and set a plate of food before the king. Then a strange thing happened. A man standing next to the king started eating the king's food before the king or anyone else had taken a bite.

"Why is that man eating the king's food?" I asked Baba.

"Not now," my father whispered, and I immediately held my tongue.

After we left the Palace, I asked my father about what I had seen.

"When the king travels from the Palace in Kabul, many who work in the kitchen are unknown to him. The man you saw is the king's food taster, who makes sure the king's meal has not been poisoned."

"The king must not think much of him if he doesn't care if he gets poisoned," I said.

"Nay," Baba said. "The king's taster is a very powerful man from the Panjshir Valley. His job is an honor, and most important, he has the ear of the king."

17

Jalalabad, Afghanistan, Winter 1963

Duck Hunting

Abo, who was my refuge, my confidante, the one I always turned to, the one who did not judge but listened, was gone. Her death was announced on Radio Kabul. For three days following her death, Abo's body lay in a wooden box in our house as relatives came to pay their last respects. On the fourth day her sons carried her casket to a hearse parked outside our house. The limousine in which Baba, Babu, and I rode was so long, Baba could stretch out his prosthetic leg while seated in the back seat. Hundreds and hundreds of cars followed behind us as far as my eyes could see. In the family plot at the base of a mountain outside Kabul, we laid Abo to rest.

That winter, as we did each year, Baba, Babu, and I made the journey to Jalalabad from Kabul's bitter cold. Jalalabad was named for Jalaludin Mohammad Akbar, a Mughal emperor—*Jalal* plus *abad*, "city" in Urdu. The surrounding Safid Koh Mountains shelter Jalalabad from the winds, making a perfect climate to grow oranges, rice, sugarcane, and olives for olive oil. It is a green oasis in a country of barren deserts and snowy mountains where the winters are mild. Afghan families have always sought refuge there from Kabul's freezing winters, and we were no different. Baba bought a house there. It was a two-story brick house painted white, with seven bedrooms upstairs for our family and our many visitors, including all of my uncles, aunts, and cousins. Each winter we trucked our furniture from Kabul to Jalalabad—even the red-patterned tribal rugs that covered the stone floors. Rugs are as important as gardens in Afghanistan. They bring color, warmth, and softness to what is often a harsh, cold environment—especially where the floors are dirt or stone. Each year at the end of our stay in Jalalabad, the rugs returned with us to Kabul.

Now we needed a garden, and for this we needed water. Baba

found a local landscaper, Mohammad, who installed pipes to irrigate the land and repaired them whenever they broke. Baba and Mohammad became good friends, and I would walk with them to the marketplace, stroll around our gardens with them, and visit Mohammad at his house with my father. Sixteen years later Mohammad would risk his life for me.

When a general's family came to visit Baba, I could not take my eyes off the rifles his two teenage sons carried. "What are you doing with the guns?" I asked them.

"Going duck hunting," the older one replied.

"Where are you hunting ducks here?" asked Baba, sounding surprised. I was surprised as well because I thought Baba knew everything.

"There's a pond behind the hills across the river where ducks come to feed."

"What do you do with the ducks?" I asked.

"Our mother makes pillows from the feathers," said the younger boy.

"And duck stew," added the older.

Duck stew! We never ate anything as interesting as duck stew. "Can I go?" I asked Baba.

"Nay. You're too young." I loved Baba, but at times like this I hated him.

"Please, Baba!" I cried. At that moment hunting ducks was the only thing in the world that mattered to me.

"Nay! We are not duck hunters." Baba was the most stubborn father anyone ever had. Perhaps that was why I was the most stubborn child anyone ever had.

I would go duck hunting no matter what he said.

After the brothers departed, I sneaked out of the house and followed them. The older one turned around and waved me away.

"Go home!" he shouted.

"I want to go with you."

"You're too young. Don't you listen?"

"I know how to swim," I said.

"The river isn't a pond. The current is very strong, and you're too small."

My eyes filled with tears; my lips quivered.

"All right," the boy said. "You can come with us, but you can't cross the river."

My face instantly brightened.

When we reached the river, the older boy said, "Stay here and wait for us to return."

They swam across, trailing special gun cases attached to ropes, then climbed the bank on the far side and walked until they disappeared around a low hill. I waited.

A shot rang out, then another. Soon the boys reappeared around the hill. They emerged from the river, each holding a duck, which hung loosely, still dripping blood.

A few days later they headed for the river again. "I'm going to cross the river with you today," I told them.

"Nay, you are not," they said.

"Baleh, I am!"

"Nay!"

"Baleh!"

"Nay!"

I followed them to the river, and when they were halfway across, I dove in. The water was cold, but the sun was warm. Just as they reached the opposite bank, the river's strong current caught hold of me. I waved my hands and called for help.

"You're so stupid!" the older brother yelled. "You don't listen!"

The boys took off running, following me down the river. I paddled desperately, fighting the current. The younger one jumped in and swam out to me, put his arm around me and swam me back to shallow water. The older one hauled me up onto the bank.

I sat soaking, dejected, awaiting their anger.

"You're a strong little fellow," the older one said. "You can come with us when you catch your breath. Walk behind us very slowly, the ducks scare easily and will fly off at the faintest sound."

The path led to a pond guarded by cattails, reeds, and tall grasses. As the older boy climbed up a small hill overlooking the pond, I followed the younger one to an opening in the reeds. Four ducks were feeding. They bobbed their heads underwater, then raised their bills to the sky and swallowed. The boy raised his rifle. *ping* . . . *ping*. Two ducks took off in a burst of glistening water and beating wings. Two lay floating dead on the pond.

I was a duck hunter.

18

A Farm North of Kabul, Afghanistan, 1964

Buzkashi

Uncle Ali's farm was not far from Kabul to the north, where his farmers grew grapes that made the sweetest raisins in all Afghanistan. Shabir and I always looked forward to our trips to the farm because we could ride horses, which Uncle Ali forbid because he thought it was too dangerous. We paid the farmer to let us ride his horses—and added a little extra so he would not tell Uncle Ali.

Afghans are by necessity a warrior culture. The men enjoy dogfights, kite battles, and buzkashi—a violent and chaotic competition, a kind of war. Even when Afghanistan is not at war, the men still play at war. The same strength, craftiness, teamwork, and communication required by buzkashi would help the mujahideen defeat the Russians. It is Afghanistan's national sport and a passion of all Afghans—Pashtuns, Uzbeks, Hazaras, Tajiks, and Turkmen. In the cool winter months thousands of men (never women) watch hundreds of riders compete as Afghan musicians play above the noise of the crowd and the grunts of the horses. The horsemen try to grab a burlap sack containing a disemboweled, decapitated goat carcass, carry it around a post, and drop it into a chalk circle—the "circle of justice." Most of the riders never get near the goat carcass.

Shabir and I made up our own game of buzkashi using a burlap bag stuffed with rotten grape leaves for the goat's carcass. Our horses' hooves kicked up clouds of dust as we galloped into each other, hitting and kicking—often ignoring the burlap bag altogether. We played for the sheer joy of it, but real buzkashi players—the *chapandaz*—play for money, special turbans, and clothing as well as the honor of their village. They know their horses and the tricks of the trade: having the horse spread its legs so the rider can grab the goat; head butting a competitor to knock him off his horse; pulling the horse's ear with scarred hands and gnarled fingers so it will kick a player and knock him off his horse. So many players break limbs getting thrown from their horses, the elders have become experts at fixing broken limbs. Shabir and I were great chapandaz. And eventually, like a great chapandaz, I broke a rib.

I had to tell Uncle Ali.

"How could you break a rib?" he demanded.

"I fell out of a tree."

"Well, what do you expect if you go around climbing trees?" he said. "Don't climb any more trees."

Shabir and I didn't climb any trees—but we continued to play buzkashi.

19

Kabul, Afghanistan, 1965

Lessons

Baba Naeem never let anyone near my father's shiny black Mercedes—which Baba Naeem thought of as his car—so when our cook asked Baba Naeem to teach him to drive, Baba Naeem refused. One day I overheard Baba Naeem complaining loudly to the cook, "Ever since I refused to teach you to drive, my food has been worse than ever!"

Baba Naeem finally gave in and agreed to teach the cook to drive. "When can we start?" the cook asked eagerly. "In the morning after breakfast," Baba Naeem replied.

That night Baba Naeem had the best lamb shish kabob he'd had in a long time.

"Learning to drive is a process," Baba Naeem explained to the cook the next morning as if he were lecturing at a great university. "You can't just get behind the wheel and go." He led the cook to the front of the car and lifted the hood. "Here is the engine," he said, pointing. "And this is the carburetor, which mixes the gas and air." Then he slammed the hood shut. "Tomorrow I'll teach you more about driving."

The cook kept waiting to get behind the wheel, but at each lesson Baba Naeem only demonstrated how to turn on the lights or how to use the windshield wipers. The cook continued preparing delicious meals for Baba Naeem in the hope that things would change.

After several weeks Baba Naeem's lessons hadn't change, but the taste of his food suddenly did. The next day the cook sat behind the wheel in the driver's seat. He put the car in gear and slowly steered it out of the garage and into the street as Baba Naeem talked excitedly, pointing this way and that. The huge smile never left the cook's face as he and Baba Naeem wove down the street together.

A few weeks after the cook learned to drive, Baba Naeem was at the wheel of our black Mercedes driving Baba and me to Logar, where my grandfather Mukarram's family had settled after their exile to Gandamak. Baba was going to visit old friends. Suddenly the engine lost power, and Baba Naeem was forced to pull the car off the road. He opened the hood, poked around, disconnected something, then flagged down a truck heading back to Kabul. While Baba Naeem returned to the city for a new part, Baba and I stood next to the car.

"I haven't heard of anyone dying in the very cold winter this year, Bari, have you?" Baba asked me.

"Nay, I have not," I answered.

"Why is that, do you think?"

"Because everyone is healthy?"

"Nay. It is because everyone has warm clothing to wear and a roof over his head." He paused to let this sink in. "And I have not heard of anyone dying of hunger this year," he said. "Why is that?"

"Because they have enough to eat?"

"Baleh, that's right. All year round the mountains are covered in snow, which melts and flows into rivers that nourish the farmers' crops to feed our people. Of course, we have our wealthy and our poor like all countries, but the people with money share with those who have less. If we create a good, honest government that will use the money to build schools and hospitals so the people are educated and healthy, the poor will have the means to improve their lives. That is why it's important that government be honest and use its money for the people."

I nodded to show I was paying attention.

"If you look carefully," Baba went on, "we live in a kind of natural paradise. We are surrounded by the most beautiful mountains and fruit-filled valleys in the world, given life by the mountains' waters. We have cities where we can escape winter's cold grasp. Afghanistan is like a gift from heaven, with a beauty created by nature, not man."

Baba was not a man of much passion. It seemed he saved it all for his beloved Afghanistan, and I felt it too: the pride in my country, the love of this gift from God.

Suddenly men in gebis and turbans of white, brown, and black emerged from a grove of trees. Although we were not far from Kabul, here was a world apart. No one here dressed in Western clothing, especially not the suit and tie my father was wearing, which was common in Kabul. In Kabul women walked about freely in dresses and skirts. Here women rarely ventured outside, and when they did, they were concealed under a shawl and accompanied by a male relative.

"You must come be my guest and share my food and drink," one of the men offered.

"Nay, come to my house," invited another, "we have food in abundance and chocolate."

Others offered their hospitality as well, and soon they were vying among themselves to host these two strangers from the city.

"I have a bad leg," Baba the diplomat explained, "and cannot walk very far. We will rest under that walnut tree and would be honored if you would bring us something to eat and drink."

The men stopped arguing and rushed off.

When they returned, Baba invited them to eat with us, but only a few did so and only because Baba insisted. As we ate, Baba stopped frequently to ask questions: "What kind of work do you do? Does everyone here have a house? Do you have enough food? Are there any sick?" Baba saved the most important question for last: "How are your horses?"

The men said they grew potatoes, apples, and nuts, which they shipped to Kabul on trucks.

"It is difficult to find trucks to take our goods to market in Kabul," one farmer complained. "The roads are very bad, and there is not enough water for our crops in the summer."

"Do you have someone to represent you in Parliament?" Baba asked.

"Baleh," they replied, "but he's no help."

"Then you should elect someone who will help," Baba said. He was always the diplomat, always the scholar, and most important, always the listener.

The sound of an approaching truck interrupted our conversation. The truck stopped. Baba Naeem got out, proudly holding up a set of spark plug wires in his hand.

As we continued on our journey, Baba looked as content as I'd ever seen him. He turned to me with a smile and said, "Tell me Bari, where else on earth can you find hospitality like this?" When I did not respond, he said. "We learned a lot today, Bari."

I hated having to take these trips with my father, hated having to sit and listen to him talk to elders and village people about their problems. I wanted to be kite flying or riding a horse or playing with Shabir. "Nay, I learned nothing," I said.

Baba was silent for a moment, letting my answer hang in the air. Then he repeated, "We learned a lot today, Bari." And though he said nothing more, I could hear in my mind the words "whether you liked it or not."

20

Ghazni, Afghanistan, 1967

Sia

My mother came from a tribe of great horsemen who lived in a valley to the west of Kabul, near Paghman. Ever since I first rode a horse in Faizabad, I wanted nothing more than a horse of my own. When I was eleven, I asked my mother to buy me a horse. "It pleases me to hear that you want to follow in the footsteps of your ancestors," she said. And I was so happy. But then Baba butted in: "Why do you need a horse? Kabul is no place for a horse."

Babu held much power in the family, but when it came to getting me a horse, Baba won.

Every Independence Day people from all over Afghanistan gathered outside Kabul with their best horses. There was buzkashi and horse racing, Afghan style—riding very fast while shooting at targets. Owners came to show off their magnificent beasts. Although it was called "Independence Day," it wasn't celebrated on August 19, the day Afghanistan gained its independence, because August in Kabul is too hot for horses. The king moved the celebration to the cooler days in September. It was at one such celebration when I was fifteen that I saw the most beautiful horse I'd ever seen. It was shiny and black as obsidian, with a blazing splash of white on its forehead. I had to have it. I asked around to find out who the owner was. "He's over there," someone said. "He's from Ghazni."

I walked up to the owner. "I want to buy that horse."

"He's not for sale," he replied.

"But I must have that horse!" I implored him.

He stared at me for a moment as if he could not believe his ears.

"Are you crazy?" he said. "Why should I sell you that horse? My great joy is owning beautiful horses. I want to buy more of them, not sell them. Nay, I will never sell that horse."

A couple of months later I still could not get this horse out of my mind. Two cousins of mine, Abdul and his brother Pirooz, who were police officers, came to visit. I told them the story of the horse. "I'm working in Ghazni," Pirooz said. "I can find out where the owner lives."

"That would be very good," I said. "I will call him and offer him money for that horse."

"Nay, that won't work," Pirooz said. "You must send an elder to ask for you."

"Nay, I want to do this myself," I insisted.

My plan was to keep the horse on a large vacant lot in the rear of our compound and take him to the warmth of Jalalabad on winter break. I knew Baba would not agree, so I did not tell him. I would rely on Babu to help me convince him that it was a good idea. But first, I had to go to Ghazni to get my horse.

The next weekend Abdul and I drove to Pirooz's house in Ghazni. The city is situated on an elevated plateau seven thousand feet above sea level, with winters so severe, it is said, that on more than one occasion the entire population perished in snowstorms. Worse, its strategic location between Kandahar and Kabul put it on the route of all conquerors. Like many Afghan cities, it has seen great power and great destruction. The king of Persia arrived first, followed by Alexander the Great. In the eleventh century Sultan Mahmoud of Ghazni (the Sultan Mahmoud of my father's story in Badakhshan) created an empire larger than Afghanistan today. He brought Islam to northern India, enriching himself, as all great rulers have done, by conquering and looting. But Sultan Mahmoud was also a man of culture who used his wealth to support scholars, philosophers, and poets. In 1747, under Ahmad Shah Durrani, Ghazni became part of the new Afghan kingdom. But this once beautiful, wealthy city, the only walled city in Afghanistan, was destroyed by the British in the First Anglo-Afghan War. The Taliban would use Ghazni as a base from which to attack Kabul.

Pirooz greeted us warmly and brought us food and drink. After we spoke a while, I talked him into calling the horse's owner. The owner agreed to meet us at a local restaurant.

"You must let me talk with him first," Pirooz said, and I reluctantly agreed.

The owner was already seated when we arrived—and he did not look happy. We joined him and introduced ourselves. After Pirooz explained the situation, the owner raised himself in his seat, glared at me, and shook his head. "Remember our discussion in Kabul?" he said firmly. "I said 'Nay.' My answer remains exactly the same: 'Nay.'"

"But I insist," I said.

The owner looked at me first in disbelief, then in exasperation. Then he walked out.

"You should not have insisted," Pirooz said. "I told you to let me do the talking. Why did you do that?"

I ignored his question and said, "I will go to his house. Then he cannot deny me."

I would use Pashtunwali, the Pashtun code of honor. If someone is a guest in a home and admires something, Pashtunwali compels the owner to offer it to him. The tradition was to be thankful but turn down the offer. I would ignore tradition and accept.

The next day Abdul and Pirooz reluctantly agreed to drive with me to the owner's house. When he saw us at the door, he had no choice but to invite us in, and we all took seats on mats on the floor.

"I have come all the way to your house from Kabul and am willing to pay whatever price you ask for that horse," I said.

"It's not good to put a price on that horse," he said. "My horses are my joy. I buy only the best, the top, the most beautiful horses. If I sell that horse, I will be selling part of my joy, and that is bad luck. I love that horse." He stopped as if he were carrying a heavy burden and needed to rest. "But you have come to my house, and you leave me no choice. So take it. If you want it that badly, it's yours. I don't need your money."

"Tashakor, tashakor," I said. I had brought a lot of money to pay for the horse but could not insult his hospitality by handing it to him in front of my cousins. Before I left, I slipped the money under the mat, trusting he would find it.

When we arrived at my compound in Karta-i-Char, I tied the horse to a tree far in the back, where Baba never went. The horse was as beautiful as I remembered. "I will name you Sia," I told him, "for you are as black as midnight."

In truth I knew my father would not approve of what I had done. I also knew the secret could not be kept from him for long. "Babu, I need your help," I said to my mother. She often prepared my father for requests for things we knew he would otherwise refuse me. "I bought a horse."

As often as possible after this, Babu would say to Baba, "It's getting very expensive to rent a horse for Bari in Jalalabad every winter. We should just buy him one."

But Baba would have none of it.

Then one day he discovered Sia on his own. "Whose horse is that?" he asked all my relatives. "I don't know," they all lied. "It just appeared one day."

Having run out of relatives to ask, it suddenly dawned on Baba whose horse it was. "Bari!"

"Baleh, Baba?"

"I thought you were crazy," he said, "but not this crazy." Then he laughed—and there was not much that would get my father laughing.

Sia traveled with us to Jalalabad every winter. One morning I decided to take my rifle and ride Sia across the Kabul River. Sia was an ornery horse, who, like me, had a mind of his own. An elderly man with a long white beard sat on the riverbank watching me approach the river. I guided Sia into the water until it was so deep he had to swim. He rolled to his side. Holding my gun above my head, I tried to roll with him, but my feet slipped out of the stirrups, and I felt my body being dragged underwater. Somehow I managed to right myself and ride back to shore.

"Are you diwana?" the old man said. "You might get yourself killed crossing the river on a horse when you don't know what you're doing."

"I know what I'm doing," I said.

"Good. Then drown yourself."

I sat shivering, waiting for the sun to warm me, as the old man stared across the river. He startled me when he spoke. "Your horse rolled onto his left side to swim, and you rolled with him," he said. "That's why you almost drowned. As soon as he starts to roll left, slip your feet out of the stirrups and roll the other way until his feet touch bottom, and he'll right himself. Don't worry, your horse knows how to swim."

Sia and I were soon clambering up the far bank, his muscled body moving easily beneath me. We followed dirt paths cut through the farms separated by tall stands of cypress trees.

Then I let Sia lead me.

He seemed to know where he was going as he headed toward a set of low green hills in the distance, then through a notch in the hills. When we emerged on the other side, I gasped. Below me lay a beautiful, broad, green valley. When we reached the valley floor, I tied Sia to a tree and headed off with my gun. A dove spooked. *Bang! Bang!*

As I watched it fly off unharmed, I suddenly felt like the luckiest person in the world to be alive in this place, at this time.

21

Kabul, Afghanistan, 1967

The Mystic

In 1964, when Zahir Shah's new constitution made political parties legal for the very first time, all his enemies took advantage. Russia backed the communist People's Democratic Party of Afghanistan (PDPA); China supported the Maoists; Shia Iran backed the Shia religious parties; Pashtuns who wanted to regain Pashtunistan formed the Afghan Social Democratic Party. But the PDPA was the most organized and had the strongest backing: the Union of Soviet Socialist Republics.

The New Great Game between the United States and Russia continued. The United States built an airport in Mazar-i-Sharif and a highway across Afghanistan. Russia built irrigation ditches, power projects, and a new Polytechnic Institute—for which it provided the teachers. The U.S. ambassador-at-large met with Zahir Shah and the prime minister in Kabul. Soon afterward Russian leaders met with Zahir Shah in Moscow. But Zahir Shah was ignoring the reality of what he had set in motion when he forced Daoud to resign and created his flawed constitution. The people were angry that their political desires were constantly frustrated by the king and his cabinet. The anger of the people often surfaces most strongly in the young, and Afghanistan was no different. After the Wolesi Jirga excluded the public and voted in secret, students at Kabul University rioted. Zahir Shah's cousin and son-in-law, General Abdul Wali, military commander of the Kabul region and head of the palace guard, ordered his troops to fire on the students, killing three of them. Schools were closed. Public meetings were banned.

In October 1965 Prime Minister Yusuf resigned. The king appointed a new prime minister, but it did nothing to quell the anger of the students, whose passions were stoked by Russia, Iran, China, and the religious parties backed by Iran and Pakistan. All of Afghanistan's neighbors were allied against it, determined to bring down the government. The new prime minister was unable to control the Communists or students and resigned in November 1967, to be replaced by Nur Ahmad Etemadi. Uncle Ali became first deputy prime minister and minister of education. It was during this time that I asked my father if I could go with Uncle Ali's wife, Aunt Deeba, to see a mystic she often consulted. Baba did not want me to go, but I pleaded with him, and he relented. "If that is what you want," he said, "then go, but it's a foolish waste of time."

With his tall, thin figure, flowing white hair, and long, wispy beard, the mystic exuded magical powers as he walked beside the Kabul River, trailed by a huge following. Suddenly the mystic stopped and extended his hand toward the riverbank. All eyes followed it. What did the mystic know that we did not? What could he see that we could not? Several people ran to the riverbank where the mystic had pointed. Hidden in the reeds lay the corpse of an old man. Everyone started shouting. How could the mystic have known this?

When the mystic arrived back at his house, he invited Aunt Deeba inside.

As I sat on the floor on a silk cushion, the Mystic's eyes seemed to peer into me. "How is it you could see the dead body?" I asked him.

He looked at me intently. "In my mind's eye," he replied, and I felt his power. "You know, Baryalai, the eyes are not the only way of seeing."

As soon as I got home, I told my father what had happened, how the mystic could see what others could not. "They say there is an invisible hand behind the universe and truths that our eyes alone are not strong enough to see," I said, trying to impress Baba.

But Baba was not impressed. "You should not believe what you cannot see or touch," he said. "You should not believe in anything without proof."

"You don't think you need to know about worlds beyond our own?" I asked.

"I know as much as I have to for my daily needs and my work. I leave to God those things I do not understand. Believing in things without proof only confuses you."

"But doesn't Islam say that your story is written before you walk into this life? There are those who know what lies ahead for us."

"Bari," he said gently, "there are those who are content to lead small, simple lives and be swept along like leaves down the Kabul River. But we make our own destinies. One day you will discover this for yourself."

"As you say, Baba," I said. "I'll believe it when I see it."

22

Kabul, Afghanistan, 1967

Basketball

When I was a student at Habibia High School in the late 1960s, Afghanistan was still a relatively stable country. Zahir Shah had been king since 1933, the longest anyone had ruled Afghanistan without being deposed or assassinated. We had good relations with the countries of the West, including France, Germany, and the United States, all of which sent professors to teach at Kabul University. And there were schools such as the American School set up for the children of Americans and others working in Afghanistan. Many of my neighbors in Karta-i-Char were from the United States. Grocery stores sprang up to feed them, the shelves full of strange foods. I became addicted to Kellogg's Corn Flakes.

Walking home from high school one day, my friend Ahmad and I met a tall, handsome American who had come to Afghanistan with the Peace Corps. I was immediately taken with Tom Gouttierre, this outgoing American who seemed so carefree and happy in his T-shirt, blue jeans, and sneakers. Mr. Gouttierre noticed my interest in speaking English and invited me to come see him. I went to his house a few days later. As soon as the door opened, a large black dog jumped on me, pawing at my chest. Mr. Gouttierre rubbed his hands into the dog's fur as it licked not only his hands but his face. I was disgusted and horrified. The Angel Gabriel had refused to speak with Allah's Messenger until a puppy hiding beneath a bed was taken outside, admonishing, "We do not enter a house in which there is a dog." This is why Afghans consider dogs unclean and never let them inside. Dogs are used only for guarding and fighting.

I was surprised when Gouttierre offered me food and drink in Dari. "What has brought you all the way from America to Afghanistan?" I asked him.

"I want to bring our cultures together," he said. "If we all know each other better, the world will be a better place. That's why I not only teach at the American School but coach basketball for the Afghan national basketball team and Habibia High as well. Where do you go to school, Baryalai?"

"Habibia High," I answered.

"Have you ever been to a game?"

"Nay, I have not."

"Ah, then you must come watch one. Habibia plays the American School this weekend."

Three days later the gym echoed with dozens of conversations and friends calling to one another as Ahmad and I entered. The American School band played loudly as both teams ran onto the court. The players shook hands, then took seats on opposite sides. A referee tossed the ball into the air, and the two teams ran back and forth in a frenzy. I found it strange and confusing, though in some ways it was not unlike buzkashi, each player trying to grab a ball (instead of a goat carcass) and throw it into a metal circle (instead of a circle drawn with quicklime).

We sat behind Habibia High's bench while attractive girls in short skirts and tight tops jumped up and down shouting encouragement to the players. "These cannot be Afghan girls," I said to Ahmad.

"Nay, they are called cheerleaders. Professor Gouttierre brought them over from the American School. Some of them are cheering for Habibia."

I did not miss a game after that.

In 1967 the Afghan Communist Party split into two factions: Khalq (The Masses), led by Nur Taraki; and Parcham (The Banner) led by Babrak Karmal, who was backed by Russia. By November 1968 the situation in Afghanistan was deteriorating rapidly. I had often hung out at Kabul University with my high school friends—now it was too dangerous. Communists, Maoists, Nationalists, and the Islamic religious parties were all using university students to challenge the government, encouraging them to engage in violent demonstrations to demand true democracy and freedom. The students spent more time protesting and rioting than attending class. Finally, they went on strike.

The government responded by shutting down not only the university but all primary and secondary schools in Kabul. Members of Parliament criticized the king and his government. Uncle Ali, first deputy prime minister and minister of education, who cared most passionately about his country's educational system, met with the king and Prime Minister Etemadi.

"You must do something, Your Excellency," Uncle Ali pleaded with Zahir Shah. "This is not democracy. This is anarchy. The university students no longer work to get an education; they work for a political party."

"What would you have me do?" the king responded. "Years ago when we used the military, students were killed, and nothing changed. I'm afraid I have no answers for you, Mr. Popal."

Uncle Ali was not deterred. "The students have too much freedom with this democracy," he argued. "We need to get strong teachers. We need to remind them who is in charge."

Etemadi stirred in his seat. "The students want to see change in our country, Mr. Popal," he said. "You served Afghanistan well under Daoud, but I'm afraid that when they see you, they see Daoud the dictator, and they want democracy. They want freedom to do as they please. The old ideas won't work now."

Uncle Ali fumed with frustration and anger. "No one is being educated now," he said. "There is nothing for me to do as an educator—I resign my post as minister of education."

"I'm sorry to hear that, Mr. Popal," Etemadi said. "But I understand. I too wish something could be done, but it is beyond our control now."

It was not just the Communists who were creating trouble in Afghanistan; Pakistan had its hand in it as well, supporting tribal Pashtuns who were crossing the border to attack Afghans. Uncle Ali had many connections in Pakistan's tribal areas and knew the situation well. In June 1969 Etemadi sent Uncle Ali to Pakistan as ambassador. Uncle Ali did not look forward to his new appointment. Over the next few years, however, he convinced the tribes not to interfere in Afghanistan's affairs.

While Uncle Ali was in Pakistan, Prime Minister Etemadi decided that the only way to counter the Communists was to back the conservative religious groups—the only ones powerful enough to defeat them. In the parliamentary elections of 1969, Etemadi made sure religious conservatives won the seats that had been held by urban liberals, women, and Communists.

"Do you think democracy can work in our country?" I asked Baba one evening at dinner.

"I'd like to believe it can, Bari. But democracy is a very strong force. It changes the concentration of power from one to all, giving power not just to the wise and well-meaning but also to the fanatical and evil. When the French overthrew their king, their revolution brought with it the Reign of Terror. Democracy after a monarchy is like a diver rising from the ocean's depths after a long dive. He must come up gradually or risk great pain, even death. If democracy is to succeed in our country, it must proceed gradually, or the rapid expansion of the air of freedom will kill it. Remember, Bari, even in America there was a long period of slavery, and women could not vote until long after the American Republic was founded. But no one declared America's democracy a failure. Democracy is government by the people, and people are not perfect, so you should not expect democracy to be perfect."

23

Jalalabad, Afghanistan, 1969

Afsana

I first caught sight of her in Jalalabad in the winter of 1969 on the sidewalk near the Behsood Bridge, walking with a group of girls, talking and laughing. They had walked to the riverbank from downtown Jalalabad (no doubt stopping to peer into the shops' windows). In the coolness beside the river, families picnicked on kebabs and rice beneath panja chinar trees whose leaves rustled in the breeze with a soft comforting sound. I slowed Sia to a steady gait, feeling very proud on my splendid black horse. The girls giggled as I passed by. She looked up at me, and for the first time I knew what falling in love felt like. I held Sia steady, but my heart was racing. To fall in love at first sight was dangerous in a country of arranged marriages. But I could not resist her big green eyes, sweet but mischievous. Her hair was unadorned, long and natural. She was simply dressed, wore little jewelry, and had a kind of unaffected smile on her peaceful face. My father did not like anything fancy or artificial, anything that would show off wealth or power, and perhaps I had some of him in me. To me she was the most beautiful being in the world.

After that I rode my horse to the bridge every day hoping to see her again, but when I did, I felt too shy to approach.

After our paths crossed a few more times, I got up the courage to speak. "Salaam," was all I could manage at first, then "Where are you from?" and "Where are you going?" I began singling her out, and we would speak more and more until one day the others continued walking while she lingered behind and she slid me a note with her phone number and her name: Afsana.

As soon as I could, I called Afsana and arranged to meet her at her house. Her father, Mr. Jilani Sadaqi, greeted me at the door. I should say Mayor Sadaqi because he was the mayor of Kabul. In Afghanistan unmarried men and women did not spend time together unchaperoned. Such behavior could get one killed by the girl's male relatives. But I did not have to worry about being alone with Afsana—her nine brothers and sisters as well as many aunts, uncles, nieces, and nephews always seemed to be visiting at the same time.

How did Jilani come to have such an important position as mayor of Kabul? Mustafa Kemal Atatürk, modern Turkey's founding father, wanted to Westernize the new Republic of Turkey. Transforming Turkey into a modern secular nation meant separating religion from government. Atatürk's reforms were far-reaching and profound: the emancipation of women; the abolition of Islamic institutions; the introduction of Western legal codes, dress, and calendar— even replacing Arabic script with Latin. But Jilani's father, a powerful religious leader, opposed Atatürk's reforms. Atatürk had him executed, and he became a martyr for Islam. Jilani's mother, Ozra, fled to Kabul with the young Jilani and his sister. When Jilani was a teenager, Ozra moved the family to Kandahar and arranged for him to marry the daughter of a powerful khan.

The family returned to Kabul after the marriage, and Jilani went to work for the government. There he met Daoud, and they became friends. After the king forced Daoud to resign in 1963, the families became close. Daoud and Jilani took turns driving their daughters Zarlasht and Afsana to school. The two young girls became best friends. Daoud liked Afsana's mother's cooking so much that he and Zarlasht often ate dinner with Afsana's family.

I did not tell Baba about my friendship with Afsana. But just as with Sia, my father found out. A few months after we returned to Kabul, Baba and Babu visited Jilani to see if he knew about the relationship. They went without me. My only comfort was that I knew Baba would not do anything rash—that was not his way. He would always carefully listen first, listen and learn.

I waited at the front door, anxious for their return. As soon as they arrived, my mother took me aside—the visit had not gone well. Perhaps, I thought, my father's mood was made worse by the sight of Afsana's many brothers and sisters, which couldn't fail to remind him that in a country of large families, I was his only child. Or perhaps it made him more protective of me. Babu told me Baba was polite—but that was all. Where Baba was solitary, laconic, brooding, and dour, with infrequent flashes of dry humor, Jilani was full of warmth and humor and conversation. The only things they had in common were their love of Afghanistan and their concern for its poor.

When Baba suddenly appeared, I almost jumped. "What did you think?" I blurted out.

"You are too young, Bari," he said, "and don't know what you are doing. You don't know about your family's place. You have not finished your schooling. Think about your future and family. Marriage between different cultures and families is very difficult. Later you can marry someone who is part of our family and you won't have this clash of differences."

I turned to my mother. "Babu?" I said, feeling crushed.

"The Sadaqis seem very nice, and we had a lovely tea together," was all she said.

Despite my father's feelings—warning—I invented excuses to leave the house and spent more and more time at Afsana's. She lived in a very large house in downtown Kabul on the other side of Mount Asmayi. I never tired of being in a house full of talking and laughter and music. Nor of being with Afsana. One day while I was visiting her, we heard the screech of brakes and ran outside. A city bus had stopped in front of the house—which was unusual because it was not a bus stop. We were surprised to see her father step out. When the bus driver saw the look on our faces, he said to Afsana, "I saw your father walking home from the bus stop. He's been very good to me. I could not let him walk all the way home. It was my pleasure to do this." I think it was then that I fell in love with Afsana's family. I asked her to marry me. When she accepted, I felt our happiness was complete. Except for one problem—I had to tell Baba.

"Absolutely not! I forbid it!" my father said angrily.

"How can you say this?" I protested. "They are a good family, and Mr. Sadaqi is mayor of Kabul!"

"I am not discussing this with you anymore. You are not to see her again."

My teenage brain could not understand this attitude from such a reasonable, kind, and understanding man. I knew my father felt so strongly about his Pashtun roots that he had named me Baryalai, an ancient Pashtun name, and refused to use his Arabic name, Abdul. There was only one person who could help me.

"Family is the most important thing to a Pashtun, Bari," my mother said, "even more important than tribe. Your father may be liberal in many ways, but he is a Pashtun at heart. You are from a family of position. This must be kept in the family. Outsiders are not welcome. Nay, if your father has his way, he will keep you from marrying Afsana until you are old enough to marry a girl from our own family. Then you will be able to understand and accept it."

"And you agree with this?" I said, anger rising within me.

"Nay. I think you should marry the one your heart tells you to marry."

When I told Afsana what my father had said, she replied, "You can't go against your father's wishes, Bari."

"But my father went against his father's wishes when he left Kabul to go to Paris with General Nadir. He cannot hold against me what he himself has done. I am not going to give you up for him, Afsana, just as he would not give up Paris for his father."

"If that is your wish, Bari, I will wait for you. But you must promise me you won't do anything foolish."

Although Baba had forbidden me to see Afsana, I could not stop sneaking out of the house to see her. This did not escape his attention. When I returned home after yet another such visit, Baba was waiting for me. "I know you're still seeing that girl," he said with a disappointed look. "You know I don't approve. Why can't I make you understand that as a Popalzai, you have responsibilities? Have all my years taking you to government meetings and tribal jirgas been for nothing? You can't escape who you are because of love."

"This is not on you, Baba," I said. "I do this for myself. It is my life." I ran from the house.

I did not return home until I heard the call to prayer at daybreak.

As soon as I could, I went to Afsana and asked, "What are we to do?"

"There's only one thing we can do, Bari," she replied. "Your father must speak to my father again."

"I asked him to, but he refused," I said.

"You can't continue to see me against your father's wishes." Afsana held me with her eyes. "You're his only son, Bari. You're everything he has. I don't think he wants to lose you. You must talk to him. Please try . . . for both of us."

To my great relief, my father did not cut me off immediately but sat and listened. Then, to my even greater surprise, he nodded his resigned consent.

I rushed off to see Afsana.

24

Kabul, Afghanistan, 1970

A Turkish Bride

The engagement party for two of Kabul's most prominent families was held in the late spring high on a hill in Kabul in the ball-
room of the Bagh-i-Bala, the former summer palace of the Iron
Amir that Zahir Shah had converted to a restaurant. It was a perfect setting for a party, a multi-domed structure of arcaded veran-
das, mirrored walls, and lavish interiors decorated with flowers
carved in stucco and plaster. Daoud and his wife, Zainab (the
king's sister), attended and, of course, their daughter Zarlasht,
who was still Afsana's best friend. Afsana's large family was there
in force, and I had many uncles, aunts, and cousins there as well
as dozens of friends.

As we made our entrance, the traditional Afghan marriage song
began. Afsana wore a powder blue dress, I a suit and tie. Flash-
bulbs popped; guests applauded. I still have the photo of those
two who had so much to look forward to and who were blissfully
unaware of what was to come.

At dinner we fed each other slices of *maalida*, a cake of bread-
crumbs and sugar, the symbol of the sweetness of our union. The
guests dined on a buffet of *teka kebab* (beef seasoned with ginger
and garlic), *shaami kabob* (chicken marinated in cumin, garlic,
and cardamom), and several kinds of rice. After dinner Afsana
and I took turns cutting slices of rice pudding cake for our guests.
When the band began playing again, we moved from table to table,
visiting our guests.

Near the end of the evening, everyone joined in a traditional
Pashtun dance set to the rhythm of *mogholi*, a tune of seven beats
unique in all the world. We formed a circle, dancing round and
round, clapping and whirling, as the music grew faster and faster,
until the elders grew tired and left the dance floor to the young.

Eight months later our marriage ceremony in Jalalabad was a
much quieter affair. Only my father attended as a witness for my

side, and Afsana's two brothers—representing her father, who was trapped in Kabul by bad weather—attended for Afsana. We all turned to face the mullah.

"God is God, and Muhammad is His messenger." The mullah praised Allah and asked for His protection. Afsana and I looked into each other's eyes, her brothers at her side, my father at mine.

"I, Rahman Popal, offer my son, Baryalai, in marriage to Afsana Sadaqi."

"On behalf of Jilani Sadaqi, I accept Baryalai Popal's marriage to his daughter Afsana," one of the brothers said.

"Baryalai, have you chosen this young woman for your wife?"

"I have," I answered.

"You have heard?" the mullah asked the witnesses.

"We have heard."

"Afsana, have you chosen this young man for your husband?"

"Baleh, I have. I offer myself in marriage to you, Baryalai, in accordance with the instructions of the Holy Koran and the Holy Prophet, peace and blessings be upon Him."

"You have heard?" the mullah asked the witnesses again.

"We have heard."

"I pledge my honesty, sincerity, obedience, and faith to you, Afsana."

"I pledge my honesty, sincerity, obedience, and faith to you, Baryalai."

"May Allah bless this union and be with you and protect you always," the mullah said.

My father had begun the ceremony, and Afsana's brother concluded it: "For Jilani Sadaqi, I accept Baryalai Popal to be my son-in-law."

I returned to Habibia High, but Afsana was now a married woman and had to attend a high school for married women. Every night we ate dinner with Baba and Babu in their dining room. As wonderful as my mother was, in truth she was not a good cook. She was not a bad cook but insisted on serving very bland food out of concern for Baba's health.

Baba never spoke.

Afsana knew my father's feelings toward her and tried to win his approval by coming home from school at noon to prepare his lunch. We grow rice in abundance in Afghanistan, and we love to eat it, so Afsana often cooked *qabeli pilau,* his favorite rice dish. Afsana called her mother each day to discuss new recipes and became a very good cook. Her mother helped out as well, preparing meals and sending them over for dinner. Baba so enjoyed these meals, I hoped he would soften toward Afsana like her soaked rice. But tribe and blood are very powerful things, and a coldness remained in his heart against this stranger to family and tribe whom I had married against his advice and desire.

The chill never thawed.

25

Jalalabad, Afghanistan, 1971

Daoud

In the summer of 1971, Afghanistan had yet another new prime minister. A drought took hold; the people were starving; the government did nothing. Money and supplies sent by foreign governments were misused or stolen. After Kabul Radio broadcast a demand for Pashtunistan independence from Pakistan, the United States stopped sending aid. One hundred thousand Afghans starved to death. The prime minister resigned.

That winter, as Baba and I drove along the park in Jalalabad, we saw a fedora-topped Daoud thrusting his cane as he strode along, leaning forward as if heading into a strong wind, eyes hidden behind dark glasses. It had been nine long years since the king had forced Daoud to resign as prime minister. Baba of course was much closer to the king than to the fiery, obstinate Daoud. Daoud, my father, and I often walked together to buy fruit, which Daoud loved and which he always carefully picked out himself. In those years Daoud (and even the king) often walked about the city alone, shopping or simply taking a stroll. We stopped, and my father offered Daoud a ride home.

"Thank you, Mr. Popal," Daoud said, "but I want to finish my morning walk. Drive to my house. I will meet you there."

Daoud's house sat on three hundred acres between the King's Palace and the Kabul River on land owned by Nadir Shah and his brothers. Daoud had built a house on several acres and had created a garden unlike any I'd ever seen. Most gardens in Kabul were small fruit orchards—large grassy areas planted with orange, sour orange, and lemon trees surrounded by a border of roses and other flowers. But Daoud's garden was completely filled with red, yellow, and white roses bordered by daffodils. All Afghans love gardens because they are a bit of paradise in a country of bare mountains and barren deserts. *Paradise* comes from the Persian word for "magnificent garden," *pairi-daeza*. It was said that Daoud treated his plants better than his people.

I think there is another reason Daoud so loved his garden—it was the only thing in all Afghanistan he could control.

As we sat in that peaceful spot, servants appeared with cups of green tea, silver containers of sugar and cream, naan, dates, walnuts, and raisins. Daoud broke off a piece of naan and plunged it into the cream, then into the sugar, and then into his mouth.

"It's always good to see you," Daoud said to my father.

"Good to see me but not so good to hear me, baleh?"

"I know you must always speak your mind and that you believe in what you say," Daoud said, pausing for a moment. "But you're right—we don't always agree with each other."

"Then you don't mind if I tell you I'm very worried."

"You will tell me whether I want to hear it or not."

"America and Russia are warring with each other, so we receive no more aid from the United States and little from Russia. Do you know there is a drought and people in the countryside are starving? Do you know that China and Russia use our schools to indoctrinate our students and military into communism? Do you know that the Communists have infiltrated our government and that our Parliament doesn't function?"

"I'm surprised to hear you talk this way," cut in Daoud. "You wanted to be close to the West. You wanted democracy. Why are you complaining?"

"Democracy works in Europe and the United States because the people are educated and can make choices and use democracy for good. But here the people are not educated, and Russia, China, Iran, and Pakistan use our democracy to create havoc. We are not strong enough to fight this. The result is not democracy but anarchy."

Daoud regarded my father for a moment. "Why don't you tell this to the king? You see him all the time."

"You know better than I do that the king does not want to use force. I'm very worried."

"I understand you, Mr. Popal, but the problem is that our mil-

99

itary was trained in Russia. This has given the Russians the upper hand. Because we are close to Russia, America no longer supports us. I understand all this. But what would you have me do? You know that I am no longer prime minister."

"Aren't you worried about your country? You can't just sit and do nothing while your country goes to ruin. The military may be leaning toward Russia, but it is not political and never has been. You must talk to the king and explain that his democracy is not working. Tell him he needs to be a strong leader. Tell him he needs to use the military to regain control."

Daoud did not respond but turned to me instead. "Your father never tires of discussing these things, but he doesn't understand that nothing we do changes anything." Then he turned back to my father. "Let's talk of other things. Tell me, how is your leg?"

My father replied that what was left of it was doing as well as one could expect. Then he quickly finished his tea. "We should be going, Bari."

I helped Baba to his feet. Daoud handed him his two canes and walked us to our car. As my father stood beside the open door gathering himself to enter, Daoud said calmly, "I know you are right, Mr. Popal. I'm not arguing with you. Things cannot continue the way they are. Something has to happen."

26

Bombay, India, 1973

The Wind

When my father received an invitation to the marriage of two cousins of the Karzai family in Kandahar, he was in no condition to make the difficult trip and asked me to go in his place.

I was not prepared for the difference between Kabul and Kandahar. At our engagement party in Kabul, men, women, boys and girls, ate together and danced together. In Kandahar men and women celebrated the wedding on different floors of the hotel. Wedding guests in Kabul wore suits and dresses. In Kandahar they wore gebis and burkas. This I would have expected in Pakistan but not Afghanistan in 1972. It was like visiting a foreign country.

After I graduated from Habibia High in November 1972, I should have attended Kabul University at the beginning of the New Year—March on the Muslim calendar—but I had failed to take the qualifying exam. When Baba found out, he said, "You must do something with yourself. You should go to India and study English."

India! I loved Indian music, which I had grown up listening to—especially the sitar. And I could improve my English. "Baleh, Baba. That's a good idea," I said.

"Bari!" he said with delight, "this is the first time in the whole of my life that I have heard you agree with me when I suggested something that would be good for you. Nothing pleases me more than to hear you say this. English is the language of the future."

Before I left for India in 1973, our son, Walid, was born. I went to India alone because Afsana did not want to take care of an infant so far from her mother and family.

The college was in a nondescript old building in a poor section of Bombay—very different from what I had dreamed it would be. Three beds were crammed into my tiny, shabby room; the paint on the classroom walls was peeling; and I found it impossible to concentrate in the oppressive heat and humidity.

Over five million people filled the streets of Bombay with congestion and noise. A thick haze hung in the air. It turned the sky white during the day and hid the stars at night. I missed the streets of Kabul and the clear blue sky that turned into a canopy of stars in the pure darkness. Soon after I arrived, I was walking through the school's large courtyard crowded with students. Weaving my way through the crushing mob, I saw an Indian student my age towering above the others like a mountaintop above the clouds. His eyes suggested an inner peace, a confidence, as if he were above the crowd spiritually as well. He strode along, unaffected by the sea of people around him. For a moment his eyes met mine, but he seemed to look right through me, as if I didn't exist. I took an immediate dislike to him.

With the arrival of the month-long school holiday, all of the Indian students went home. I was alone in my room. I heard footsteps in the hallway and went to investigate. There stood the tall, arrogant Indian student I had seen in the courtyard. "I thought everyone went home for the holiday," I said.

"I chose to stay," he said. Then he added in classical Dari, "You are from Afghanistan."

It took me a moment to recover from the shock of hearing him speak the ancient language of the Afghans and speak it so well. "Baleh, my name is Bar. It seems we are the only ones here."

"I am called 'The Wind.' I stayed because I prefer this quiet time so I can meditate and grow my mind. I could sense your presence and sought you out."

"How is it you speak Dari so well?"

"I studied Dari so I could read the original words of the great Afghan poets. Why? Because I want to come to my own understanding of their poems as they wrote them. It is very important to find things out for yourself and not rely on what others tell you." He regarded me as if waiting for his words to take hold. "You are Muslim."

"Baleh, that is true."

"Do you yourself believe in Islam, or do you believe because you were born into it?"

I realized I had never thought about this before. Islam had always been part of my life, the life of my family, my friends, and neighbors. I knew nothing else, as if no other possibility existed. "I believe because my mother and father believe," I answered.

"You know what is the difference between you and me? I accept something because I believe it. You accept something because someone else believes it."

I had always felt so sure of myself, but what The Wind said was true. I hadn't chosen Islam—Islam had chosen me. "Listen! Do you hear that?" he asked. I listened but heard nothing. "Listen again," he said. Still, I heard nothing. "Go down the hall and look out the window."

"You are joking with me."

"Nay. I have never joked in my life. I am giving you a lesson in believing and accepting."

I left him and wandered through the hallways until I came to a window. I looked down and saw a baby crying in its mother's arms.

When I returned, The Wind said, "Did you hear the baby's cries? I wanted to show you part of what I can hear. What I can feel. I sense you have a need for this. I can teach you to listen to the sounds around you—teach you to hear what I hear, feel what I feel, know what I know. The mind is like a muscle. Exercise your muscles, and they get stronger. Don't exercise them, and they become weak. Don't use them at all and they become useless. You have the power in you. It is only a matter of acceptance and training. I can be your guide."

Wasn't this the real reason I had come to India? I had found what I was searching for in this tall stranger who had at first seemed so repulsive. I imagined the look on Baba's face when I showed him how I could hear things he could not. I would prove to him that there's more to the world than what we can see, feel, hear, taste, and touch.

Two days later I found myself in an auto rickshaw (a small, motorized, three-wheeled taxi) traveling through villages and past farmhouses with The Wind until there was nothing but impenetrable jungle. "Stop here," he told the driver. Now I was worried.

"Indians hate Afghans, you know," Uncle Ali had warned me. "Be careful. They will rob and kill you whenever they get the chance." If I were killed, what would my family think? "How could Bar have been so stupid? We warned him. Going off into the jungle with an Indian stranger! He has only himself to blame." As if he could read my thoughts, The Wind said, "Don't be afraid. I don't ask you to trust me, only yourself."

After some time walking through thick jungle, we came upon a round fieldstone house in a clearing, where two men in white robes sat meditating on a stone patio.

"Join them," The Wind said, "and listen."

"Listen to what?"

"Listen to the silence. Forget about time. Do not move until I return."

I sat and listened. I sat until my body went numb and all sense of time disappeared. Suddenly I heard a sound. The soft beating of a bird's wings in the treetops? Or just the breeze teasing the leaves? A drumlike beat filled my ears—the rhythmic pounding of my heart. I could feel its steady pulse in my wrists.

When The Wind returned, I was almost too stiff to stand and only did so with a great effort. I looked at my watch. I had been sitting for six hours.

"If you are ready," The Wind said, "I will take you to a village high above a valley. There you will spend a month in a small room, and your mind will learn to walk. You won't have to ask people how they feel; you will know how they feel because you will feel what they feel. Your mind will become like your eyes, and you'll see and hear what is now invisible to you." He paused, then continued. "I see you are skeptical, but you can do this. It won't be easy, but if you follow my path, you will be rewarded. Each day a plate of food will be placed in a circle of sunlight. Each day that place will be different, so you will never eat in the same place twice. This will break down the body's power over the spirit. The spirit will no longer be the body's servant, and you will be in touch with your true feelings."

All my life, it seemed, I had been attracted to the mystical: the

One Who Knows the Stars; the Mystic. Now I had a chance to experience this world for myself, something of which I had always dreamed. But if I were to follow The Wind, I would not learn English. And I had a wife and child now. "I can't do this," I told him, the words sticking in my throat. "I have other responsibilities."

"Don't think about what your family or others will say. Think of yourself and your spirit. Whatever you decide should be your choice."

That night back in my dorm room, I slept on all The Wind had said.

In the morning my feelings had not changed. I searched for The Wind everywhere, up and down the corridors and throughout the whole dorm and campus. But he was nowhere to be found. It was as if he'd never existed—as if I had only imagined him.

I never saw The Wind again.

When I returned to Kabul, my father wanted to hear everything about India. I told him the story of The Wind. "Thank God you did not accept his offer," he said.

"You should not dismiss The Wind so easily," I said angrily. "He is a very powerful man."

Baba gave me that look of his. "There are many powerful men in this world, Bari," he said, "but that does not mean you should follow them."

27

Kabul, Afghanistan, April 1973

Coup d'État

The king called my father to the Palace.

"You will find His Excellency in the library," the king's secretary told my father.

Baba went to the library, but the king was not at his desk, nor could he be found among the rows of bookcases. Baba had given up all hope of finding him when he came upon Zahir Shah sitting behind a cabinet reading a book. "What are you doing there, Your Excellency?" Baba asked, surprised.

"I wanted to speak with you but realized it was useless."

"So, you know what is going on outside?"

"Of course, Ustad," the king said. "I know students are protesting. I know Russia is trying to control us. I know China is trying to control us. Tell me, Ustad, what can I do about the students? What can I do about Russia and China? What can I do to restore order to our country? Declare martial law? How many people will I have to jail? How many people will I have to kill? Communism is very attractive in a poor country. Those who have nothing are given housing, clothing, food, land."

My father was silent. He knew the United States had helped Islamic religious fanatics fight the Communists. Whichever one took over, it would be a disaster. "What about your Constitution? What about democracy?" my father finally asked.

"You can't eat democracy," the king replied.

Zahir Shah seemed to have given up on democracy, but he set dates for parliamentary elections. Russia, which had been stung by the last election when most of the Communist Party members lost their seats, was not one to accept defeat. If it could not control Afghanistan through elections, it would find another way.

On July 18, 1973, while Zahir Shah was in Italy receiving medical treatment, Daoud, with the help of Russia and the Afghan Communist Party, ousted the king in a coup d'état. The Russians backed Daoud because he had the support of the Pashtuns. Daoud accepted Russia's help because he knew that he could not depose the king without Russia's support. But Daoud was not a Communist. He was a despot who thought that once he was in power, he could replace the Communists in government with his own people. Daoud declared Afghanistan a republic and himself its president and minister of defense, putting an end to Afghanistan's centuries-old monarchy. Still intent on modernizing Afghanistan, Daoud banned government workers from wearing gebis or shawls. Zahir Shah, comfortably settled in Italy, was only too happy to let Daoud have the reins of power.

When I returned from India, my newborn daughter, Mariam, was waiting for me. With a one-year old son and new baby girl, I enrolled in Kabul University.

In the 1960s Germany, France, the Soviet Union, and the United States, all vying for influence, expanded the university, each erecting buildings in a different style: one for the study of law and political science; one for engineering; another for agriculture; one for languages; another for economics. Scholars from abroad taught about communism, capitalism, and feminism. In Kabul girls went to school, and women attended university with men and worked in government and business.

I had wanted to study architecture, but it was not offered, so I chose government instead. Maybe I would follow in my father's footsteps after all. My classes in political science, international law, international economics, and history were held in a two-story, red-brick building a fifteen-minute walk from my house. There were forty students in each class, six of them women. We all dressed in the style of the West, the women even perming their hair in the current fashion. Most of my professors were Afghans who had received their doctorates in France. Having returned with the French notion of "liberté, égalité, fraternité," they encouraged free and open discussions. When I arrived home one evening to find my father and his brothers discussing the dangers of communism, I could not resist jumping in. "I think the PDPA was right to try to bring Communist ideas here," I said. "And I heard that too many poor people here are in need and that the Communists want them to share in our country's wealth."

"It's good to see that you want to join our conversation, Bari," Baba said, "but conversations are like houses—you shouldn't enter unless you are invited. When you do speak, if you say, 'I think,' you must be prepared to back up why you think that way. If you say, 'I heard,' you must be able to say where you heard it and why it should be believed. If you talk without backing up what you say, people won't trust you, and they shouldn't listen to you."

"You don't think giving power to the farmers and workers and redistributing land is a good thing?" I asked.

"You must open your eyes, Bari. Communism will destroy Afghanistan's agricultural system. Now the owners provide the equipment, the farmers provide the labor, and the two share the profits equally. Daoud wants to let the farmers grow crops on land the owners are not using. But the farmers have no money for equipment and no experience in running a business. Islam forbids stealing land from its owner. The Communists are trying to make Afghanistan into Russia. They think all they have to do is pass laws and announce them in the countryside to create their Communist paradise. But they don't know Afghanistan. The tribal leaders will never accept this."

28

Kabul, Afghanistan, 1974

Sitar Lessons

When I told my father I wanted to learn to play the sitar, he was so pleased that he insisted I study with Ustad Sarage Odine, the most renowned sitar player in all of Kabul. Ustad Odine agreed to teach me three times a week but only for four months. "Then I will decide if you are a student worthy of my teaching," he said. I ran out and bought an expensive three-string sitar made in India.

"Learning to play the sitar is a process," Ustad Odine said at my first lesson. "You cannot just pick up the instrument and begin playing. First, you must show respect for your teacher. So, before we begin, bring me food and drink."

During the first month of my lessons, the Ustad would not let me touch my new sitar. Instead, I learned to sit correctly and respect my teacher. Our housekeeper was kept busy bringing him food and drink. One day Ustad Odine called for whiskey. After several glasses he looked at me with eyes that seemed to have difficulty focusing. "The eyes see only what the brain will allow them to see," he said. "You must loosen the brain if your eyes are to see beyond what is in front of you. Only then can you begin to understand the sitar."

At the next lesson the Ustad swept into our house as if it were his own. A lapis lazuli bowl caught his eye. "What a beautiful bowl," he said.

"It's a very special bowl my father brought back from Bada-khshan," I said. "Here, you must have it." I placed the bowl in his hands, expecting him to refuse it, but instead he said, "Tashakor. I will cherish it." Each lesson after that, Ustad Odine would admire something, a silver spoon, a tribal rug. I was bound to offer it to him—and he always accepted. And he was drinking all of our expensive alcohol, while I had not yet touched a single string on my sitar.

After three months Afsana's patience ran out. She was going to tell Ustad Odine that the lessons were over. I disagreed, but I couldn't blame her. Afsana, by custom, always remained out of the room when he visited. I would have to confront the Ustad myself. Before I had a chance to say "Salaam," Ustad Odine announced he was most satisfied with my progress and I was now ready to take up the instrument. He plucked one string of the sitar, *ping!* and said, "You must do exactly as I have shown you, and it must sound exactly like that." I cradled the instrument in my lap, almost too terrified to put my finger to it, but the Ustad urged me on. Soon we were both plucking the same string—*ping! ping! ping!*—over and over again for what seemed an endless amount of time. Then suddenly, he stopped. "That will be your lesson for the next month. Practice it as often as you can."

I was determined to be the best sitar player in all of Kabul. Day and night I plucked that one string: *ping! ping! ping!* Even after Afsana went to bed, I plucked that string—*ping! ping! ping!*—until she got up and pulled the sitar out of my hands. After that I was careful to play it only when she was out.

It was some time before I learned to play the next two strings, but the sound of that very first string still resonates in my head.

29

Paghman, Afghanistan, 1974

Japan

After Daoud seized power, he recalled Uncle Ali from Pakistan. Daoud knew that Uncle Ali disapproved of the coup d'état and his alliance with Russia, so in the summer of 1974 Daoud appointed Uncle Ali ambassador to Japan. That summer our large family of uncles, aunts, and cousins made the short drive to Paghman. It was a world away from Kabul's steamy heat where in the 1920s King Amanullah built his Summer Palace. On his tour of Western countries, he'd been captivated not only by Western social ideas but also Western architecture. He hired Western architects and built Paghman in classical designs. The village entranceway and gardens were modeled after the Arc de Triomphe and the Gardens of Versailles. The Summer Palace was built high on a hill above a verdant valley of oak, aspen, and mulberry through which flowed cold mountain streams.

We spent many lazy afternoons picnicking in the royal gardens, listening to music from the bandstand, and watching the waters dance in the fountains off the terrace café. My cousin Shabir and I were walking home from the gardens one evening when we heard Afghan music coming from a compound. We peered in through the door to see young men and women dancing in the glow of lanterns that hung from cherry trees. A friend called out, "Bar! Shabir! Come join us."

As we took seats beneath the cherry trees, he handed us cups of pomegranate juice. In the soft light of the flickering lanterns, we talked and laughed with our friends until late in the evening. As we walked home, Shabir's face lit up. "Bar," he crowed. "I've found paradise! All I need in life is here, and I never want to leave."

When I went to see Shabir the next morning, Uncle Ali was shouting at him. "Nay, Shabir! You're coming to Japan with your family. That's final!"

Not long after we returned to Kabul, Shabir was gone. I did not know then that it would be many years before I would see him again.

The only good thing that came of Uncle Ali's posting to Japan was his convincing a Japanese company to install a television system in Kabul. Baba bought a television for his room. There were only a few programs, but it was the first time I'd ever seen television, and I looked forward to watching it each night in the cushioned armchair in Baba's room. One night I heard a loud crash and rushed upstairs. Our new television lay on the floor, its screen shattered. "Ali should never have brought television here," Baba said angrily. "People were making fun of Hashim. Television is only a means of showing disrespect. That is intolerable."

"But you didn't even like Hashim when he was prime minister," I said. "You said the way he used Daoud was scheming and manipulative."

Baba pushed himself up in his bed. "That's no excuse. You must respect authority. This younger generation doesn't. They don't take things seriously. That is very dangerous. If they don't respect our government, we will have anarchy."

He pointed to the remains of the television on the floor. "Take it away."

That was the end of television for me.

30

Moscow, USSR, 1977

Daoud and Brezhnev

If Uncle Ali thought he would end his political days in Japan, he was wrong. With the increased involvement of Russia in Afghanistan, many Afghan students and military personnel were studying in Moscow. Daoud called Uncle Ali back from Japan and sent him to Moscow as ambassador to the Soviet Union. Shabir, now twenty-four, remained behind in Japan, where he married a Japanese woman and raised a family.

Daoud's rule did not begin well. Earthquakes and massive flooding left one hundred thousand Afghans homeless. To legitimize his self-declared presidency, he met with Pakistan's president, Ali Bhutto, and India's premier, Indira Gandhi. When Daoud met with U.S. secretary of state Henry Kissinger, Kissinger complained about Afghanistan's close ties to Russia. Daoud assured him that Afghanistan was not Russia's puppet and wanted good relations with the United States. When Daoud asked for U.S. help with Pashtunistan, Kissinger turned him down.

Since the 1965 war between Pakistan and India, the United States had maintained an arms embargo against Pakistan. After Daoud refused to distance himself from Russia, the United States shipped arms to conservative religious groups in Pakistan that were upset by Daoud's reforms. They used the weapons to stage attacks across the Afghan border. Daoud accused Pakistan of trying to overthrow him and arrested dozens for plotting a coup against him. He was besieged on all sides: by Russia, by the United States (through Pakistan), by Islamic conservatives, and by supporters of the deposed Zahir Shah who could not forgive Daoud for overthrowing the king. His attempt to legitimize his government by meeting with world leaders had failed. Needing to show that he had the support of the Afghan people, Daoud called a loya jirga. To ensure it would vote to confirm his presidency, he stacked it with people loyal to him.

In March 1977, Russia forced the Afghan Communists to unite against Daoud. When Daoud disbanded the Communist Party and removed Communists from his government, Leonid Brezhnev called him to Moscow. Uncle Ali, as ambassador, sat next to Daoud, across the table from Brezhnev. When Uncle Ali returned to Kabul, he told us about the meeting.

"Brezhnev spoke first, looking old and feeble. He was so excited, he talked too fast for the poor interpreter, who had trouble keeping up. He accused Daoud of allowing NATO and U.S. spies to work near Russia's border and angrily demanded that Daoud remove them immediately. After pausing to let these words have their effect, Brezhnev offered Daoud Russian aid if Daoud would comply. But no one can tell Daoud what to do. The more Brezhnev talked about the United States and imperial powers trying to influence him, the more upset Daoud became, until he exploded. 'No one is going to tell us how to run our country. We will employ foreign experts whenever and wherever we choose.' Then Daoud got up from the table and began walking toward the door. I rushed after him and urged him to take leave of Brezhnev in a proper manner. Brezhnev appeared at Daoud's side. He smiled and extended his hand and offered to meet with Daoud at his convenience. 'There is no need for a meeting,' Daoud replied, and he walked out."

"This worries me, Ali," Baba said. "Russia is a dangerous foe."

31

Kabul, Afghanistan, April 1978

Daoud Is Overthrown

After Daoud disbanded the Communist Party, Party members and students rioted. Daoud began to lose control. He jailed hundreds of political opponents he believed were plotting to overthrow him and return Zahir Shah to power. He imprisoned thousands of other political opponents and military and police officers in Pol-i-Charki Prison. Daoud feared not only Russia but Pakistan (which had the huge financial support of the United States). My cousin Abbas, a patrol officer on the Pakistan border, was arrested and imprisoned.

In April 1978, a founder of the Afghan Communist Party was assassinated in Kabul. When his supporters turned the funeral into a massive demonstration against Daoud, Daoud had the Party's leaders arrested and imprisoned.

On the night of the twenty-seventh of April, the scream of jets and the boom of explosives jolted us from our sleep. Our family gathered in the living room, confused and frightened. We turned on the radio but heard only an eerie static.

While Babu and Afsana comforted Walid and Mariam, I climbed to the rooftop, where I used to battle with my kite. Now those kites had been replaced by Russian jets and helicopters attacking the Presidential Palace. Daoud's forces responded with a barrage of antiaircraft fire. The deafening noise seemed to last all night.

By early morning the fighting had stopped, the sound of jets replaced by loud rumblings of tanks and personnel carriers in the streets outside our compound.

The Afghan Communists called the coup the "Saur [April] Revolution," as if it were a wonderful thing inspired by the people. But it was not a revolution. A revolution is an uprising of the people against their government. The Communists who overthrew Daoud did not have the support of the majority of Afghan people. That is why it was doomed to fail and at a terrible cost to Afghanistan.

When the radio finally returned a few days later, it was broadcasting the Afghan National Anthem. I walked downtown and joined the throng of people outside the Presidential Palace. It seemed like the entire population of Kabul was there. Smoke hovered in the cool, still air. A terrible stench rose from the bloodied streets, where bodies lay strewn about as if deposited by a great windstorm. The charred remains of military vehicles and tanks with gaping holes surrounded the Presidential Palace like a frightening necklace. The Palace walls were riddled with bullet holes and rocket craters. From the top of the stairs, military commanders and armed soldiers eyed the hundreds and hundreds of people who slowly circled the Palace, undaunted by the soldiers on tanks brandishing their bayoneted Kalashnikovs.

Grim-faced commanders and soldiers emerged from the Palace, where Daoud and his family had been. The great throng of people parted as the commanders quickly entered their waiting vehicles and sped off.

The next day we all understood the reason for their hasty departure: Daoud, his wife, all of their sons and daughters (including Afsana's best friend, Zarlasht), and their four grandchildren were dead—gunned down by the Russian-backed Afghan Communists as the family clung to each other in the Palace basement.

At dawn the next day, Afghan Communist soldiers emerged from the Palace carrying the canvas-wrapped bodies of Daoud and his family. They tossed the canvas bundles into the back of an Afghan military truck and disappeared. I thought, "If these people could murder women, children, and babies, what hope is there for my country?"

32

Kabul, Afghanistan, 1978

Professor Wazir

In the weeks leading up to the Saur Coup d'État, many Western and Western-trained professors fled to Pakistan or France. Others could not leave or wanted to continue teaching despite the risk. By the end of the summer of 1978, they had all been replaced by professors trained in the Soviet Union. You could tell the difference in the way the new professors dressed. Our old professors wore tailored suits and fashionable ties, the new ones ill-fitting, poorly made suits. Our new professors never looked at us, their noses always in books or papers from which they read monotonously. Our open discussions about democracy and civil rights were replaced with lectures and readings on Communist dogma. We were to memorize what we learned, not discuss it. Before the Communists came to power, all that had mattered was the final exam. Now attendance was mandatory; records were kept.

Then students began disappearing. A Party member accompanied by National Guards would enter the classroom, point to students, and the guards would seize them and drag them away. We never saw our friends again. Women stopped coming to class because imprisonment for a woman was the worst of fates. Our political science course was renamed "The History of the Revolution." Our professor was a Communist from the countryside, the most fanatic Party members, who despised the intellectuals of the city—students like us. He couldn't wait to retrain us. You could hear his country roots in his Pashto-tinged Dari.

Our two official languages, Dari and Pashto, say much about Afghanistan. When Afghanistan's Durrani Empire stretched from Persia to India, Persia was considered the great civilization, the mighty empire of history. Persian was the language of priests and scholars, of great cities and the king's court—a symbol of culture and royalty, which is why the Durrani adopted Persian as the official language of their court. It served to distinguish the royal family from the Pashto-speaking masses. Dari, the Afghan dialect of Persian, came to identify and separate the educated, sophisticated city dwellers from their Pashto-speaking relatives in the country-side. When King Amanullah came to power, with his new ideas of equality for men and women, and the rich and poor, he replaced Dari with Pashto because it was the true, native tongue. After Amanullah was deposed, Nadir Shah and his son Zahir Shah, who were closer to the people, used both Dari and Pashto. The words of Afghanistan's national anthem are in Pashto, but Dari is the tongue most Afghans have in common.

Our new professor was much more comfortable in Pashto than Dari. "I'll be teaching this class from now on," he announced. "You are to forget everything you've been taught about Parcham and Khalq. Many lies and misconceptions have been spread by your old professors. You are very fortunate to be in Afghanistan now when the Party is here to look after the people."

We moved uneasily in our seats.

"Some of you look concerned. Your only concern should be that you have been fed propaganda about communism. Now you will learn the truth about the Soviet Union's socialist democracy."

A few students laughed.

"You in the front row—what do you find so amusing?" the professor demanded.

"I thought you were joking," the student said.

"Joking?" the professor asked, surprised. "Tell me, how do you think I was joking?"

"Everyone knows the Soviet Union is not a democracy. The Communist Party is the only party. It's like saying there's a horse race when there's only one horse in the race."

Some students nodded in agreement. I kept still.

"I see," the professor said. "It appears your minds have been poisoned by your Western professors. If you won't listen to me, I know someone you will listen to." He stormed out of the room. All the students began talking at once. We waited and waited—but he did not return.

At the beginning of the next class, a man briskly entered and stood behind the professor's desk. We all knew from his tight-fitting black suit, white shirt, and skinny black tie that he was a member of the Party. No one laughed or joked.

"I am Professor Wazir," he told us. Then, glaring at a student in the second row, he said, "You, what is your name?"

"Abdul, sir."

"I understand some students found the professor's discussion of democracy in the Soviet Union amusing. Tell me, Abdul, is the Soviet Union a democracy?"

"They hold elections, but they are not real elections."

"I see. That's one opinion. Stand up if you agree with Abdul." Several students rose from their seats. "Remain standing."

I feared for these students. I had grown up seeing people fall in and out of favor with the government and knew that opposing those in power could get you exiled to Badakhshan or Japan—or worse. I stayed in my seat. Suddenly several National Security guards entered and hustled the standing students out of the classroom.

"I have a list of all your names," Professor Wazir continued. "You will all be here for the next class, and you will learn everything I teach you about the Soviet Union and the Communist Party. You will take notes, and you will be tested. I'm not interested in your ideas. I'm not interested in your theories. I'm not interested in what you think. Everything I teach you, you are to take into your hearts." He paused and glared at us before continuing. "Is there anyone else who thinks the Soviet Union is not a true democracy?" His eyes swept slowly from one side of the classroom to the other. "Good, I know that from now on I will have your complete attention."

Suddenly I felt a great fear in the pit of my stomach that I would be the next student to "disappear." Afsana's family had been close to Daoud's family, and Uncle Ali had worked with him at the highest levels. The Party considered anyone with such connections to Daoud to be an "Enemy of the People." I knew I had to fight my fear and stay because it was my last year at university, and I desperately wanted to graduate, but I also knew it was too dangerous to do so. Then the decision was made for me. Afsana's cousin, who worked for the Party identifying Enemies of the People, uncovered my father's journal in the Foreign Ministry. In his final entry after he resigned from the foreign ministry, my father had harshly criticized Russia and the Communists. National Security guards came to arrest Baba, but when they saw the condition of his leg, they placed him under house arrest.

"What are we to do, Baba?" I asked after the guards left.

"I'm afraid there's nothing we can do, Bari," my father replied. "My worst fears have been realized. But politics is a fickle wind. Let's hope it soon blows in our favor."

The next day in class I explained my situation to my close friend Amjad, who was in charge of taking class attendance, and he agreed to mark me "present." It was the last day I attended classes at Kabul University.

1. *Back row, from left*: Uncle Ali, Abdul Rahman Popal (Baba); *front row, from left*: Baba's sister, Abo, Tajwar (Babu). Courtesy of Baryalai Popal.

2. (*Opposite top*) Abdul Rahman Popal (*front, center*), ambassador to Iraq, Baghdad, 1944. Courtesy of Baryalai Popal.

3. (*Opposite bottom*) King Zahir Shah (*left*) and Prime Minister Daoud.

4. (*Above*) Afghanistan cabinet, Prime Minister Daoud at the head of the table and Uncle Ali, third from Daoud's left, on right side of table.

5. (*Opposite top*) Soviet premier
Nikita Khrushchev (*left*) and Daoud.

6. (*Opposite bottom*) U.S. president
Dwight D. Eisenhower (*left*) and Daoud.

7. (*Above*) Camel caravan.

8. Chapandaz with goat carcass being pursued in buzkashi, Kabul.

9. Biology class, Kabul University, 1960s.

10. Home of Baryalai, Karta-i-Char, 2002. Courtesy of Baryalai Popal.

11. Home of Baryalai, Karta-i-Char, 2009. Courtesy of Baryalai Popal.

12. From left, the author Kevin McLean, Abbas, and Baryalai in Frankfurt,
Germany, 2009. Courtesy of Kevin McLean.

33

Kabul University, December 1978

The Final Exam

I breathed a sigh of relief when I saw my name on the exam list for Professor Wazir's History of the Revolution class—Amjad had not forgotten to mark me present after I stopped attending class. I entered the law building, headed down the long hallway lined with the offices of administrators and professors, and stopped to take a deep breath.

Wazir's frightening face looked up from his work in a room barely large enough for his desk and the empty chair facing it. He still wore the same dark suit, dark tie, and white shirt of the Party. I was still dressed as a student—dress shirt, sports jacket, and blue jeans.

I quickly sat down, full of nervousness. Three rows of folded papers rested on Wazir's desktop, each containing questions on the history of the Revolution. The questions in the row closest to the professor were easy—questions for students who were Party members or the sons of Party members. The questions in the second row were harder; they were for students with no Party connections but who were not considered threats. The third row of questions was intended to trap students who were out of favor with the Party.

"You look nervous, Mr. Popal," Wazir said, eyeing me closely. "I don't recognize you from class."

"I always sit in the back," I said.

"I have a good memory for faces," he said, still staring at me. "The poor students sit in back. I know them. I don't recall seeing you sitting in the back."

"I'm sorry if my face is so unremarkable," I replied, managing a weak smile.

He hesitated, then reached into a drawer and pulled out the attendance records, studying them carefully as I sat terrified.

Finally, he put the records back in the drawer and closed it.

"Choose a question," he snapped, pointing to the third row. He smiled an unsettling smile as I opened the paper with my question. "Read it aloud!"

"As first president of the Republic, Daoud was a good leader because he was a nationalist who was not interested in private gain but what was best for Afghanistan. In pursuing these goals, however, he lost touch with the principles of the Revolution. Discuss."

I hesitated. The professor looked impatient. I knew if I did not answer soon, I would be in trouble. "Daoud was a good leader," I began—but before I could say another word, Wazir cut me off.

"So, you think Daoud was good?"

"That is what the question says."

"Nay! That's not what it says! It says he was against the Revolution!" He looked at me hard, then stood up and leaned into me, his clenched hands pressed against the desktop.

"Do you think the Revolution is good for Afghanistan?"

My strong head got the better of me, and I said defiantly, "I think the Afghan people know what's good for Afghanistan."

Wazir reached for the phone. "I think some time in prison will help you understand who the good leaders are."

"But I wasn't finished," I protested.

A student from the copy center suddenly entered the room and, with a loud thud, dropped a large box of papers on the desk. Wazir gave the student an annoyed look. "Didn't you see that the door was shut? I'm conducting an exam."

"I have a lot of copies to deliver. If I hadn't delivered these, I'd be in trouble for that."

His response took Wazir by surprise—he wasn't used to students talking back to him. "You people are always making mistakes," he said coldly. "I'll have to look these over."

Suddenly I thought of Lemar, who was in charge of university security for the Party. Lemar's older brother was Uncle Ali's brother-in-law and head of Party Security. Although he was ten years older than me, I had often visited Lemar at the university when I was young and had done him favors over the years.

While Wazir examined the copies, I quickly scribbled on the

back of my exam question, "Get Lemar." As I was slipping it into the student's hand, Wazir looked up from the box of copies. My heart stopped. But Wazir was too annoyed at the student to notice.

"You can go now," he barked at the student. "And close the door behind you!"

Then Wazir turned to me and spoke with venom. "You think I'm stupid? You think I don't know who you are? You think I don't know you lie to us while you scheme against us?" I sat frozen as his cold eyes pierced me to my bones. Then he picked up the phone and dialed. "I have found another student against the Revolution," he said, still holding me in his gaze. "He thinks Daoud is a national hero. Come and take him away."

I wanted to run—but that would prove I was guilty. I sat silently for what seemed an interminable time, waiting for National Security to arrive. Loud footsteps approached the door.

"What's going on here?" Lemar demanded, looking hard at Wazir.

"Mr. Popal is an enemy of the Revolution. He thinks Daoud was a hero."

Lemar looked at me. "Wait outside." Then he turned to Wazir. "You and I will discuss this."

As I got up to leave, Wazir hissed at Lemar, "People like him are dangerous. He will talk with others about the Party and change their minds. I've already called National Security. It's better he stay here until they arrive."

"Are you questioning my authority?" Lemar said coldly.

"Nay, forgive me," Wazir said, sounding humble for the very first time. "I only thought you had more important things to attend to than this student."

Lemar turned to me. "Go! And close the door behind you."

I stood outside, ear pressed against the door, listening as shouting erupted and continued for several minutes.

Then all was silent.

The door flew open. I leaped aside to find myself staring into the beet-red face of Wazir. He glared at me, seething. "I promise you in the name of the Revolution that if it were not for your friend, you would never see the face of your father again."

34

Kabul, Afghanistan, 1979

Hiding

In March 1979, President Taraki of Khalq, the independent-minded Communist Party of the Pashtuns of the countryside, executed hundreds of political opponents and imprisoned thousands more, including many tribal leaders. His rival, Babrak Karmal of Parcham, the Russian-backed party of upper-class Communists from the city, fled to Russia. An Afghan resistance group declared a jihad—a holy war—against Taraki's regime. In Herat rebels murdered over a hundred Russians and paraded their decapitated heads around the city on poles. When Taraki responded by killing thousands of Afghans, Afghan soldiers deserted and joined the rebels. I received my diploma from Kabul University and should have registered with the military, but I would not do this—I would not take part in the killing of my own people.

In the middle of April a National Security guard delivered a frightening letter to my house: "Dear Mr. Popal, National Security records show that you failed to register for military service or provide proof that you are employed in an approved position. You are to report to our office immediately." I no longer could leave my house for fear I would be arrested.

When National Security guards knocked on the door one day, I ran upstairs and hid in the small space above Baba's bedroom used to access the chimney. They didn't find me. A few days later three National Security guards broke down the outside door of our compound, marched across the yard, and pounded on our front door, demanding entry. When my mother opened it, she found an AK-47 pointed at her.

"Where is Baryalai Popal?"

"He's not here," she said.

"You're lying. We know he lives here. It would be better for both of you if you bring him to us."

"Nay, I tell you the truth," Babu insisted. "He left after he graduated. I haven't seen him since."

The security guard gave her a threatening look. "If you know what's good for you, you'll tell us where he is."

Babu looked at the gun, then at the men. "I cannot tell you what I do not know."

"We're not done here. We'll return, and we will keep coming back until you turn him over."

The government curfew kept Kabul locked down from dusk until dawn. Anyone foolish enough to venture out after dark risked imprisonment or death. Only National Security walked the streets, making surprise visits to houses to grab young men like me who hadn't registered for the military. I could no longer risk staying in my house at night. I had to find a safer hiding place.

After the Saur Coup d'État, a British embassy official who'd been renting the house next door went back to England. A Russian general moved in. Afghan soldiers stood guard outside the general's house. The guards had long shifts, and my mother frequently brought them food. We came to know and trust them. When the Afghan guards saw that National Security was searching all the houses for young men my age, they told me they would hide me. Each night after this, I climbed my back wall and hid in the guards' sleeping quarters in the rear of the general's yard.

A few weeks later the National Security guards returned to our house.

"Bring us Baryalai Popal," they demanded.

"What are you talking about?" Babu asked them. "You people came and took him away. I don't know what has become of him. What have you done with him?" She began to cry. The guards talked among themselves, then left.

We prayed that would be the end of it. But a few weeks later they returned again, this time pushing past Babu. They searched for documents showing my family was against the Revolution or against the Party. They searched for weapons that would prove we were supporting the mujahideen. When they found nothing, they broke furniture, scattered books from our bookshelves, and shattered plates and glasses on the floor.

Afsana's father was ill, so she took Walid and Mariam with her to visit her parents on the other side of Mount Asmayi as often as she could. It was only a half-hour drive but a nerve-racking one because the roads were full of military vehicles, and there were soldiers and police everywhere. As a woman with small children, Afsana was not seen as a danger to the Party. Having been close to Daoud, Afsana's parents would have been in danger, but they had connections with people who held important positions in the Communist Party. Every time Afsana left her parents, they all feared it would be the last time they would ever see each other again.

I was not the only one confined to my house. Baba and Babu were as well—my father, an ailing seventy-eight-year-old, under house arrest as an Enemy of the People. When Afsana became despondent, my mother would assure her that things would get better, that everything would be all right. None of us believed her.

In September, as the country spiraled out of control, Taraki traveled to Moscow at Russia's insistence. In his absence his deputy prime minister, Hafizullah Amin, seized control of the government. Taraki immediately returned to Kabul, riding to the Presidential Palace with the Russian ambassador, Alexander Puzanov, on a road that was strewn with flower petals—a token of welcome from Amin. Puzanov and Taraki met with Amin, seeming to accept Amin's presidency, and agreed to meet with him again to discuss the new situation.

The night before the meeting, Amin received a coded message saying Taraki intended to kill him. Amin told people he could trust in the military and security forces about the plot and called Puzanov to express his concern. Puzanov assured him that there was no need to worry—Russia would guarantee his safety.

Taraki arrived at the meeting with several men. As Amin approached to greet him, one of Taraki's men pulled out a gun. One of Amin's men jumped in front of Amin and was shot and killed. Taraki fled. He was captured a short time later.

We passed the hours in our living room listening to Radio Kabul. Taraki had resigned "because of bad health and nervous weakness," the announcer said. A few weeks later Taraki was "definitely sick." Then, at the beginning of October: "We are sorry to report that Nur Mohammad Taraki has died of a serious illness." Everyone in Kabul knew Taraki had been executed.

"Taraki was no good," Uncle Ali said. "Amin has good intentions and will be good for Afghanistan." Baba gave his much younger brother a disgusted look. Ali continued, "I've known Amin all my life, and he's not a KGB puppet like Taraki was. He's a Nationalist and has only Afghanistan's interest at heart."

My father raised himself slightly in his bed. "Pashtuns are naturally independent people who place themselves and their interests first. Amin is trying to make Afghanistan into Russia, and we are not Russia."

"That is only by necessity," Uncle Ali persisted. "Like Daoud, Amin is concerned about Pashtunistan and still believes the only hope is with Russia's help. Say what you will, but I tell you Amin is not on Russia's side."

"True," said Baba, "and that is why the Russians will take care of him. He'll be dead in a month." For once Baba was wrong—it took the Russians a little longer.

After the attempt on his life, Amin moved his family out of the Presidential Palace to the Queen's Palace. The Queen's Palace had been constructed on a knoll for protection—as much fortress as palace—and was heavily guarded by Amin's tanks. Afghans were told to cover their windows with cardboard at night so they would not be targets for helicopters and jets. We all knew only Russians flew helicopters and jets.

Toward the end of December 1979 three Russian army divisions massed on Afghanistan's northern border. On December 26, 1979, hundreds of Russian planes appeared in the skies above Kabul— the "Sky Bridge." Amin knew this buildup of Russian forces was not to protect him, as Russia claimed, but he could do nothing. That evening in celebration of the fifteenth anniversary of the founding of the Afghan Communist Party, Amin held a dinner for Russian

Politburo members, Afghan government ministers, and their families in the warmth of the Presidential Palace, with its marble staircases, golden elevator, and crystal chandeliers. My family sat huddled together under blankets against the frigid cold of our living room.

After Amin and his family toasted their guests with pomegranate juice, they began to feel ill. They staggered into the hallways and collapsed onto the marble floors and staircases. Amin lapsed into unconsciousness. Palace guards rushed Amin and his family to the safety of the Queen's Palace.

The following day the city was full of rumors that the KGB had poisoned Amin and his family. That night we heard a great explosion and saw the dark winter sky illuminated with blindingly bright red flares. A barrage of shells smashed into the thick granite walls of the Queen's Palace. Tanks and armored personnel carriers snaked through the fire and smoke, relentlessly making their way up the slopes of the knoll. Afghan tanks battled Russian tanks. The Russian-trained Afghan tank commanders knew their enemy and, despite being greatly outnumbered, continued battling for hours until their last tank was destroyed.

Afghan Communist and Russians troops stormed into the palace, tossing grenades, "cleaning" every room until they came upon Amin and his family sitting terrified on the floor in the basement. With a blast of their automatic weapons, the Russians killed Amin, his wife, and their young children.

The next morning we turned on Radio Kabul to hear Babrak Karmal, the new president of the Democratic Republic of Afghanistan, speaking from Tajikistan.

"Today the torture machine of Amin and his henchmen, savage butchers, usurpers, and murderers of tens of thousands of our compatriots, has been broken. The great Saur Revolution, accomplished through the indestructible will of the heroic Afghan people, has entered a new stage. The bastions of the despotism of the bloody dynasty of Amin and his supporters—those watchdogs of the princes of Nadir Shah, Zahir Shah, and Daoud Khan, the hirelings of world imperialism, headed by American imperialism—have been destroyed. Not one stone of these bastions remains."

35

Kabul, Afghanistan, 1980

Pol-i-Charki Prison

Afghans were horrified by the murder of Amin and his family and the Russian invasion of their country. In an attempt to win support, Karmal released thousands of prisoners from Pol-i-Charki Prison, including my cousin Abbas. We were all overjoyed to see Abbas, especially his wife, Nadara, who had suffered so much in his absence. Nadara had worked for USAID, an American agency that pulled out of Afghanistan when the PDPA came to power. Now that the Russians had arrived, everyone feared her connection to the Americans would prove dangerous. No sooner had Abbas and Nadara been reunited than Nadara fled with her sister to Germany. Abbas was devastated. He wanted to go with Nadara but feared he would be arrested, imprisoned, and tortured again if he tried to leave the country.

Late one night Abbas and I were sitting in the darkness of my living room.

"When I was in prison," Abbas said, "I'd given up all hope of being released. There were fifty prisoners packed in a small cell. There was no space to lie down. Over time you became too weak to care. Every night a guard appeared and called out ten or fifteen names. Then these prisoners were taken to the 'cleaning room.' We never saw them again. There were always others to take their place. One night a guard called out my name. I knew it was my turn for the cleaning room. The guards were walking us down the corridor when someone called out, 'What's he doing here?' It was a high-ranking Communist Party official visiting the prison. The guard said he was taking me to the cleaning room. The official told him, 'Nay. Not him. I know him. Take him back.'

"I looked hard at the official, and though his name escaped me, I recalled his face from my military days. Then they took me back to the cell.

"I thought that after I was released, I would never be sad again.

Walking out a free man into the blinding light, I felt reborn. But my time there, the faces never to be seen again, are always with me, ready to pop into my head, and I feel like I'm still in prison."

Russian Special Forces and troops seized Bagram Airfield north of Kabul. They found themselves surrounded by mujahideen. Russian helicopter gunships staged major attacks in the countryside. In the Kunar Valley near Jalalabad, more than a thousand men, women, and children were killed. But the only part of Afghanistan the Russians occupied was Kabul. They did not control Herat to the west, they did not control Kandahar to the south, and they did not control Mazar-i-Sharif to the north. As foreign powers have discovered over the centuries, taking charge of Kabul is like grabbing an octopus by one tentacle and thinking you have the octopus securely in your grip. Your fight has only begun.

The Russians were facing fighters who knew the mountains, caves, and deserts far better than any outsider. These men lived to fight. When they weren't battling an invader, they were fighting each other, as they had been doing for centuries. To the mujahideen, who were fervently religious and intent on establishing an Afghan government ruled under Islamic law, the Russians were worse than the British. The British believed in God and had many of the same prophets, but the Russians were atheists. The mujahideen would never rest while the Russians occupied Afghanistan.

As the months dragged on, I said to Baba, "This is a crazy war the Russians have started. They are spending hundreds of millions of dollars but have no chance of winning."

"You're right, Bari," Baba replied. "We have an old saying: 'You can occupy Afghanistan, but you can't keep it.'"

"What really worries me, Baba," I said, "is another saying you taught me: 'What the bear takes into its mouth, it never spits out.'"

That night my father and his brothers got into a debate. Baba said the Russians could not hold on for long, but Uncle Ali disagreed. "I don't believe that. Why do we read history? To learn from it and know the future. Whenever Russia has invaded a country, it has never pulled out."

Baba was not impressed. "Show me a country the Russians have ever invaded that is like Afghanistan. We are a country of high mountains and few roads. Those other countries have networks of highways and railroads and countryside suitable for the movement of tanks and military vehicles. And the people are educated and not driven by religion."

Uncle Ali quickly replied, "Chechnya."

Baba laughed. "Where are the mountains? Show me on the map of Chechnya how the mountains interfere with occupation. They are in the South, where few people live. The rest of Chechnya can be occupied as easily as Hungary or Czechoslovakia. Russia will not last more than a few years here."

But even Baba did not understand the crazy will of the Russian leaders or how much money Russia was willing to spend to save face. It was only when the money started running out that Russia was forced to leave.

That took ten long years.

36

Kabul, Afghanistan, 1980

Kandahari

One February night in 1980, I went to seek help from Kandahari. I had met Kandahari as a boy. When my father took me to see the king, I would leave them and go explore the Palace and visit Kandahari, who calculated the calendar of religious holidays. Because the religious celebrations fell on different days each year, it was an important and challenging task. Kandahari explained to me how he made his calculations, and though I did not understand a thing, I knew he was very wise. On one such visit, Kandahari told me the king had come to see him as three men were leaving. Kandahari predicted that one of the men would die soon. "Is he ill?" the king asked. "Nay, Your Excellency, he is fine at the moment, but his death has been revealed to me."

The man died a few days later. That is another reason why I believe in the mystical.

Although Kandahari did not live far from our house, it was a dangerous walk for me. But I had to risk it because a friend had asked me to seek Kandahari's advice for his brother, who was having such violent epileptic fits that the friend was afraid his brother would die.

The night air was freezing, and my hand stung as I knocked on Kandahari's door.

"What are you doing here at this time of night?" he asked, surprised to see me. I told him about my friend's brother. Kandahari thought for a moment. "This is what you must do. Stand him up for two nights. Do not let him sit or lie down. That should cure him."

"Tashakor, we will do as you say."

As I turned to leave, I felt Kandahari's touch on my shoulder and turned to look at him. "One more thing," he said. "You will leave Afghanistan in October."

His words confused and troubled me. What he said was impossible. I wasn't going anywhere. I had too many responsibilities. I would never leave Baba or Babu, Afsana, Walid, or Mariam. They were all I had.

Our family spent our days together reading and talking, afraid to be alone. Baba remained upstairs in his bedroom. Radio Kabul broadcast nothing but propaganda now, so we listened to the Voice of America and the BBC each day to find out what was happening in the outside world. We never stopped worrying that someone might turn me in.

The war for us was sleeplessness, fear, worry, hopelessness, sadness, and endless boredom.

37

Kabul, Afghanistan, October 1980

Leaving

I was surprised to see my cousin Kader Popal at my door on a cool and breezy October day, the kind of day that used to be for flying kites. He looked much older than I remembered, his hair thinner, his once smooth face now lined with worry. Kader walked like Daoud—always leaning forward as if charging into life.

My cousin was a well-known political and short story writer who had worked for the Ministry of Education before the coup. For generations his family had been one of the most important in Kabul, and at fifty he was one of the most respected people in the city. Kader looked at me with his deep-set black eyes and spoke in a frantic voice, which was not like him.

"Bar, you must leave immediately. National Security and Russian soldiers are now searching house to house. The Russians don't even respect our women. They break in unannounced. They have searched half of Karta-i-Char. You must come to my house. It's the only place that will be safe for you now."

I did not know what to think. I wondered if I could trust him—he could have given in to the Communists, or he could be telling me this because they were holding someone in his family hostage. I hated the Russians for making me doubt him, and I hated myself for doubting him. I thanked him for his concern and explained that I had a special hiding place where National Security guards never searched.

"You must come to my house," he insisted.

"Tashakor," I said. "I will have to think about it."

"There's no time!"

"I have to think of my family—Afsana and the children."

"You won't be much use to them dead."

"What you say is true, Kader," I said. "But first I must speak with my father."

Looking dejected, he said, "I understand . . . God be with you."

Baba always told me that one should make decisions with the head, not the heart, and that one cannot make a decision with the head if one has no time to think. That night I lay on the floor unable to sleep as National Security guards in the street outside my house shouted, "What is tonight's password?" If there was no response, there would be the sound of gunfire, and I would flinch as if the bullet had ripped through me.

As soon as the sun appeared, I went up to my father's bedroom and told him about Kader's visit. "Things have changed," I said. "Every house is being searched now—they will search the general's house. There's nowhere for me to hide from these crazy people any longer."

"So you think you should go stay with Kader?" Baba asked.

"We don't know who's honest anymore," I replied. Then the words I had dreaded saying for so long escaped my lips. "The time has come for me to leave."

Baba didn't say anything at first. He just lay there.

This unsettled me—Baba was never at a loss for words. When he finally did speak, his voice was weak. "I was afraid it might come to this." Then he looked at me as if considering his next words. "I've spoken with Abbas. He's agreed to go with you. I will get word to him. You can leave at first light."

That night Walid and Mariam slept on the couch cuddled next to Afsana. I lay on the floor next to them, listening to their steady breathing. I had to tell Afsana I was leaving—but couldn't find the tongue to do it. Finally, I whispered, "Afsana?"

"Baleh?"

"It's not safe for me here anymore. . . . I must leave tomorrow."

"What do you mean?" she asked. I could hear the panic rising in her voice.

"Kader came to see me. Things have become too dangerous now. Abbas is coming for me in the morning. He'll make sure I get out safely. I'll send for you and the children as soon as I can."

Afsana stared at me in shock, as if she were looking through me to the shattered remains of her life. She tried to speak, but words failed her.

Then I told Babu. Her whole body shuddered. My mother was never able to sit still when she was nervous. Now she began pacing. She walked from one room to the other, pacing back and forth and peeking out the front door until I could take it no longer.

"Sit!" I told her. But she never sat.

As dawn approached, my mother and I climbed the stairs to Baba's bedroom. His door was closed—as if he wanted to shut out the reality of what was happening.

I went in alone.

Baba raised himself up, looking old and tired. "Ah, the time has come," he said. He seemed to be searching for something to say. "Be careful" was all he managed.

Suddenly I knew I could not leave my family. "I won't go without you!" I said. "We'll all go together!"

He looked at me for a moment before he spoke. "Nay, you know that's not possible."

"I can get friends to help us. They can take all your things. We'll go to Jalalabad. Everything will be all right."

"Nay, Bari. I'm too old. And they won't hurt Babu or Afsana or the children. We'll be safe here. If we try to leave, none of us will survive. Things are very bad, but I still have my house and my writings. It's no longer safe for you here. You must leave. Let's pray that in a few months, things will change."

We both knew they wouldn't.

"If that's your wish," I said.

"Say good-bye to me now," he said. "I'm afraid you won't see me again."

"How can you say that?"

"My father said the same thing to me just before I left for Paris. It was the last I saw of him. History has a way of repeating itself."

How could I leave everything I had ever known, everyone I had ever loved? It was out of the question, as impossible as tearing out one's own heart.

Baba hugged me with what little strength he had left.

At the door to his bedroom I turned for one last look, one final snapshot of him to hold in my memory. He just stared straight ahead, shrunken and defeated. Then, suddenly, he roused himself. "One more thing, Bari. The Russians have been here a year. We have been here for over a thousand and have always found a way to prevail. We are survivors. Remember that. Never give up."

I could barely find the voice to speak. "Don't worry, Baba. I won't. I will always think of you."

My mother stood crying outside the bedroom door. She hugged me close as if she never wanted to let me go. I helped her down the stairs.

A sharp knock at the front door like a gunshot. Afsana leaped up from the couch, looked at the door, then back at me, staring. Babu woke up Walid and Mariam. "Say good-bye to your Baba."

I kissed Mariam and gave her a last hug, then took Walid into my arms and hugged him close, his tears falling on my face.

Suddenly Abbas was standing next to me. "Let's go," he said. "We must hurry."

I quickly handed Walid to Babu. Afsana stood there as if in a trance. I took her by the shoulders and looked into her eyes. "Don't worry," I said, "I will send for you and the children as soon as I can." But even as I said these words, I knew she would worry every minute of every day and every night. A married woman without a husband in Kabul in the middle of a war with two young children to care for and no end in sight—how could she not?

"See you soon," I whispered and kissed her cheek for what I feared would be the last time.

"Baleh . . . soon . . . ," she said, but her words rung as hollow as the feeling in my heart.

38

Back in the Minefield

The longest night of my life was spent in that minefield in the Hindu Kush covered in the blood of our young guide, Afzel. We could not move, afraid of stepping on another mine. I stared into the darkness until a faint glimmer appeared in the sky. Then a strange sound: "*ting . . . ting . . . ting.*" At the edge of the minefield where the land sloped upward—the beginning of the trail to the Khyber Pass—swaying shaggy shapes transformed into a caravan of camels. A camel puller guided the lead camel by a rope attached to its nose. Four more camels trailed behind, tied nose to tail, each bearing a bundle. With every stride the large bundles of firewood rocked from side to side as if on the deck of a ship at sea.

"Over here!" Abbas called out to the camel puller.

The camel puller stopped and peered down at four miserable figures staring up at him with desperate eyes. "What are you doing down there?" he called to Abbas.

"We were on our way to Pakistan when our guide was killed by a landmine. We're trapped."

"Baleh, your guide led you into a minefield. That was very foolish."

"Can you get us out of here?"

"What can I do against a minefield? I will only end up like your guide. I have to get these camels to the village."

"Then what are we to do?" Abbas asked.

"Walk back out the way you came and pray God will protect you. I'll wait here for you. If you survive, you can follow me to Landi Kotal."

We all turned around. The old man was now in front, then the younger, then Abbas, and finally me. The old man's tired eyes searched the ground for signs of footprints, but the soil was firm, and the wind had erased any guideposts. The old man hesitated but had no choice. He took a first cautious step. We all flinched. Then another and another, and we followed him, like figures in slow motion.

"We are the lucky ones, eh, Bar?" Abbas said as we began our perilous journey back through the minefield.

"Lucky?" I asked. "Tell me. How are we lucky?"

"We're not in front."

Step by painful step, one tentative footstep at a time, the old man made his way back through the minefield. With each step he took, we were playing Russian roulette. I stared at the ground as I took each step, my chest pounding with fear. I did not even realize we were out of the minefield until I looked past Abbas and saw the camel puller.

"God must have been with you," the camel puller said, "Follow behind the camels. Don't worry—you're safe now."

I fell in line behind the last camel and was immediately overwhelmed by the stench of stale urine wafting from the shaggy fur. We made our way up the mountainside along the rock-strewn path, a frigid wind our constant companion. To my right the mountain plunged straight down a thousand feet. A sudden gust of wind. A bundle of wood shifted, jerking a camel toward the edge of the cliff. It instinctively dropped to its knees. The camel puller halted the caravan. He rushed back, secured the kneeling animal's bundle, and guided it back to its feet.

As we slowly advanced up the mountain, thousands of feet of climbing ahead of us, each pebble, each depression, wore on me, and I thought of all those who for thousands of years had traveled the same path. Another gust of wind, and the stench of the camel urine hit me again. I turned aside and gagged. A treeless landscape of crumbled rocks lay far below me.

Why did the Russians want this empty desert?

The camel puller's route was long and torturous in order to bypass Torkham, the border town where we would have been turned back by Pakistan border guards. The landscape was relentless, the mountains colorless piles of jumbled rocks, the vegetation sparse. We trudged upward for hours, then the camel puller called out, "We are now in Pakistan."

I looked around me. The landscape was indistinguishable from Afghanistan.

We didn't stop but plodded on. A few isolated farmhouses appeared in the distance. As we approached the ancient town of Landi Kotal, we began to encounter people: a man guiding a donkey, another leading a small horse, a lone man shuffling along the dusty trail. We arrived in Landi Kotal to find a collection of flat-roofed, mud brick buildings surrounded by walls, like every small Afghan village. There were several two-story buildings framing a main street just wide enough for two vehicles to pass—a mud-plastered version of a frontier town in the American West with a backdrop of stark gray mountains beneath a blue sky made brilliant by the altitude and dry air.

The streets were crowded with farmers leading sheep, cows, and camels. A sudden gust of wind lifted the dry earth in a miniature dust storm, coating humans and animals alike in a fine powder, the pungent odor of manure hanging in the air.

"I must leave you now," the camel puller said. "The bus to Peshawar leaves from here. God be with you."

Our two travel companions and the guide headed toward town. Their figures grew smaller and smaller, until all that remained was a strangely comforting sound resonating in the thin air: *ting . . . ting . . . ting.*

Abbas and I took seats at the back of the bus, joining the other ragged, exhausted men crowded on board. I leaned my head against the window and closed my eyes, my head rocking with the swaying of the old bus as I settled in for the short journey to freedom.

Suddenly the bus lurched to a halt. "A Pakistani guardhouse," Abbas said in a tone that frightened me. Two soldiers with bandoleers strapped across their dark gray vests boarded the bus. They walked slowly down the aisle, coldly eyeing each passenger. I froze. Then I desperately tried to cover my dirty, blood-spattered gebi with my arms but realized my arms were as filthy and bloody as the rest of me.

The soldiers continued down the aisle. I sank down in my seat and stared out the window. "You!" a soldier shouted in Pashto, his voice right in my ear. I turned to face the barrel of a pistol.

"*Ho* [Yes]?" I answered in my poor Pashto.

"Get up!"

"It's all right. He's with me," Abbas said.

The soldier turned and pointed his gun at Abbas. "Out! Both of you!"

We were shoved into the back of a dark green military van. It made a U-turn and sped back toward Landi Kotal.

39

Landi Kotal, Pakistan, 1980

Prison

The van stopped at a single-story mud brick building somewhere near the Afghan border. Before we were taken inside, a guard searched us. He did not find my passport hidden inside my muddy, worn-leather shoe, but he did find Abbas's papers—including his military documents. After a frantic, hushed discussion with another guard, he returned them to Abbas. I prayed that would be the end of it and we would soon be on our way.

We spent the night in a small, cold prison cell. In the morning a flap at the bottom of our cell door opened, and a plate of food and a little jug of water appeared. Starving and thirsty, we devoured both. Suddenly a pain hit my gut as if something were squeezing me from the inside. I looked at Abbas. He was a blurred vision. I passed out.

When I regained consciousness, I was staring into the face of the post's commander. He was clean-shaven except for a carefully trimmed mustache and he wore the gray dress shirt and gray pants of a commander from Peshawar. The commander was small in stature but swollen with authority.

"Who do you work for?" the commander demanded as the two guards held me up by my arms.

"I don't work for anyone," I replied. "I'm a refugee." A sharp slap burned my face.

"I want the truth," he shouted. "It will be better for you if you tell me who you are working for."

"I told you. No one. I had to leave because of the war."

The commander raised his arm higher this time and whipped the back of his hand across my mouth. "The truth!" he shouted.

"That is the truth," I mumbled through bloodied lips. "I cannot tell you anything else unless you want me to lie."

"We know you are spies—admit it."

I felt a sudden blow to the head from one of the guards' pistols and slumped in my chair, groggy from the drug and the pain. But the guards hoisted me back up as the commander regarded me with hard, cold eyes. He stared at me for a moment, considering what to do next, his body tense. Then he suddenly relaxed. "That's enough for today. Give him some time. I'm sure he'll be more honest tomorrow. Take him away."

That night I lay awake in fear of what the morning would bring. But the next day no one came, not even to bring us food. All Abbas and I could do was sit and watch the light of the sun trace its way across the walls until it disappeared again. I became resigned to my fate. Baba had been right: I would never see him again. Or Babu or Afsana or my children. I looked at Abbas. He had come with me for the sake of my father, and now he was going to die in prison with me.

A few days later we were driven to a small military base in Landi Kotal. Two armed guards motioned us through massive doors. We emerged into a large garden area, the only fragrance the stench of outdoor toilets. The new prison was much larger, a solid-brick, two-story building with four cells on each floor. Each cell was designed to hold two prisoners, but most held eight men crowded together. The first night we were fortunate—we were placed in an empty cell.

Early the next morning Abbas confronted the guards. "I know important people in Peshawar who would be upset at what has happened to us. Let me send word to them that we are here. It will be better for all of us." The guards ignored him.

The guards prodded us with their rifles and led us to another cell, barely lit by sunlight filtering through a small, dusty skylight. There were five other prisoners, all young male Afghans. One, his face dirty and worn despite his youth, stared at me with empty eyes. I looked away. The others sat unmoving, patoos covering their faces.

Each day we were given one plate of rice and dal. Our only exercise was a daily trip to the outdoor toilet escorted by a guard. Abbas and I were still wearing the same filthy clothes we had been wearing since we left Abdien. The guards, either taking pity on us

or, more likely, no longer able to bear our smell, let us wash ourselves and our clothing. The only measure of our weeks there were
our beards, which grew longer by the day.

Although we were seven men trapped in a small cell, hour after
hour, day after day, no one spoke. We all thought it would be easier to survive if we kept our mouths shut, our thoughts to ourselves. Who knew if there was a spy among us or guards listening.
When someone did speak, it was only a weak voice desperate for
food or water.

Whenever a guard appeared, Abbas demanded to know why
nothing had been done to release us. The reply was always the
same: "Everything is under control."

One day Abbas demanded to know how long they intended to
keep us. "Until we get our orders from Peshawar," the guard replied.

But the orders from Peshawar never came.

After several more days had passed, I said to Abbas, "You've
talked to them and talked to them, and nothing's happened. What
kind of people are they? They are never going to release us. It's
time we do something. When the guard comes with food tomorrow morning, I will do something they will regret."

Abbas gave me a stern look. "Nay, Bar, let me handle this. I have
more experience in these matters."

The next morning Abbas confronted the guard. "I demand to
speak to the commanding officer," he said with the authority of
the officer he once was.

"Shut up, sit down, and eat," the guard said.

Abbas did not do any of these things. "I've served in the Afghan
military," he said. "I insist on speaking to someone in charge."

"And I insist you shut up," the guard said.

"I won't be quiet until I see the commander!" Abbas shouted.

"Sit down!" the guard commanded, getting in Abbas's face and
bumping him with his chest. Abbas shoved the guard backward.
The guard caught his balance and came back at Abbas, shoving him
harder, but Abbas stayed on his feet. The guard grabbed Abbas's
shirt and tried to force him to the floor, but Abbas held him in
a bear hug. The guard tried to shake him off, but the harder he

fought, the firmer Abbas gripped him. They began wrestling, knocking into prisoners and sending food flying. Abbas started squeezing the air out of the guard's chest. "Help!" the guard managed to scream. Several guards rushed in. They wrestled Abbas to the floor and pinned him down while another kicked him as he lay curled up on the floor, his arms covering his head.

"Take him away," said the guard who was attacked.

Then he looked at me. "And take him too."

We were shoved into a very small cell by ourselves. When the light faded from the tiny barred window, we were left in utter darkness. We lay on the cold stone floor. "I'm sorry," I said.

"Don't be," Abbas replied. "You were right. We needed to show these jackals who they are dealing with."

On the fourth day the guard Abbas attacked entered like a dark cloud, then quickly moved aside. In strode the commanding officer. "Why have you come to Pakistan?" he demanded.

"The Russians have made life in Afghanistan hell," Abbas told him. "We almost died getting here when our guide stepped on a landmine."

"That's not my problem," the commanding officer said. "We are flooded with refugees with sad stories. My job is to protect Pakistan."

"There are millions of Afghan refugees in Peshawar," Abbas said. "Why do you keep us here?"

"I don't have time for this," the commanding officer said, and he turned to leave.

"Wait!" Abbas called. "We have many friends in Peshawar. We know many powerful people here. Call them—it will make things easier for all of us."

The commanding officer's boots echoed down the stone floor of the corridor.

40

Landi Kotal, Pakistan, 1980

Connections

"You say you know important people here," the commander said a few days later. "Give me their names." After this, every time we heard footsteps outside our cell, we were full of hope. But it was only our daily food and drink.

Just when we'd given up hope, the cell door opened and the commanding officer strode in; to our great surprise he said, "I apologize for your captivity and treatment here." The guards took us out and led us to another building. Now we were housed in a clean, spacious room used for guests visiting the prison. There were two beds with real mattresses, and in place of our meager daily meal, we were fed three good meals a day.

An officer wearing the gray uniform and trimmed mustache of Peshawar appeared in our room. "You have a visitor," he said, then he stepped aside.

"Abbas! Bar! It *is* you," Dr. Ahmad exclaimed. "I can't believe it! Don't worry. We'll take care of you now." Dr. Ahmad and Abbas had been stationed on the Pakistan border together. Dr. Ahmad became family physician to the high-ranking political and military families in Kabul, many of whom, like him, had fled to Peshawar. Blond and green-eyed, an unusual combination in Kabul, he was considered one of Kabul's handsomest men. You would call him a ladies' man, though he had a wife in Kabul and another in Jalalabad. He knew how to have a good time and how to make the time better for all around him.

"These two men have been our guests here," the officer said to Dr. Ahmad. "If there is anything more we can do for them, or for you, please don't hesitate to ask." He turned to us. "You are free to go."

"Thank God I found you," Dr. Ahmad said as we drove away in his old Toyota." Most Afghans arrested as spies die in prison. We'll go to my house where you can rest."

"Tashakor, we are in your debt," I said.

"Don't thank me. Thank Hazrat Sepgotolah. I've been his family doctor for many years. I left Kabul six months after the Russian invasion, hoping to get to Canada, Europe, or the United States. Instead, I find myself stuck in Pakistan taking care of Sepgotolah's family. It was his letter to the commanding officer that got you released."

Although I was grateful to Hazrat Sepgotolah for saving me, I still shivered at the name. Hazrat signifies one who is descended from the Prophet Muhammad and thus entitled to great respect among all Muslims. But Hazrat Sepgotolah was a warlord and religious leader who had opposed the modernization of Afghanistan and agitated against Daoud. When Uncle Ali was deputy prime minister, he invited Sepgotolah to come to his office to talk. But after Sepgotolah arrived, he was arrested by National Security and imprisoned. When he was finally released, he traveled to Pakistan and headed an organization that fought the Russians.

Dr. Ahmad told us a local khan wanted to meet with us and that we would stop at his compound before going to Peshawar.

The khan controlled an area his family had ruled for generations. Just as in Afghanistan, he held a position of power handed down from father to son, settling disputes among tribesmen and providing law and order. The khan's compound was a complex of buildings covering several acres near Landi Kotal. We drove past armed men into an extensive garden of flowers, fruit trees, and wide stretches of grass. Hundreds of men occupied the garden. Some were guests of the khan; others travelers who had sought refuge there; still others were mujahideen who were fighting the Russians. The men sat against the walls or at small tables, smoking and talking. People from nearby villages waited patiently to speak with the khan.

At the far end of the garden were the sleeping quarters for the khan, his guests, and the khan's goats and sheep. In Afghanistan and Pakistan the ruler of a village is truly a man of the people—and his farm animals. The women slept in a separate building that had a small outdoor cooking area.

The soldiers all stood as the khan entered, accompanied by sev-

eral armed men. Those standing in his path parted like doors opening. A dark brown gebi covered the khan's tall frame. He took a
seat on a cushion on the floor—hard-packed dirt covered in rugs
in patterns of deep red and black—then motioned for us to join
him on the floor. We sat and listened attentively, giving him the
respect due his position.

"Don't be upset at the Pakistan police," he said. "They were only
doing their job. I understand your anger and frustration. I know
things are very bad for you in Afghanistan and that you are fighting against a very bad enemy. There are bad enemies and good
enemies—do you know the difference? When my family fought
against the British, the British soldiers fought fairly. If there were
women and children inside a house, the British soldiers would not
enter. They respected us, and we respected them. They were a good
enemy. But you in Afghanistan are fighting a very bad enemy. The
Russians have no principles. They want to take everything from
you, even your dignity. They want to hurt you in every way. They
will use any means to humiliate and kill you. They don't respect
women or children and kill them without remorse. They are infidels. I'm afraid a battle against such an enemy can only end badly."

41

Peshawar, Pakistan, 1980

Pir Gailani

It was a nerve-racking downhill drive to Dr. Ahmad's house in Peshawar through a barren landscape of dry valleys and bare mountains. The view did not change until we approached the city, where the waters of the Kabul River turned the landscape green. Peshawar was larger and cleaner than Jalalabad, but like Jalalabad, it was crowded with Pashtuns in gebis and turbans. Dr. Ahmad lived in a small, old house on a narrow street near the ancient city center—one in a long row of such houses. It was only a temporary house, he hoped, because like millions of other Afghans in Peshawar, Dr. Ahmad wanted to leave. Dr. Ahmad employed as many people as possible—a cook, a gardener, a driver—because there were so many war refugees who had nothing. Each night his cook made us a wonderful meal of rice, meat, and fruit, served with a warm basket of soft, round bread. We never saw Dr. Ahmad's wife and children, who kept to the rooms in back.

Abbas and I slept on mats in the entrance room. Sleep was never easy. A dog barking, a door creaking, a footstep outside—any sudden noise unsettled me. We did little more than rest and eat for the next few days as we recovered from our ordeal, and we always looked forward to our breakfast with Dr. Ahmad. "What are your plans?" he asked Abbas one morning.

"I'm going to Germany. I'm trying to convince Bar to come with me."

Unlike Abbas, I had not been educated in Germany and had only bad memories of it. I still remembered how the Germans had treated us when my father was in the hospital. And I'd long forgotten the little German I had learned.

"What will you do, Bar?" Dr. Ahmad asked me.

"I want to go to America."

"Good luck," he said. "I waited over a year just to get an application. Now I have to be interviewed. Do you know how long I've been waiting for that? Three years! And there's no end in sight." My insides collapsed at his words.

The next day Abbas and I went to downtown Peshawar, a city of narrow, ancient streets crowded with people, animals, and auto rickshaws. We wandered through Peshawar's many bazaars tucked between buildings on narrow, winding alleys. We strolled past stall after stall of vendors selling blankets, copperware, and gold jewelry, all shouting, "Highest quality, lowest prices!" The aroma of kebabs and freshly baked bread mingled with that of tea, cardamom, sandalwood, incense, and tobacco. Shrill voices speaking Hindi, Urdu, and Pashto assaulted us from all sides. It was not difficult to find inexpensive gebis and pakols—every store seemed to be selling them. We changed into our new clothes behind a curtain, then stepped out into the street and blended into the crowd.

For the next few days we flowed along with the stream of people as we explored the city. At one restaurant Abbas encountered many men he had known at Pol-i-Charki Prison who regularly gathered there to eat and talk—compatriots of the closest kind. They recognized him immediately and were among the few in Peshawar Abbas trusted. We began eating there often, hoping to hear about a way out.

I went to look up an old friend of my family, Payam, who had worked with my father. Payam had fled to Peshawar with his two sons, who had formed an organization to fight the Russians and were doing very well with the money they received from the ISI— the Pakistan Inter-Services Intelligence agency. Their men were constantly shuttling back and forth between Peshawar and Kabul with weapons, supplies, and documents. They were so well-known in Peshawar, it was not difficult to find them. I had promised my father I would get word to him once I arrived in Pakistan and thought they could help me.

"We would be happy to let your father know you are safe," one of the brothers said. "We can get anywhere in Kabul." He asked me to stay and work for them, recruiting fighters.

"Nay, tashakor," I replied, politely turning him down.

Several weeks later I checked back with the brothers to see if my father had received the message. "Baleh. He is happy to hear you're alive, and everyone there is well. He said you should stay in Peshawar as long as you can." I had the opposite idea, of course. I wanted to leave Pakistan as quickly as possible. I discovered that Omed, a close relative of mine who had left Kabul just before the Saur Coup d'État, was working for the mujahideen in Quetta and came to Peshawar several times a week to discuss weapons and funding. He greeted me warmly. "I have many friends in Quetta," he said. "I could get you a place to stay and a job recruiting mujahideen for the ISI."

I knew Quetta, Pakistan, a mile-high city of more than a million, mostly religiously conservative Sunni Pashtuns. I had heard about how these recruiters for the warlords made money getting paid by the ISI for recruiting two or three hundred fighters when they had only recruited a handful. The ISI had so much CIA money that they paid without question. War profiteers were becoming wealthy sending young men to their deaths. Worst of all, they did not want the war to end because that would stop the flow of cash. I wanted no part of this blood money made by recruiting young Muslim men to die in a "holy war."

"Let me think about it," I said.

"Come with me to see Pir Gailani," he said. "I'm sure he can help you."

Pir Gailani (*Pir* is a religious title) was the father of my high school friend Hamid. The family had moved to Peshawar after the Communist takeover. Pir Gailani founded the National Islamic Front for Afghanistan, which supported Zahir Shah. It was far more moderate than the religious parties, perhaps because Pir Gailani was more a businessman than a religious leader. He rejected communism and rule by Islamic law in favor of Afghan nationalism and democracy. Pir Gailani believed that women and men had equal rights in work and politics, just as in the time of the Prophet Muhammad. Unfortunately, Pir Gailani received far less CIA money from the ISI than radical Islamic groups such as Gulbuddin Hekmatyar's Hezb-i-Islami Party.

Hamid was surprised and happy to see me. I told him how I'd come to be in Peshawar. "I'm sorry to hear that," he said. "The war has made life miserable for everyone." We stood there in silence for a moment before he continued. "Stay with us and have something to eat and drink, then I will take you to meet my father. He can get you a job here."

We met with Pir Gailani after lunch. I told him that if I was ever going to see my family again, I would need a visa. "I'm afraid even I do not have that power," Gailani said. Then he offered me work recruiting men to fight the Russians. I thanked him but, once again, turned down an offer to do this. "Then I wish you all the best," he said. "May God be with you and your family."

Outside Omed looked exasperated. "What are you going to do, Bar? You have turned down every job offered you." When I told him I wanted to try to get to India, he asked me if I had a passport. I showed it to him. "It's expired," I said.

42

Peshawar, Pakistan, 1980

Hazrat Sepgotolah

"No problem," Omed said. "I know someone who can fix it." We rode to the old marketplace in an auto rickshaw, then got out and walked as the streets became clogged with people. The three-story brick building was on a block lined with similar guesthouses. We walked up to the second floor and entered a small room with faded green walls. Several men were speaking with a fat middle-aged man seated behind a battered desk. He had little hair on his head and a thick, dark mustache and breathed with a labored, noisy breath. When he saw us enter, he told the men to leave. I took a seat on a chair near the desk and handed the old man my passport as Omed looked on. The fat man unlatched the brass locks of a heavy, ancient-looking leather briefcase, which contained a neatly organized array of rubber stamps and inks, each in its own small compartment, then pulled out a few stamps, pressed them one at a time onto an ink pad, and stamped my passport. "Your passport is now current," he said.

I held out some bills to him, but he waved them away.

After we left, Omed said, "When the old man fled Afghanistan, he took a business with him. Most of those stamps came from the consulate in Kabul. I must get back to Quetta now." He held out a fistful of bills and offered them to me.

"Nay, I cannot accept this," I said.

"I insist." He shoved the money into my pocket.

I met Abbas at the restaurant where he could now almost always be found. The first thing he said to me was, "If you won't come to Germany with me, you must come with me to see Hazrat Sepgotolah." I knew Abbas thought I needed a job. I did not want to go with him, but I couldn't refuse.

Like Pir Gailani, Hazrat Sepgotolah—the same Sepgotolah who had secured our release from prison—controlled a mujahideen organization. He had been imprisoned by Daoud and came to Pakistan after his release. Sepgotolah's compound was twenty minutes outside Peshawar, down a long, dusty road. It was very large, with several gardens and houses behind its high walls. The main garden was filled with men, some lying on cots beneath trees spread around the edges of the yard. Most were mujahideen seeking aid, weapons, jobs, or advice. Others were tribal leaders who had come to seek his counsel. Hazrat Sepgotolah himself sat on a chair behind an enormous desk at one end of the garden. He was a thin man in his sixties with a thin beard. Unlike Pir Gailani's large white turban, Sepgotolah's turban barely covered his head. He wore a dark gray waskat over his white gebi. He gestured for us to sit, peering at us through glasses perched on his beak of a nose. Abbas and Sepgotolah spent some time exchanging stories before Sepgotolah turned his gaze on me. "Would you like to work for us?" he asked.

"Tashakor," I replied. "Give me some time to decide, and I will let you know."

Sepgotolah looked at me and then at Abbas and said, "Rise with me."

Abbas and I stood up, facing the great gathering of men in the garden.

"I would like to introduce my guests," Sepgotolah called out to the crowd. He took one of my hands and one of Abbas's in his own and raised them above his head. The crowd began to stir, their voices rustling like the leaves of a panja chinar tree in a strong wind. "These two men are nephews of Ali Ahmad Popal, the former deputy prime minister of Afghanistan." I felt a sudden chill. "The man who imprisoned me."

The crowd became agitated, their voices loud.

"But I hold no grudge against them," he continued. "They are my guests here and will be treated as such." He dropped our arms, which smacked against our sides. I stood there, dumbfounded. Suddenly Abbas blurted out, "Uncle Ali would never have done that!"

There was a stunned silence, then Sepgotolah said in a powerful voice, "You are wrong! When I was in hiding, Ali asked me to meet with him to discuss my opposition to Daoud. He guaranteed my safety. But after I arrived, I was arrested by Daoud's security police. I spent years in prison because of your uncle. But do not worry, I did not tell my people this because I hold it against you, only to remind them of the truth."

The encampment of armed men raised their guns, shaking them, less willing to forgive and more inclined to revenge. I prayed that no one knew that Uncle Ali's brother-in-law had been head of Daoud's security police. Then Sepgotolah's voice softened, and he was once again a good *hazrat* host. "You must stay and join me for lunch," he said.

"Nay, tashakor," we both replied. Then we left as fast as we could.

Many years later, when I told Uncle Ali what Sepgotolah had said, his voice flashed fire. "That's a lie! I asked Sepgotolah to meet me, but we never agreed on a date. I had no idea he was coming. He just appeared in my office one day. When the security forces entered and arrested him, I was as surprised as he was. They must have followed him. It was his own fault. He should have been more careful. He knew he was a wanted man. Besides, it was foolish of him to think I could protect him from National Security."

43

Peshawar, Pakistan, 1980

The United Nations Humanitarian Aid Office

The German consulate called Abbas and told him to come to the consulate to apply for his passport and visa. Abbas made one last attempt to convince me to go with him, but I stood firm.

The next day the two of us made the four-hour bus ride to Islamabad, over an undulating ribbon of highway bordered by farmlands. Islamabad is literally a city of the twentieth century. Unlike the cities in Afghanistan and the other cities in Pakistan whose histories extend back thousands of years, Islamabad was built after the creation of Pakistan in 1947. The new Islamic Republic of Pakistan (Land of the Paki—those who are spiritually pure) wanted a capital city that would reflect the central role of Islam in their country. The government chose to build the new capital, Islamabad (City of Islam), on a broad, flat plain near the foothills of the Himalayas, far from the coast (which was vulnerable to attack from the Arabian Sea) and far away from Karachi's summer weather, which was unbearably hot and steamy. Islamabad's climate was mild year round. The new capital was close to Rawalpindi, home to Pakistan's military. From the very beginning the military and civilian governments constantly battled each other for control, the military often taking power by force.

We were impressed by Islamabad's broad, well-organized, clean streets, which had been constructed in a grid pattern—a complete contrast to Kabul, Jalalabad, and Quetta. Most people in Islamabad worked for the government, making Islamabad a prosperous city, full of trees and well-built homes. It was a world completely apart geographically and every other way from the Pashtun tribal lands to the west that lie beneath towering snowcapped mountains.

A clerk at the German consulate welcomed Abbas and took his papers.

"Go over there and get your photograph taken," he said. "We'll call you in a few days when your passport and visa are ready."

With German efficiency, the documents were ready two days later. Abbas was anxious to depart. As soon as we left the consulate, we took a taxi to Rawalpindi, where he could get a train to Karachi for his flight to Germany. I could not remember seeing him so happy.

"I'm glad for you, Abbas," I told him just before the train left. "I owe you my life and wish you only the best."

"Come to Germany, Bar," Abbas said. "You know you don't want to stay here. Trying to go elsewhere is just a waste of time. I'll take care of all the paperwork in Germany and call you."

"That would be good." I lied.

Abbas looked at me, perhaps, like me, wondering if it would be for the last time. He broke the silence. "Remember, Bar, this is a dangerous world. Don't trust anyone. The Pakistanis are as bad as the Russians."

I left Dr. Ahmad's house early each morning, taking an auto rickshaw to downtown Peshawar. I spent my days among other Afghan refugees in the Sadar Bazaar, a long stretch of three-story buildings with small shops on the ground floor. The noise of auto rickshaws, motorcycles, cars, and buses mixing with the constant din of shoppers and merchants in that canyon of a space was deafening.

At a restaurant where refugees like me gathered hoping to find some way out, some way to get a visa to another country, we talked endlessly about what to do and got nowhere. But breaking bread and drinking green tea with fellow Afghans made my situation bearable.

When I heard it might be possible to get a visa at the Indian consulate, I decided to try. The consulate was packed with so many people seeking visas, it seemed that every Afghan refugee in Peshawar was there. After hours of waiting in line, I handed the clerk my passport. "I cannot issue you a visa," he said. "Next!"

"Why?" I asked.

"You have no entry stamp. You are here illegally. Next!"

"There are four million Afghan refugees in your country," I said loudly. "Do you think they all have entry stamps?"

"You should have stayed in Afghanistan," he said, then added in a softer tone, "Please don't blame me. I'm only a clerk. India does not want to deal with four million war refugees."

The next day at the restaurant, one of the men asked me if I had registered as a refugee. When I said I hadn't, he told me I needed to. "It's the first step to getting a visa—or at least having your application considered by a consulate," he said. "The United Nations aid office will help you apply for a visa and give you money."

The United Nations Humanitarian Aid Office was a huge one-story concrete building with a yard the size of a large field. Even though I arrived early, five or six hundred Afghan refugees were already lined up outside, talking and shouting. After we waited for several hours, a man came walking down the line. "Anyone who can read and write, go to that line," he said, pointing.

Only fifty or sixty of those hundreds followed him. At the new line the man said, "Those who can speak a foreign language, go over there." Only five of us left. At a table a man pressed my thumb onto an ink pad and rolled it onto the page of a book. He handed me food coupons and money and directed me into the building.

"What languages do you speak?" a woman behind the desk asked me in Dari.

"English and a little Pashto."

"Wonderful! Would you like a job?" she said in English. When I heard these words, I thought my English was not as good as I thought. Surely she had not just offered me work. When I did not respond right away, she repeated the question more slowly.

"Baleh—yes, that would be very good," I said.

"Go talk to those men," she said, indicating three middle-aged men dressed in slacks and short-sleeved shirts. "They are reporters looking for an English translator."

Two of the men had light complexions and hair, the third, shorter and darker, wore gold wire-rimmed glasses. All had thin faces and beards. Expensive-looking cameras with long lenses hung from the necks of two of them. I took a deep breath and introduced myself. It had been a long time since I'd spoken English.

"Hello. My name is Baryalai Popal. You are in need of a translator?"

"Jones," one of the blond men said with authority, extending his hand. He spoke with an Australian accent, which I found difficult to understand. "We're headed across the border into Afghanistan— not very deep. We just want to take some pictures."

Afghanistan! This I had never considered. The thought of returning gave me a sick feeling in the pit of my stomach. "Afghanistan . . . ," I muttered.

They stared at me, waiting for me to say something, but I couldn't.

44

Afghanistan, Somewhere Near the Pakistan Border, 1980

Mujahideen

While my mind was fighting the idea of returning to Afghanistan, one of the men broke the silence. "Didn't she tell you? We're reporters doing stories on the mujahideen. Bill MacAfee from New Zealand. Nice to meet you." He nodded toward the reporter wearing gold-rimmed glasses. "That's Henri. He's French. We work for different newspapers and need to get to where the fighting is. We're going across the border to get some stories and photos."

"What you ask of me is impossible," I said.

Jones regarded me with impatience. "We don't have all day," he said. "There are plenty of other people who will take this job, you know."

I took an immediate dislike to him. "If I go back, I could be killed by the Communists," I said.

"There won't be any Communists where we're going. We're not going anywhere near Jalalabad. We're only interested in the mujahideen-controlled areas. We ask questions; you translate. Simple."

I had heard that foreign journalists could help in getting visas, but I needed time to think.

"Who do you work for?" I asked.

"That's not your concern," Jones said.

"How much does it pay?"

"Two thousand dollars for two weeks."

I found myself doubting my English again. "Two thousand dollars? You're joking with me," I said.

"No, mate, that's the rate."

The money was too good to believe. But it wasn't only the money—I needed to get out of Pakistan. Maybe these men could help me if I helped them.

"Do you want the job or not?" Jones said.

My dislike for Jones grew stronger every time he spoke, and I began to have second thoughts. Who were these men anyway? There were so many organization here—the UN, foreign governments, the mujahideen, warlords, the Pakistan ISI. You never knew who someone was working for. They said they were reporters, but didn't Abbas tell me not to trust anyone? What would he think if I returned to Afghanistan only to be killed?

The three started talking among themselves, then Jones turned to me and gave me a look that made me uncomfortable. Maybe they worked for the CIA and were going to use me for their own purposes? What good would a visa be to a dead man? "I'll have to think about it," I said.

"We have papers and passwords. We have our own car and guide. The mujahideen want the world to know of their struggle. Are you in or not?" Jones said.

"What you ask of me is very difficult."

"We leave tomorrow. Meet us here in the morning if you want the job."

I spent a sleepless night at Dr. Ahmad's guesthouse. There was the money and a chance that if I helped them I could get a visa. There was also a chance I could die—but my life was the living death of a refugee stuck in Pakistan.

"How do I know I'll get the two thousand dollars in two weeks?" I asked Jones the following morning, hoping my demands would make them withdraw the offer and it would not have to be my decision.

"We work for big news organizations. Don't worry, you'll get paid."

"I need some money now," I insisted.

Jones reached into his pocket and peeled off five one hundred dollar bills from a thick stack. "You'll get the rest when we get back."

That afternoon I met the reporters outside the UN Humanitarian Aid building. They were standing next to an oversized jeep, now like me dressed in gebis and pakols. I took a seat in front beside a mujahid who was cradling a Kalashnikov in one arm, an anti-tank gun at his side—he was our guide. The reporters sat in back.

"Where will we spend the night?" I asked.

The look on Jones's face told me he didn't like questions.

"The mujahid will decide," he said.

We left Peshawar on the Grand Trunk Road, then turned onto Jamrud Road in the direction of Landi Kotal. Long before we reached the town, we veered onto a dirt road, enduring a jarring journey before the driver pulled over and stopped.

After walking for an hour down a wide dirt path framed by bare mountains, we reached a mujahideen guard post. The guards seemed to know our guide and waved us through. After another few hours of walking, the guard announced, "We've entered Afghanistan. We must be more careful. Walk quickly and stay alert."

This was Pashtun tribal land, with no distinction between Pakistan and Afghanistan. The dirt path opened onto a broad stretch of level farmland. In the distance we could see the walls of a farmhouse and walked toward it. The farmer greeted us and showed us to a small two-room building not far from the main house. "This is where you will sleep," he said. He fed us soup and round bread. As we ate, Henri turned to me. "The hashish here is very special, *mais oui*?" he said with a tobacco-stained smile. "You will find some for me to try, eh?"

The farmhouse was really a kind of base, a way station between Pakistan and the battlefront where mujahideen would come to obtain weapons and ammunition, get medical care, or simply rest before returning to battle. There were three groups of mujahideen at the farmhouse. One consisted of almost a dozen fighters who would go deep into Afghanistan—as far as Jalalabad. Another six would venture not quite as far but far enough that it would be difficult to escape if there were a problem. We would follow a third group of six who would patrol the territory in the area of the farmhouse.

The next morning the reporters were out early taking pictures. After devouring a small breakfast, we followed the mujahideen along a mountain path for several hours. When we finally stopped, we found ourselves looking down on a road snaking alongside a small river.

"That road is used by the Russians," a mujahid said. "When we attack, Russian helicopters will come. You must take cover over there." He gestured toward a shallow cave in the rock face nearby.

But to the disappointment of the reporters (and to my relief), no vehicles came by that day or the next. On the third day a small convoy appeared, and the mujahideen let loose with their Kalashnikovs as the camera shutters snapped.

The deep thump-thump of helicopter blades soon followed.

"Go!" a mujahid shouted. "Get to the cave."

As we crouched in our hideout, I could feel the blasts echoing off the surrounding mountains pounding inside my chest. The helicopters disappeared over the mountains, and we returned to the farmhouse.

The next day we struck off in another direction. After walking for hours, we came to a heavily damaged farmhouse. Several bloodied and disfigured bodies of mujahideen lay on the ground. MacAfee and Henri immediately started taking photographs. I began walking away, but a mujahid grabbed my arm. "Be careful," he said. "There are landmines everywhere." I froze, turned, and walked back to where we'd entered. I watched MacAfee and Henri do their work from a distance.

The following day we were awakened by the distant sound of Russian MiG fighters. We saddled up horses and rode in the direction of the explosions. After riding for some time, we stopped and tied our horses to a tree. A half-hour walk brought us to another farmhouse, where two dozen mujahideen, many wounded, sat or lay on the ground amid the pungent smell of exploded shells. As I approached, my foot slipped on something—a human leg in a pool of blood. I looked around and to my horror saw body parts scattered about the wet, rust-colored dirt. I thought of Afzel's charred body and started to retch, turned away, and stared at the mountains in the distance.

"Be careful of unexploded bombs," a mujahid called out. "Russian bombs are poorly made. For every five, two don't detonate—but they can still be deadly."

Henri and MacAfee took pictures as fast as their fingers could press the buttons on their cameras. When they were finished, the two reporters starting making a video of Jones interviewing a mujahid as I translated.

"How's the war going?" Jones asked.

"War is always very difficult, but *inshallah*, we will triumph," the mujahid replied.

"It must be difficult fighting Russian tanks and helicopters with small arms."

"Nay. We are very happy that God has brought us this war."

"What do you mean?" Jones asked.

"It's our one chance in a lifetime to fight for Allah against infidels who have invaded the land of Islam." The other mujahideen nodded in agreement, then began loudly chanting, holding up their weapons and pumping them as the cameras rolled. Another mujahid jumped in front of the video camera. "We look forward to death," he said. "When you die fighting the infidel, you die in glory for Allah and go to heaven."

Jones stopped recording. "We got what we came for," he said.

As we rode back to the farmhouse, Henri turned to me. "I don't understand," he said. "How can they not be afraid to die?"

"They've given themselves to God," I replied. "In their minds they're already dead."

Back at the farmhouse several wounded young mujahideen lay resting on the floor. I crouched down to one and asked if there was anything I could do for him. He whispered in a voice full of pain, "I have a favor to ask of you."

"I'll do whatever is in my power," I told him.

"My friend was badly hurt in the fighting. We could not carry him back. We hid him in a grave. Please, go find him and bring him back. One of us will show you the way."

"Don't worry," I said. "I will find your friend."

I struggled to keep up with the young mujahid as he quickly ascended the mountain trail. Large, flat rocks framed by upright stones appeared—the shallow graves that dotted the landscape as if they had sprouted from the soil itself. The mujahideen could not match the firepower of the Russians, but they were more than a match for them in cleverness. A mujahid would slip into a grave waiting for a Russian patrol to pass, then fire his Kalashnikov at the rear guard, slaying dozens in the confusion before he was gunned down himself, another martyr.

I began to doubt we would ever find the grave. Just as I had given up hope, the mujahid called out, "Over here!"

He shoved aside the stone cover, and the face of a mere boy stared up at us with lifeless eyes. I was transfixed by his unblemished skin, fresh as when he was alive—perhaps he'd just died. His mouth was frozen in a smile, as if he'd welcomed death.

It was with great disappointment and sadness that I told his friend back at the farmhouse what we had found. "Don't be upset," he said. "He died for Allah. I'm happy for him, as you should be."

We returned to Peshawar. When Jones handed me the rest of my money, he said, "Good luck, mate," then paused for a moment, as if he'd forgotten something, and added, "Oh . . . and thanks."

"Can you help me get a visa?" I asked.

"Sorry, mate. Can't do that. Tell you what, though—I could write a recommendation about the good work you did and how you risked your life for us."

"Will that help me get a visa to America?"

"Good luck getting one to the U.S.," he laughed, "or anywhere for that matter. There are millions of Afghans here trying to get out. It takes years to get a visa—if you survive. And there's nothing that I or anyone else can do about it."

I had made it out of the minefield, but I was still trapped.

45

Karachi, Pakistan, 1981

Train Ride

Steam rose from copper kettles in the Turkish café tucked down a side street in the Sadar Bazaar. As usual, it was crowded with Afghan men, most dispirited, cradling glass cups of green tea nestled in metal holders. It was a place I'd come to often, hoping to find a way to get a visa, any way out of Pakistan. Others came to buy guns or fake passports. I took a seat and found myself staring into the cardamom-laced froth of my tea as the rising steam warmed my face. Soon this cup would be as empty as my life.

"Salaam," said a voice in Dari tinged with Turkish. I looked up to find a man standing next to my table. He appeared to be just another Afghan refugee, but his accent intrigued me. "Forgive me, my name is Gul. You look lost."

"Baleh, in a way I am. Would you like to join me?"

"Tashakor. Tell me, how did you come to be here in Peshawar?"

I told him of my escape, the minefield, the prison, the reporters. "I want to go to America," I said, "but I'm just one of millions of Afghan refugees in a country that doesn't want us. No one wants us. I have no entry stamp, so I have no way of leaving, no way to get together with my family again."

"Why don't you go to Turkey?"

I thought he hadn't been listening. "I told you, I have no entry stamp. I cannot get a visa."

"You don't need a visa to fly to Turkey, only a passport. In Karachi you can buy a plane ticket and fly to Ankara."

"Why has no one told me this before?"

"Very few risk the trip to Karachi. Those who do don't return. I lived in Turkey. Here is the address and phone number of my cousin Hadir in Ankara. Call him when you arrive. For five thousand dollars he can get you to England."

Now I was suspicious. Was this man Gul (if that really was his name) just trying to find refugees with money to steal? Was what he said about flying to Ankara true? I didn't know what to think. So much one heard in Peshawar was unreliable, and even if what he said was true, there was nothing simple about it. Karachi was a thousand miles away. To leave my fellow Afghans and the relative safety of Peshawar and travel all that way across Pakistan to a city of Muhajirs and Punjabis involved great risk. So many things could go wrong on the fifteen-hour train journey. I did not want to be imprisoned again, and without Abbas I would not be so lucky a second time.

"Nay, Gul, tashakor," I said.

After several more weeks at the Sadar Bazaar, I realized I had only two difficult choices left: stay in Pakistan until the war was over (though there was no end in sight) or risk going to Karachi. Karachi was the best of my bad options.

I thanked Dr. Ahmad for all he had done for me and told him I was taking the train to Karachi. "I wish you luck," he said. "Keep your belongings close. Pickpockets roam the trains looking for dozing passengers."

At the end of January 1981, three months after I'd left Kabul with Abbas, I boarded the train. Three hours later the train pulled into Rawalpindi station, where the gebis and pakols of Peshawar gave way to the colorful silk robes and turbans of the Punjabis. The British had built Pakistan's railway system to connect all its major cities, even the remote Quetta. Afghanistan had no railways—none. Rawalpindi station, built in the manner of British imperial architecture, could have been mistaken for a miniature castle with its turreted stone construction.

The train journey from Rawalpindi to Karachi, Pakistan's main seaport on the Arabian Sea, descends from mountain highlands to hot, humid jungle. Each car of the old coal-fired train was crowded with families. The cries of babies almost drowned out the noise of the train. At each stop the train was set upon by men selling fruit, bread, and drinks. The farther south we traveled, the bigger and more crowded the stations became. The interior of the train became a steam bath. The suffocating aroma of spices, shouting of adults, and wailing of babies permeated all, like the soot from the coal-fired engine that coated everything in a fine black dust. I wanted to sleep, but I hadn't forgotten Dr. Ahmad's warning about pickpockets. Even if I could have understood my fellow passengers' Urdu, I would not have trusted them. I did not want to lose the hard-earned money I had hidden on me. And I worried about what lay ahead. Would I be able to get from the train station to the airport? Would I be able to buy a plane ticket to Ankara? Once I was in Turkey, would I be able to get out?

And my biggest worry of all, a worry that never left me: would I ever see my family again?

After a seemingly endless journey, the train pulled into Karachi station, another monument to the British presence. Even before the train came to a stop, a throng of vendors advanced on us, imploring the passengers hanging out the windows to purchase their breads and fruits and drinks. I fought my way down the aisle to the doorway, got off, and bought biscuits, bread, and orange soda. As I found some breathing room, I ate and drank, then joined the rush of humanity flowing down the street thick as water after a monsoon rain.

Men, desperate to drive me to the airport in their taxis, assaulted me, almost dragging me to their vehicle. I shared a taxi to the airport with several others. Pedestrians mobbed the streets. The taxi stopped and started constantly, trying to navigate through the sea of humanity. How could one country produce so many people? Afghanistan was sparse in every way: landscape, infrastructure, population. Pakistan was so crowded; I could have walked faster than this taxi was moving.

The situation at the airport was no better, the crowd of people so dense I could not see the ticket counter. An old floor sweeper working nearby was constantly being interrupted by questions. When I heard him answer someone in Dari, I approached him and asked him where I could buy a ticket to Ankara. "You are Afghan," he said, his eyes lighting up. He pointed toward a counter that I could barely see in the distance through a gap in the crowd. "There is the ticket counter. God be with you."

The long line to buy tickets moved at a glacial pace. Each person seemed to have some great difficulty that could only be resolved through a long, heated discussion. When it was finally my turn, I approached the ticket seller.

"Passport!" he demanded. I handed it to him. "Where is your visa?"

"I was told I don't need a visa to fly to Ankara."

"That's true—but only if you have an entry stamp. You have no entry stamp, so I cannot sell you a ticket."

"No one said anything about an entry stamp."

"That's not my problem. Next!"

As I stood there, the people behind me became more and more restless. They began shouting, "Step aside!" The ticket seller kept waving me away, but I refused to move. I had nowhere else to go. Suddenly I felt a poke. There, resting on his broom handle, was the floor sweeper. He motioned me closer. I bent down to him. "Baksheesh," he whispered.

I turned to the ticket seller. "How much for an entry stamp?"

He quickly replied, "Five hundred dollars U.S."

It was an outrageous amount. But wasn't my freedom worth five hundred dollars? Everything has a price, I thought. Then my pride took over. I had risked death going back to Afghanistan for this money, and I was not going to turn it over to this ticket seller for simply stamping a piece of paper. The voices of the crowd behind me grew louder, and the floor sweeper gave me another poke with his bony elbow. "You must pay him," he said. "Hurry!"

I gave the ticket seller a determined look and told him I only had one hundred dollars.

"Next!" he shouted.

The floor sweeper pulled my sleeve and whispered into my ear, "Two hundred."

I ignored him and said to the ticket seller, "I will find another agent who will take my money, and you will lose one hundred dollars. What do you want to do?"

He motioned me away impatiently.

I stepped aside and stared at him as others bought tickets. After twenty minutes he motioned to the next person in line to stop and gestured to me to come to the counter. I handed him my passport with the hundred-dollar bill inside. He reached under the counter and retrieved an ink pad and stamps. "Whack! Whack!" He handed me my passport with its newly inked entry and exit stamps.

My seat on the plane was as dirty and worn as a seat on a Peshawar bus, but I didn't care. I plopped down and buckled my seat belt, so tired that I took little notice of the strange rumbling from the plane's engines, which grew worse as the plane taxied down the runway. As we lifted off, the engines groaned in defiance, but the plane's tired, hulking body soared into the sky over the Arabian Sea.

The straining sound of the engines was drowned out by the drone of passengers running their fingers along their prayer beads as they rhythmically chanted, "God is greater, God is pure, praise be to God; God is greater, God is pure, praise be to God." The plane leveled off, and the praying stopped. Vast quantities of food and drink appeared from vests and bags, and I understood why my waskat had so many pockets. The plane's interior smelled like a Pakistani restaurant.

Then the plane plummeted, tipping from side to side as if it were trying to shake us off. I broke into a cold sweat, and my stomach leaped into my throat. Food and drink flew everywhere; overhead bins popped open; baggage toppled out; flight attendants were knocked to the floor as screams of "Allahu Akbar! Allahu Akbar!" filled the cabin.

What a cruel fate. I'd survived the Russians, the mujahideen, the landmine explosion, and prison only to discover that just when I thought I had escaped, God's plan for me was to plunge to my death in the Arabian Sea. The plane rose and plunged, rose and plunged, as the passengers screamed and prayed, screamed and prayed, and my last thoughts were of my family, who I would never see again: Baba, Babu, Afsana, Walid, and Mariam, my cousins, uncles, and aunts. I closed my eyes and accepted my fate, awaiting the impact of the plane slamming into the sea.

The plane swooped back up, leveled off, and the pilot regained control.

"We appear to have a problem with the right engine," the pilot announced. "We're returning to Karachi."

Hours later our new plane rose smoothly over the Arabian Sea. We flew above the vast, glistening, empty deserts of southwestern Pakistan, across the Pakistan border, and over the belly of Iran, before setting down at the Ankara airport.

Rain pummeled me as I stepped off the plane, but it was Turkish rain, and as I ran to the terminal in the downpour, there was no one on earth who was happier than me.

But having had nothing but problems with government officials, my happiness turned to fear as I handed the customs officer my passport. "What's this?" he asked, holding up the dripping wet document.

"My passport," I replied. "It's raining very hard outside."

He shook his head. My heart sank.

Then he smiled and said, "Wait over there until it dries."

I returned, and he gently turned each page, smiled, and waved me through—and he had not demanded a bribe. I liked Turkey already. As I headed out of the terminal, I thought, "This is the land of Afsana's family," and I felt suddenly close to her, and my step grew light.

If only such happiness could have lasted forever.

46

Ankara, Turkey, 1981

Shoeshine

There were no crushing crowds of pedestrians; no dirt roads jammed with cars; no mud bricks; no dirt floors; no animals; no gebis, pakols, or turbans. People lived in new apartment houses and worked in glass and steel buildings. In the department stores, people purchased goods from women as well as men. On the streets, women dressed and walked about in ways that would not be tolerated in Jalalabad or Quetta. There was an atmosphere of freedom I had not experienced in a very long time.

Hadir (the cousin of the man I'd met in the tea shop in Peshawar) lived in a four-story building ten minutes from the city center. Before entering his apartment, I removed my worn, dirty shoes and placed them by the door next to his new, polished ones. He was a light-haired middle-aged man with a well-manicured blond goatee—even the beards here were different. After seeing so many grocery stores and restaurants, I was surprised by how thin he was. He greeted me warmly. I shook his hand and thanked him for his hospitality. He smiled a broad, friendly smile. Another remarkable thing about Turkey: smiles seemed to come easily here.

"Where's your luggage?" he asked. When I showed him the plastic bag containing my clothes and papers, he shook his head. A maid sprayed my hands with a fragrant mist whose powerful scent made my head spin. She misted Hadir's hands, and he brought them to his face, breathed deeply, smiled, then turned to me. "You must be hungry," he said. "Do you like fish?"

"Yes, very much."

"What kind?"

"Any kind."

"Then we'll go to the fish market."

Having come from a world where people in bare feet sold their wares on the street, where goods were displayed in stalls along dusty roads and in small, grimy shops, I found the cleanliness, the orderliness, the clinical display of food, almost too much to take in. The fish were laid out on carpets of ice, their eyes still glistening, their mouths puffed out as if for a kiss, the iridescent colors of their bodies still gleaming. That night I ate like a shah.

The next day, Hadir insisted on taking me to a *hammam*, a Turkish bathhouse. After a short drive, we arrived at a huge gray stone building. Inside, men sat in brown leather armchairs quietly sipping tea beneath paintings of horses and sheep. We put on cotton robes and wooden shoes, then lay face down on white marble "sofas," joining other men being washed by attendants. The attendant looked at my body as if to say, "I can see it's been a very long time since you've been to a hammam," then he began pounding my back like a chef trying to tenderize a slab of meat. Every muscle in my body melted painfully beneath the onslaught. I was scrubbed with a rough sponge until I thought I would have no skin left. When the attendant finished, my whole body felt aglow—as if I were floating above the table.

Hadir and I relaxed with small cups of black tea as the unmoving horses and sheep in their painted meadows stared down on our rejuvenated bodies. When I asked for a larger cup of tea, the attendant looked confused, and Hadir laughed. It was another reminder that I was no longer in Kabul, where green tea is served in cups the size of bowls.

Just outside the hammam's door, a young boy sat on the stoop next to a wooden box of brushes, cloths, and tins of shoe polish. He leaped up when he saw us and started shouting. I followed his eyes down to my shoes—the same shoes that had hiked up and down the Hindu Kush and walked through a minefield; that had sat in a prison in Landi Kotal; that had made the long train ride to Karachi and the harrowing flight to Turkey—the same ones that had been drenched in rain at the Ankara airport.

"Shoeshine, mister?"

My shoes were in such terrible condition, it seemed pointless, but the boy grabbed a brush from his box and with an irresistible grin invited me to take a seat on his worn wooden stool. He began scrubbing my shoes' tired leather with his small, quick hands, constantly spitting on them and brushing them as if he could force them back to life. As he polished, he looked up at me and asked, "Where do you come from?"

"Afghanistan," I replied.

"Afghanistan!" he beamed. "Then you are fighting the Russians!"

"Baleh. That's true." The boy applied more polish, brushed and brushed, spat and spat, even more furiously, then buffed with a soft cloth until my once sad shoes shone. "What do I owe you?" I asked.

"Nothing."

"Nothing? Nay, that is not right. You've done a good job. I want to pay you something."

"Nay," he said, still smiling.

"I don't understand."

He started talking excitedly, waving his polishing cloth around as he spoke. "You are a *mousafer*—someone who has traveled far from home. If I had money, I would give it to the Afghan people to fight the Russians. And if I were older, I would go fight them myself!"

I slipped several dollar bills into his shoeshine box as we left.

47

Istanbul, Turkey, 1981

U.S. Consulate

That night I decided I would go to the U.S. consulate in the morning to apply for asylum. But sleep could not find me, so I took a blanket, walked to the consulate, and slept in the park across the street.

I awoke to a pomegranate sunrise to find dozens of people already outside the consulate. The line, mostly young men, soon grew to resemble a human serpent. Just before nine o'clock, a consulate official directed us to the rear of the building, where we stopped before a huge wrought iron gate. A spacious yard with towering trees and grand gardens loomed beyond. Consulate employees awaiting the swarm of refugees sat at tables scattered around the yard.

The official approached the first man in line. "Nationality?" he asked.

"Iranian," the man answered.

"Nay," the official said and waved the man out of line. The man was confused at first, but the official made it clear he was not welcome. This poor man had had nothing to do with the Iran hostage crisis, but he was paying for it. As the official continued down the line, the interaction became a rhythmic drumbeat.

"Nationality?"

"Iranian."

"Nay."

"Nationality?"

"Iranian."

"Nay."

Then he stopped before me. "Nationality?"

"Afghan," I replied. The official looked surprised, hesitated, then pointed me to the consulate entrance.

Inside was a long, wide hallway with small, glass-walled offices on either side where consulate employees were conducting interviews. At the far end, a short staircase led up to another set of offices. I walked the length of the hall and up the stairs to a desk where a blonde, blue-eyed woman was sitting. I asked her for an application for asylum. "Over there," she said, gesturing to a table. "Let me know if you need help."

I sat down and started to read the form, so nervous my hand started shaking. "Is there a problem?" I looked up to see the woman from the desk.

"My English is good," I said, "but sometimes not that good."

She sat next to me, asked me the questions, and filled in the answers. When we were finished, she said, "Come back tomorrow for an interview with the assistant consul."

The next day I sat in a hard wooden chair in the consul's office, nervously awaiting my interview.

"Baryalai Popal?" asked a slightly built, oval-faced young man with light-colored hair and metal-framed glasses that made him look like an owl. I followed him to his office and sat down before a desk covered with stacks of papers. "My name is Delan. I see you are a Popal," he said.

"Yes, that's true."

"I heard a lot about your family when I was stationed in Kabul. Tell me, how did you come to be here?"

If ever there was proof of destiny, I had found it—our two lives intersecting under the most unlikely of circumstances. What else could it be? For the next half-hour we discussed Afghan politics like old friends. When I told him I wanted to live in America, I was certain he would make it happen quickly. But to my great disappointment he said, "If you want to live in America, you must apply for a green card. It takes a year or more to process. In the meantime my secretary will give you a letter to take to the UN aid office. They'll give you money for living expenses while you're waiting."

Now I was trapped in Turkey.

48

U.S. Consulate, Istanbul, 1981

Hazaras

The sound of the phone ringing in my hotel room jarred me awake.

"Mr. Popal?" I could barely hear the voice of Delan's secretary above the noise in the background. "Come to the consulate immediately. We need you."

As I entered the courtyard, I was greeted by angry shouting. Delan stood at the entrance of the building staring at dozens of agitated Hazaras. "Thank God you're here," he said. "What do they want?"

I called out to the Hazaras, but they erupted in such an uproar of demands and complaints that I could not understand a word they said.

"Do something!" Delan shouted at me impatiently.

When I saw an elder near the front of the crowd, all of the trips I had taken with Baba to visit elders in the countryside, all the knowledge of diplomacy, politics, and tribal customs that he had tried to instill in me—knowledge I had fought against with youthful disdain—came back to me. "You must choose three men to represent all of you," I told him. "The consul will see them in his office. The others must wait here."

The elder disappeared into the crowd of Hazaras. Soon he reappeared with two other elders. Delan led us to his office. One of the elders immediately began talking. "We don't want asylum. We want to go to America so we can work and buy weapons. America gives the ISI money for weapons, but the ISI only gives them to Pashtuns. This is not right. We want to get weapons and return to Afghanistan to fight the Russians. That is all we ask."

"You shouldn't say this," I told the elder. "If you ask for weapons, they'll reject you."

Delan looked at me impatiently. "Why aren't you translating?"

"They want visas," I said.

"What are you telling him?" the elder cried. "Tell him what I told you!"

I looked at the elders, then at Delan, everyone upset with me. I said to Delan, "They want to go to America to work so they can buy weapons to fight the Russians. They say the Pashtuns are getting all the weapons."

"That's absurd!" Delan said. "Tell them this is the U.S. consulate, not a weapons dealer. Tell them we're here for people who need help, not people who want to fight." When I hesitated, Delan burst out, "Tell them!"

When I had finished, the elder said, "Is this the consul's answer?"

"Baleh," I replied.

The three elders quickly turned and walked out of Delan's office, down the long hallway, and out the entrance, where they stood before the throng of Hazaras gathered outside the building. Delan and I followed and stood at the head of the crowd beside the elders. One of the elders spoke out to the Hazaras in a strong and determined voice. The crowd murmured more and more loudly as he spoke. When the elder finished, all the Hazaras began chanting: "Down with America! America is no good! Down with America! America is no good! Give us visas, give us weapons." Then they began a new chant: "The translator is bad!"

Suddenly a group of reporters with video cameras appeared and started filming. The Hazaras began jumping up and down, whooping and waving their arms above their heads as if they were holding invisible weapons.

"You must do something!" I said to Delan. "It's not good to make so many people your enemy."

Delan disappeared back into the building; the reporters left; the Hazaras grew quiet.

When Delan reappeared, he handed me a bullhorn and told me what to say.

"The Australian embassy has agreed to consider your applications for asylum," I said through the roar of the bullhorn.

As soon as the Hazaras heard this, they erupted in shouts of joy that drowned out my next words. "Don't mention guns."

49

Frankfurt, Germany, 1981

The Parcel

I awoke the next day more determined than ever to get to America. Surely Delan would help me after I helped him with the Hazaras. I went to see him.

He said there was nothing he could do.

Ever since I was young, I wanted to go to America. I knew that if I settled in Germany, that dream would end. It was with a heavy heart I called Abbas. I had not spoken to him since we parted ways in Pakistan. He was surprised and happy to hear my voice. "I'm so happy to hear that you're finally coming to Germany. I will arrange to have the German consulate in Istanbul issue you a visa. The German consulate in Kabul can prepare the paperwork for Afsana and the children. I can't wait to see you."

Abbas was there to meet me when I arrived at the Frankfurt Airport. "I'm so happy to see you, Bar. When I saw you enter the terminal, I still couldn't believe my eyes. I feared this day would never come. Destiny has brought us together again."

"I'm happy to see you as well, Abbas. But you know this is not where I want to be."

"Destiny had a different plan for you. It's more powerful than your own desires. You should not swim against the current, Bar. You should swim with it. Accept your destiny and be happy."

Waiting to hear that my wife and children had left Kabul made each day long and painful, so I focused my energies and attention on news about Afghanistan, spending hours listening to the Voice of America broadcasts in Dari and Pashto. My body was in Germany, but I had never really left Kabul.

A few weeks later Uncle Gholam received a telegram from Kabul: "The parcel will be arriving soon." The next day, before the sun had risen, Abbas and I left for the long drive to the Frankfurt Airport, where the "parcel" would be arriving. At the terminal hundreds of Afghans were sitting under trees or leaning against cars, many chain-smoking. They had camped overnight, awaiting the daily flight from Dushanbe, Tajikistan—the stopover from Kabul. Inside the terminal hundreds more sat waiting for a loved one, a relative, or a friend. Many came simply hoping to recognize a familiar face. There was always cause for hope, but there was always worry as well. Had they been caught by the police in Kabul? Were they stopped by airport security and turned back? I was all hope and no certainty.

We went to the airport terminal, but no "parcel" arrived on that flight nor on the flights over the next two days. All I could do was return each day and hope to see the faces of my wife and children.

As we waited in the terminal on the fourth trip, someone shouted, "The plane is landing!" and a wave of excitement surged through the crowd. We all stared through the glass wall at the corridor where the passengers would appear.

"They're here!" someone shouted. The Afghan refugees looked in amazement at the throng of Afghans cheering their arrival. More followed, all peering at us through the window, as anxious to see a familiar face as we were. Then the stream became a trickle. Then it stopped.

I stared at the glass wall feeling empty.

A woman appeared, struggling with a cart piled high with suitcases and bags. Two small children clung to its sides. It was Afsana, preoccupied with the cart, and Walid and Mariam. As soon as Walid and Mariam saw me, they started running. Walid was older and faster than his sister, and I caught him in my arms. Mariam quickly followed, hugging me even harder than her brother. I set Walid and Mariam down and looked up. There stood Afsana. Our eyes met.

When we embraced, my world was once again complete.

50

Frankfurt, Germany, 1981

The Interview

We were settled in Aachen, a small city an hour west of Cologne on the Netherlands border. Our new home was a small two-bedroom apartment furnished with old furniture from a government warehouse. As soon as we were settled, we enrolled Walid and Mariam in school. Their teachers took an immediate liking to these two young Afghan refugees, particularly Mariam, who couldn't wait to learn to speak German because talking was what she liked to do most. In Afghanistan, the teachers were very strict, very severe, and the schoolwork was very hard. Here the teachers were kind and friendly. They treated the children with cakes and chocolate. Walid and Mariam went on school trips to a park, the zoo, and a forest, where they went swimming in a lake for the first time. Change is easy for the young. Within a few months, Walid and Mariam were talking German with new friends. My son and daughter's last years in Afghanistan had been terrible for them, especially after I left. They were trapped in our home with no father, everyone terrified, security guards constantly at the door with their guns and shouting. They came to love their new home.

Life for Afsana and me was the opposite. Until I received a work permit for a regular job, I laid television cable in the streets at night. In the winter, breaking the frozen soil with a pickax before digging the trench made each night seem endless. During the day, Afsana and I both struggled to learn the language of our new country. When her German improved, Afsana worked as a stock clerk in a department store, quietly resigned to her fate. She volunteered at the local hospital, where dozens of Afghan children injured in the war arrived each week with every injury imaginable: broken limbs, puncture wounds, missing arms and legs. Afsana tried to comfort them. It gave her great pleasure and broke her heart all at the same time.

One morning after work, I arrived home to find Afsana standing terrified on a chair as mice scurried around the kitchen floor. I grabbed a broom and banged it hard on the wooden floor and chased them away. Afsana started shaking and covered her ears. After I helped her down, she looked at me and said, "After you left Kabul, National Security guards came looking for you all the time, demanding to know where you were—where I was hiding you. They threatened me. I shut Mariam in the bedroom—you know how she talks—but she let herself out. When they asked her where her Baba was, she started to talk, and I had to put my hand over her mouth, scoop her up, and shut her in the bedroom. When the guards threatened me again, I told them Mariam had started making up stories about you after you disappeared. Finally, the guards left. Now, whenever I hear a loud banging, it's as if I'm back in Kabul and security guards are pounding on the door again."

Since neither of us spoke German, a trip to the doctor's office meant waiting for Gholam or Abbas to take us. I could not get government permission to work full-time until my German improved, so I quit my job laying cable at night to attend German classes full-time. I took as many part-time jobs as I could, painting houses, moving furniture, anything that paid. At a party for an Afghan friend, I heard that I could make good money buying and selling used cars. "Look for one for sale by an elderly woman who no longer drives," I was told. "Such cars are always in very good condition." I started buying and selling used cars. Having no place to store them, I parked them on the street until they were sold. One day I answered the door to find two German policemen staring at me, looking grim.

"We've received complaints that you have been storing cars in the street," one of them told me. "Move them, or they'll be towed."

"Yes, I will take care of it." I was relieved the police didn't seize them or fine me, but now I had to find a place for the cars.

Later that week I met Mohammad. He was my age—thirty—dark-haired, thin, with confident eyes. He had been in Germany for only a couple of years but managed to operate multiple businesses, including a large used car lot in Aachen. There was much he could teach me. I told Mohammad my problem. He introduced me to an Afghan friend of his who was willing to rent a dirt lot for me under his name and let me use his business license—one of the many things refugees do for each other when it is not possible to do things legally and survive at the same time.

I could afford to rent only half the lot. The few cars I had for sale looked like vehicles that had been abandoned in a field. I paid an Afghan friend to look after the lot while I searched for used cars to buy.

When my German improved enough to receive permission to have a full-time job, I applied for a position as a night clerk at a hotel in Cologne and got an interview.

The four-story hotel was near the cathedral, a short walk from the railway station. The street, a mixture of modern and old buildings, was German-clean. A heavyset German woman, her hair pulled tightly against her skull, eyed me suspiciously.

"Baryalai Popal?" she asked.

"Yes."

"You are from Afghanistan?"

"Yes."

"Your people are fighting the Soviets."

"Yes."

"Afghans must be very stupid to think they can defeat the Soviet Union. Running around in the mountains with guns just makes life miserable for everyone. You should be grateful to be here."

"Stupid" is the worst of insults to an Afghan, but I held my tongue. I would have liked to have told her that I did not feel grateful to have lost everything, to have found myself in a country where I could not speak my own language, a country where I was disliked simply because I was a foreigner, a country where someone with a degree in law and political science should be grateful to be applying for a job as a night clerk an hour and a half from my tiny, mouse-infested apartment. "Yes, I'm very grateful," I said.

"Life here must not be so bad for you, eh? The German government provides well for you refugees."

"Yes, life here is very good."

"I watch the television. I see your people with no shoes in the snow, no food on the table, no milk to drink. Here in Germany the shops are full."

I wanted to defend my people and my country, but she was right. The Germans had an abundance of goods in their shops and could afford to buy them. People lived in cities and villages connected by roads and railways, bringing them close and giving them a sense of national identity. In Germany everyone is a German. Afghanistan has few roads and no railways. People live in walled compounds in small villages scattered among deserts, mountains, and valleys. Most important to them is family and tribe.

"The job is from 8:00 p.m. to 8:00 a.m.," she said. "Our guests are executives of big companies from all over Europe here to attend conventions. You must be polite and on time. Can you do this?"

"Yes," I replied.

"Good, then you're hired. The girl at the front desk will explain everything to you. I expect you to work hard. I had to fire the last two night clerks. One got drunk and slept the whole time. The other rented out rooms to prostitutes and kept the money. You want to work, yes? I hope I won't have to fire you."

"Don't worry, I'm very thirsty for work, and I don't drink alcohol."

When Uncle Gholam called me to tell me Baba had died, a wave of sadness came over me. I felt a great weight had suddenly been put on my shoulders, and I realized how much I had depended on Baba to carry the burden of life for me. I was surrounded by family, but I felt terribly alone.

"He was a great man," Afsana said. "After you left, he would look at pictures of you all the time and would often talk about you. He loved you very much. What more can a child ask?"

51

Frankfurt, Germany, 1989

Warlords

In February 1989, the stone that Russia had tossed into the air when it invaded Afghanistan came crashing down on its head. Russian soldiers perched on tanks and in troop carriers crossed the Termez Bridge back to Russia carrying TVs, cartons of cigarettes, drugs, and souvenirs of the war. The Russians had constructed the Termez Bridge—the "Friendship Bridge," as they called it—in the early 1980s to connect the Russian republic of Uzbekistan with Afghanistan. But they used the Friendship Bridge to send tanks and troops to war against the Afghans and force young Afghan men into the military to fight against their own people. This senseless war had cost the lives of thousands of young Russian men. More than a million Afghans had died. Some two million refugees had fled into Pakistan, two million more into Iran.

Mohammad Najib, former head of the Afghan Communist Party and KHAD, the Afghan secret police, was left in control. Russian soldiers were gone, but Russia controlled Najib. The bear still had us in its mouth.

But Najib's government was weak, and Afghans took up arms against it. Najib had the support of Russia, but the rebels had the support of the United States, Pakistan, and Middle Eastern countries. In an attempt to distance himself from the infidel Russians, Najib changed his name to Najibullah, "honored of God." He passed a new constitution that declared Afghanistan an Islamic state. But after the collapse of the Soviet Union in December 1991, Russia's support to Najibullah stopped. When his government fell the following spring, Najibullah took refuge in a UN building in Kabul, where he remained for the next five years.

Tajik, Uzbek, and Hazara warlords from the North took control of Kabul, fighting Pashtuns backed by Pakistan who wanted to create an Islamic state. In order to gain the support of southern Afghans, Hamid Karzai, son of the leader of the Popalzai tribe in Kandahar, was appointed deputy foreign minister. Gulbuddin Hekmatyar, head of Hezb-i-Islami, the Party of Islam, refused to accept the new government and attacked the warlords in Kabul with rockets. The Russians had destroyed the countryside. The war of the warlords would destroy Kabul.

This new war arose out of the different factions organized to fight the Russians. Some, like Pir Gailani's National Islamic Front for Afghanistan, were non-Pashtuns who hoped to establish a moderate Afghan nation encompassing all ethnic groups. Others were Pashtun factions, such as Jamiat-i-Islami, led by Burhanuddin Rabbani, and Hekmatyar's Hezb-i-Islami, which wanted to establish a fundamentalist Islamic state under strict Sharia law. Pakistan hoped it could exercise control by backing the radical Islamic Pashtun groups and placing them in power. The United States wanted to defeat the Soviets and backed whomever Pakistan favored.

In 1980, several of these groups had gotten together in an attempt to form an Afghan government in exile to gain international recognition and support. But as is the way with such disparate groups, the alliance fell apart. Another attempt to unite was made in 1985, when a combination of moderate and radical groups formed an Islamic unity party, but Hekmatyar refused to participate. That year the United States increased its aid to the mujahideen to over a quarter-billion dollars. Other attempts to form an interim government failed over the next few years because of ethnic and religious divisions.

Hekmatyar's severe black eyes glowed with the intensity of an extremist, which is just what he was. His only interest was establishing a fundamentalist Islamic state in Afghanistan to the exclusion of all other groups. Sharia law would be the law of the land. In the years ahead, Hekmatyar's group, Hezb-i-Islami, would be involved in assassinations and the destruction of Kabul. But it would continue to receive the support of Pakistan and the United States.

Hekmatyar was opposed by the moderate Ahmad Shah Massoud, the Tajik warlord from the Panjshir Valley north of Kabul. During the Russian occupation he had returned to the Panjshir

Valley and defended it against wave after wave of Russian attacks and became known as the "Lion of Panjshir."

The United States had spent billions supporting the mujahideen to drive out the Russians. Now that the Russians were gone, I waited anxiously for the United States to bring order to Afghanistan. Surely it was not going to abandon us now. But the United States did nothing.

In Germany in May 1990 my used car dealer friend Mohammad stopped by my car lot. I had rented the whole field, though there was still plenty of room for more cars. "I'll be gone for a few days," he said. "I'm off to East Germany to trade deutsche marks."

"What do you mean?" I asked.

"You don't know about the black market in deutsche marks across the border?" he said, surprised. "I trade one deutsche mark for three ostmarks."

"I don't understand," I said.

"East and West Germany cannot stay divided for long. They will have to reunite, and when they do, East Germans will have to be allowed to exchange their ostmarks for deutsche marks. I'll triple my money! I'm making one last trip."

"Let me come with you. I have twenty thousand deutsche marks saved from my used car business."

"Nay, you shouldn't do this. It's too risky."

"Why not? You are."

"True, but I have a house and many businesses. I can afford to be wrong. But that's all the money you have. Things may not turn out as I expect. I don't want to see you lose everything."

"And if I don't do this, I could lose the money some other way," I said.

"It's a five-hour drive to the border. If you want to go, meet me at my car lot at dawn."

The next morning I told Afsana I would be gone all day looking at used cars.

The border town was small, with just a few shops. Mohammad parked the car on the main street near a park. When I handed him my money, he looked at me and said, "Are you sure you want to do this, Bar?"

"Baleh. Very sure," I said, then watched Mohammad walk across the border and disappear.

When he returned an hour later, we sat down to a lunch of bratwurst. As I counted my sixty thousand ostmarks, I had an uneasy feeling in the pit of my stomach.

Months passed, and each day I feared Afsana would find out what I had done with our life savings. Then, in the middle of May, East and West Germany united. With the sixty thousand deutsche marks I received for my ostmarks, I filled my used car lot with cars.

I arrived at the lot a few weeks later to find dozens of former East Germans waiting impatiently outside. When I opened the gate, they rushed in. Each one ran to a car, pulled off the sales sticker, and shoved money into my hands without even examining it. They didn't care. They were going to sell the cars in East Germany for double what they paid because everyone in East German was desperate to own a car and would pay anything to get one.

Now my car lot was empty.

For the next few weeks, I looked for more used cars to buy, but there were none to be had. As soon as I became successful, I was out of business. I went to see Mohammad. "I have no more cars left in my lot," I told him, "but your lot is full of used cars. Where did you get them?"

"California," he replied.

"California?"

"There are plenty of used cars in California—and no snow. That means no salt on the roads and no rust. You don't have to spend money on body work."

No rust? No body work? Here I always probed a car with an iron rod to see how bad the rust was—and it was usually very bad. I was determined to go to California.

My cousin Oman, who had worked in the Foreign Ministry under Daoud's government, had been assigned to the United Nations in New York. After Daoud's overthrow and murder, Oman lost his job. He moved to San Francisco, where he found a job with the

U.S. government helping Afghan refugees seeking asylum. With the UN refugee passport I had received in Germany, I got a tourist visa to the United States and flew to San Francisco.

As my plane approached San Francisco, with its bay of sparkling water and its majestic bridges, their towers poking through a shimmering fog, I had a vision of the smoke rising from the Jalalabad Airport terminal when I began my escape from Kabul a lifetime ago.

When Oman greeted me at the airport, we talked all the way to his apartment and late into the night.

An Afghan friend of Oman was familiar with buying used cars, and with his help I purchased several Japanese cars I could sell in Germany.

When Afsana met me at the Frankfurt Airport, I was as excited as a child as I told her, "I flew to California to buy cars but discovered something more. I discovered Americans. They don't care about foreign looks or foreign accents. Why? Because America is full of people from different countries, people of different colors, people with different accents. It's a place where no one fits in, so everyone does."

52

San Diego, California, 1992

SpeeDee Oil

In 1992 a door to America opened for me. If I bought a business and hired a certain number of workers, I could get a green card. Afsana was reluctant to go. With an enormous effort, she had learned German and had come to accept Germany as her new home. But I did not want to stay in Germany. The risk I had taken in buying ostmarks with our life savings had paid off. I bought a SpeeDee Oil franchise in San Diego.

Before we left, we had dinner at Uncle Gholam's. "Your father is not here, Bar," Uncle Gholam said solemnly. "So it is my obliga-tion to say what he would say. You are making a big mistake. Your children are comfortable in Germany and have many friends and relatives here. Why do you want to go to America? I don't under-stand this. There's no government health care, no help if you're unemployed, and the cities are full of gangs."

"Baba said I should make decisions that would give me the most opportunities," I replied. "America may not be perfect, but it's still the land of opportunity."

"If you go to America, you'll never see Afghanistan again," Uncle Gholam said, his voice rising—which was not like him.

"My Afghanistan doesn't exist anymore," I replied defiantly. "And it's my fate that I should go to America. When I was in Tur-key, Abbas told me, 'You should not resist your fate; you should swim with the current.' I swam with the current of the Kabul River when I left Afghanistan. Now I will swim with the cur-rent to America."

On the opening day of my new business, Afsana and Mariam came to help. We arrived to find the former owner's manager and four employees waiting for us. The manager, a huge figure with dirty-blond hair and a bushy mustache, was hobbling around the shop, delivering orders in a booming voice. When he saw us, he waggled a fat finger at me.

"Come!" he said. "I need to make clear the relationship between you and me. Do you know why the last owner went bankrupt? I'll tell you why. He didn't listen to me. I paid all his expenses—his big mortgage on his fancy house, his kids' private schooling, the monthly payment on his Mercedes. I watched his wife come in each week and take money from the cash register. If you want to survive in this business, you're going to have to listen to me. And anything you want to say to the workers has to go through me, so that there are no misunderstandings. You got that?"

How could he talk to me like this? *He* was supposed to be working for *me*. I felt such shame that I prayed for the earth to open up and swallow me.

"Do you understand me?" he boomed as if I were deaf. "Do you speak English?"

I grabbed Mariam's hand and sat her down in the office, bristling with fury, trying hard to contain myself, trying to think of what to do or say.

"Don't do anything crazy, Baba," Mariam begged.

I did want to do something crazy, but I did not want to lose my business before I even started. Why was this happening? I paced back and forth in the office, feeling the sweat beading on my forehead as Mariam and Afsana looked at me with worried faces. The whole time the manager stared at me as if I were an idiot. Please God, I prayed, help me. I made a decision and waggled my finger at the manager to come. He planted his hulking frame in the doorway, oil dripping from the rag he was holding. "I live in a small apartment," I said. "I have no mortgage payments. I drive an old car. My wife and I have experienced worse things in our lives than you will ever know. She has no need for money. There's the door you walked through this morning. I want you to walk out that door right now and don't return."

He didn't move. "Who will run your shop?" he asked.

"That's no longer your concern."

"If I go, the workers go with me."

"Fine. Take all your friends with you!"

He stood there, staring, as if he did not believe what he had just heard. "I've seen many crazy people," he finally said. "But you're the craziest." Then he folded his arms across his massive chest and said, "You know corporate isn't going to like this."

"I told you that's not your problem."

He threw the oily rag on the ground, walked over to my desk, grabbed a handful of invoices, and tossed them in the air. Paper rained down like kites whose strings had been cut.

"Boys, I'm no longer working here," he shouted to the workers. "Now's the time for you to decide. Are you leaving with me or staying with this crazy guy?"

The men looked at each other. Then they looked at the manager. Then they looked at me. They followed the manager out of the shop, as the line of cars waiting outside grew longer and longer. Mariam looked at me. "He can't treat me like that," I said.

"What are we going to do now, Baba?"

"I don't need them," I said. "I'll do it." But even as I spoke these words, doubt crossed my mind. I'd watched a shop in operation during my training sessions and saw how to change oil but had never actually changed it myself. I knew that if the shop closed for even one day, corporate could take it away. I found a large sheet of paper, wrote "No Tune-Ups Today, Only Oil Changes," and taped it to the front window, then rolled up my sleeves and said to Mariam, "Let the cars in."

Crouching in the pit beneath the first car, I unscrewed the oil plug. Hot oil erupted, spurting down onto my face and body. I reached for a rag and banged my hand against the hot engine.

Seven hours later, I was covered in oil and sweat, burned, and utterly exhausted. "Tell the rest of the cars we're closed," I called to Mariam. "Tell them to come back tomorrow." I wiped the day's misery off me and then collapsed into a chair. Afsana, shaken, sat across from me trying to stay composed.

Mariam closed up the register, then entered the office and approached me on gentle footsteps. My head rested on my chest, eyes closed, too exhausted to even think. "We did it!" she yelled, and I looked up to see the biggest smile I'd ever seen. She hugged my tired, oily frame.

I placed an ad in the local paper offering to pay more for a manager and workers than SpeeDee suggested. Over the next few days, men began showing up at my shop. "You can start right away," I told each one—without even asking if he knew what an oil pan was. I hired a new manager as well.

Each day at noon I brought out containers from the small fridge and sat down to a lunch of Afsana's lamb and rice with a very large cup of green tea. I had brought a little bit of Afghanistan with me. My thoughts of home were suddenly interrupted by a loud, familiar voice, and I almost spilled my tea.

"I didn't know you were so sensitive." In the doorway stood the large figure of my former manager. "We Americans are a very up-front kind of people," he said. "We tend to speak our minds. You may not be used to that kind of thing, being Afghani and all."

"You walked out."

"Look, I saw your ad. I'll come back, and I'll respect you. And I'll only take a hundred dollars a week more."

"No. Not for a hundred dollars more or a hundred dollars less."

He looked completely surprised. "You're sure about that?" he asked.

"Yes, very sure," I said, and as he turned to walk away, I called after him, "and Afghani is our currency. I am Afghan."

53

Kabul, Afghanistan, 1995

The Taliban

The warlords in Kabul divided the city into sections, each controlled by a separate faction, each section gated and heavily guarded. Hazaras controlled my neighborhood. When the Hazaras took over the rooftop of Uncle Ali's house to launch rockets at Massoud's forces, making Uncle Ali's house a target for Massoud's counterattacks, Uncle Ali and Aunt Deeba fled, traveling through Pakistan to India and finally to Germany.

The warlords attacked not just each other but the people of Kabul as well. Kabul's residents were robbed, starved, and murdered. Women were raped. The city had descended into anarchy and chaos. In Kandahar, the birthplace of Afghanistan, Mullah Mohammed Omar, a fundamentalist religious leader, wrapped himself in the robe of the Prophet Muhammad and declared himself "Commander of the Faithful." Mullah Omar began attracting young men from the refugee camps in the border areas of Pakistan, many of whom were orphans of war with no connection to family or tribe. These young men had been trained in a radical form of Islam in the madrasas and were known as "talibs"—"seekers of knowledge." They shared Mullah Omar's religious fervor and took up arms under him to restore order to Afghanistan in the name of Allah. They became known as the "Taliban."

Supported by money, weapons, and supplies from Pakistan (paid for by the United States), the Taliban took control of Kandahar, Ghazni, and Herat. In 1997, the group captured Jalalabad. When the Taliban advanced on Kabul, Massoud and thousands of his followers fled to the Panjshir Valley. Burhanuddin Rabbani, left behind as president, appointed the Islamic fundamentalist leader Gulbuddin Hekmatyar prime minister in the hopes of appeasing the Taliban. But the Taliban wanted control and surrounded Kabul, bombarding it with rockets and artillery. When Taliban fighters entered the city, they immediately went to the UN office, seized

Najibullah, chained him to a car by his neck, and dragged him around the garden of the Presidential Palace until he was dead. They hung his body from a lamppost in a Kabul square.

The Taliban required women to be covered from head to foot. If a woman went outside, she had to be accompanied by a male relative. Men were required to wear turbans and beards and pray five times a day. Television, music, photography—even my beloved kite flying—were banned as a distraction from worshipping God. Hundreds of Afghan cultural artworks were destroyed, including two thousand–year–old Buddhas carved into the mountainside at Bamiyan. Created to honor God, they were destroyed in the name of God.

The Taliban ruled the people under oppressive religious laws, but they also stopped the robbing, killing, and raping and brought order to a city desperate for any kind of peace and security. The Taliban stopped the drug trade and the stealing of small farmers' properties.

Although the Taliban did not control Mazar-i-Sharif, the large city north of Kabul that was home to many Hazaras, in May 1997 Saudi Arabia, Pakistan, and the United Arab Emirates recognized the Taliban as the legitimate government of Afghanistan.

The Taliban attacked Mazar-i-Sharif but were thwarted by the Uzbek warlord Abdul Rashid Dostum until Malik Pahlawan, Dostum's second in command, betrayed him, combining forces with the Taliban to drive Dostum out of the city. The Taliban poured into the city, slaughtering thousands of Hazaras.

Afghanistan was now united under one leadership for the first time since the Russians left in 1989. Pakistan rejoiced in the victory of the Taliban, the group they had backed after the fall of Najibullah.

A new alliance was formed among the warlords of the North called the "Northern Alliance." The Taliban were primarily Pashtuns. The Northern Alliance included a mix of ethnic groups: Tajiks, Uzbeks, and Hazaras. Among the alliance commanders was Hazrat Ali, a military commander from Jalalabad with whom I would have my own great battle.

During all this time my thoughts never left my mother, Babu. She was still in Kabul—now without Baba to comfort her. Every day I prayed that things would improve, that it would be safe for me to return to Kabul so that I could see her one last time. But it was not to be.

When Uncle Gholam gave me the sad news that Babu had died, I thought of the last time I had spoken with her on the phone.

"I'm so afraid I'll never get back to Kabul to see you," I told her.

"Don't worry, Bari," she said. "Things here will not stay as they are. You will return one day."

"But I'm afraid you won't be there."

"It's not so important that I'm here, Bari," she replied. "What's important is that your house and all its memories will still be here for you."

54

New York City

September 11, 2001

I called my cousin Shabir in Japan, who I had not seen in over twenty-five years. When his father, Uncle Ali, left Japan after being appointed ambassador to the Soviet Union, Shabir remained behind, married a Japanese woman, and had a son, Rasoul. They lived outside Tokyo, where Shabir taught German in a Japanese school.

"Moshi moshi," a voice answered in Japanese.

"Salaam, Shabir," I said, "it's Bar. I was almost afraid to call you. It's been a very long time."

Shabir laughed. "This would be the first time in our lives you have ever been afraid of me!" For a moment I felt as if we were back in Kabul and young again.

"Do you remember the party we went to in Paghman," I asked him, "the day before you had to leave for Japan?"

"I will never forget it."

"Remember how you said you never wanted to leave Afghanistan."

"Baleh, but my life is here now. It's my destiny, as they say."

"Destiny has a way of playing tricks on us," I said. "But with all that has happened in Afghanistan, you were wise to stay in Japan."

"Do you think you'll ever go back?" Shabir asked.

His question caught me by surprise. "Nay, that's not possible. The Russians destroyed the countryside, and the warlords destroyed Kabul. There's nothing to return to."

On September 9, 2001, two suicide bombers posing as journalists traveled to the north of Kabul to interview Massoud. When they were told the interview would have to wait a few days—until after September 11—they threatened to leave, saying they had to interview him before September 10. Massoud agreed. As one of the men raised his camera and pushed the shutter, the other reached for a battery pack on his belt. An explosion rocked the room, instantly killing Massoud and the two suicide bombers.

Two days later, on September 11, 2001, Islamic extremists hijacked airplanes and flew them into the World Trade Center towers in New York City. The towers burned for hours before collapsing. Thousands of Americans died. The world was horrified.

U.S. and British forces launched air strikes against al Qaeda bases. Northern Alliance troops attacked the Taliban on the ground, defeating them and taking control of Herat, Kandahar, and Mazar-i-Sharif. The Taliban fled to western Pakistan.

Hazrat Ali took control of Jalalabad. Osama bin Laden was reported to be hiding in Tora Bora, east of Jalalabad. The United States paid Hazrat Ali tens of millions of dollars to capture him. When Hazrat Ali failed to capture bin Laden, some said it was because of Pashtunwali; others said it was because if Hazrat Ali captured bin Laden, the flow of American money would stop.

Zahir Shah was prepared to return as a figurehead monarch with a moderate government composed of many ethnic groups. He had the support of the Afghan people. But the United States backed Hamid Karzai. When Karzai was named interim president, this decision surprised me. Hamid was an intelligent man but not a strong leader, not someone who controlled many men or had the respect of the people. The United States seemed to be giving him credit for defeating the Taliban, but it was the warlords who led the fight against them, not Karzai. In Quetta, Karzai was interviewed by a U.S. television reporter as if he were the leader of the forces that had defeated the Taliban. There were many warlords there who had fought and defeated the Taliban, but no one interviewed them because they did not speak English—only Karzai did.

A few months later I said to my cousin Omed, "Things are better in Afghanistan now."

"I'm not so sure," he replied. "They may only be different."

"What do you mean?" I asked.

"The interim government is relying on the same warlords and religious leaders who caused the problems in the past. You cannot expect new beginnings from old seeds. The same people will continue to do the same things as before. I'm sorry to say this, Bar, but I'm not at all hopeful about the way things are going."

"They may not be good people," I said, "but you have to start somewhere. And there is no one outside Afghanistan who can fix things. Only those inside can. I have hopes that things will improve in time."

Omed's words made me uncomfortable—like my father, Omed was never wrong.

55

Kabul, Afghanistan, 2002

The Dance of the Dead

"I'm going to Kabul, Bar. Do you want to come with me?"

It was Haroun Karzai, Hamid's brother, who I knew from Habibia High School. When the Russians invaded, he'd moved to the United States and opened an Afghan restaurant. His question caught me completely by surprise. I had abandoned the thought of returning to Afghanistan years earlier. "I'm not sure," I answered. "The war may not be over."

"Things have settled down there now. It's safe. I'm leaving next week if you want to come with me."

At one time the chance to go back to Kabul, to Karta-i-Char, would have filled me with excitement. But now, to my own surprise, I was not sure I wanted to go. It would stir up too many painful memories. And I knew my house in Kabul had been destroyed. "Is anyone going with you?" I asked.

"Baleh, there is someone who wants to work in the new government, an Afghan from Britain named Nabil who wants to be ambassador to London, and an American friend of mine who has an Afghan wife and wants to help rebuild the country."

My father would have reminded me that every important decision should be made with the head, not the heart. Returning to Afghanistan would be a decision of the heart, and no doubt he would have considered it a foolish thing to do. In the end, I only had ears for my heart.

We flew to Dubai, where we boarded an Ariana Afghan Airline jet for the flight to Kabul. The plane was left over from the 1950s, its interior filthy, its seats threadbare, and its ashtrays stuffed with cigarette butts. There were three flight attendants. They served us plates of chicken, rice with raisins, and steamed spinach suffused with cumin and saffron. When I thought I was going to burst, they brought out lamb kebabs smothered in onions and peppers, baskets full of oranges and pomegranates, and big cups of green tea. We were cruising at thirty thousand feet, but I felt as if I were already home.

"What brings you back to Afghanistan?" the man seated next to me asked.

"I grew up in Kabul but left when the Russians came. I want to see my old neighborhood—even though it no longer exists."

"Kabul is no longer the same place, I'm afraid. It has suffered so much destruction, so much sadness." He paused as if lost in these thoughts, then turned to me and asked, "How did we ever come to be the land of the Dance of the Dead?"

"The Dance of the Dead? What do you mean?" I asked.

He pulled himself up in his seat, placed his arm on the armrest, and leaned toward me with a grave look on his face.

"After the Russians were defeated, the mujahideen in Kabul took over the abandoned buildings and began fighting each other. They were no longer mujahideen fighting for God. They were men fighting for power and control. There were no prisons, so they had to kill their prisoners. When Pakistan and the United States stopped supplying ammunition, bullets became scarce. The mujahideen did not want to waste ammunition. When they captured an enemy, they would bring him to a circle of men and tell him, 'Dance for your life,' then one of the soldiers would sneak up from behind and cut off his head."

My seatmate looked at me as if he was not sure he wanted to say more but then continued. "For a few moments the headless body would remain upright, its limbs still twitching, dancing 'the Dance of the Dead.'"

It took me several minutes before I found my voice and asked him, "What brings *you* back to Afghanistan?"

"I am old and have nothing more to live for," he replied. "And like you, I am a fool for my country."

We began our descent into Kabul airport, where my odyssey had begun over twenty years earlier. How different were my feelings now. Then I had been filled with the pain of leaving my family, the fear of being imprisoned or killed, the anguish of not knowing if I would ever see my family or country again.

Now I was filled with excitement and anticipation.

56

Kabul, Afghanistan, 2002

Karta-i-Char

We stayed in a private guesthouse in Shar-i-Naw (New Town), a new neighborhood of glass and steel high-rises built for government officials and wealthy Afghans that had somehow escaped the destruction of the war. On its broad avenues lined with shade trees and pines, men in gebis and pakols strained to push huge wooden carts from which they sold their goods. Early the next morning, Hamid Karzai's brother Haroun and I, anxious to see our old neighborhood of Karta-i-Char, went out to hail a taxi for our group. Many taxis roamed the streets because driving a taxi was one of the few ways of making money in Kabul now.

"Karta-i-Char," I told the driver.

"Nay, I will not take you there," he said.

"You're a taxi driver," I said. "You're supposed to take us where we want to go."

"You are one of those who fled. Now you have come back to see the destruction, and you want me to risk my life for you? That area is full of desperate people. Beggars and thieves who will do anything to survive. Nay, I won't get myself killed for you." He sped off.

No other taxi would take us. We offered to pay anyone with a vehicle to drive us to Karta-i-Char, but no one was willing to take us there.

"I'll try to get a hotel van," Haroun said.

A few minutes later the five of us climbed into a gray Toyota Land Cruiser supplied by our hotel. Two sat in front with the driver, and Haroun, Nabil, and I squeezed in the back. We all wore jeans and jackets, except for Nabil, who was dressed in a dark business suit and tie, starched white shirt, and polished black dress shoes because he was hoping to meet Haroun's brother Hamid, Afghanistan's new president.

The Kabul I had left was a small city of four hundred thousand, a paradise of gardens and broad, thick-leaved trees. When the Russians bombed the countryside, millions of refugees fled to the safety of Kabul. To survive Kabul's long, cold winters, the refugees cut down all the trees for heating and cooking. There was nothing to hold the moisture in the ground. The soil dried out. When the winds blew, the city became coated in a fine dust. As we drove, our car's wheels kicked up a dust storm so thick, it was almost impossible to see. Fortunately, there were almost no other vehicles on the roads. Where buildings once stood, only foundations remained. What wasn't destroyed was heavily damaged. Most of Kabul's residents were hiding within the ruined buildings, too afraid, or too weak, to come out.

We arrived at Kabul University, not far from my home, to find its buildings intact. The windows had all been blown out; broken glass lay in piles on the ground beneath them. I got out and walked to the Political Science building, where my life had almost ended at the hands of National Security so many years earlier. There was no electricity. The corridors were dark, dusty, and eerily empty, my footsteps echoing loudly on the hard floors. As I stood at the back of my classroom, I was filled with memories of young men and women students laughing and joking together. Suddenly a heavy sadness overcame me as I thought of how many of them had disappeared. I told myself that that story had ended and a new story was being written for Afghanistan.

I returned to the Land Cruiser. The closer we got to Karta-i-Char, the more destruction we saw—whole neighborhoods were gone. We stopped at an intersection. Everywhere there were ruined buildings, some with a wall or two still standing, others leveled to the ground. On either side of the street emaciated children dressed in tattered clothing climbed up and slid down large mounds of dirt. The wind gathered up the dry soil, creating dust storms around their pitiful playground.

Nabil opened the Land Cruiser's door and started to get out.

"What are you doing?" Haroun cried.

"Look at them. They're in rags. They're starving. I must give them money."

"Don't get out of the car," I warned. "You will attract many people. It's too dangerous."

"Nay, Mr. Popal, this is my country, my people. I'm not worried."

Nabil's shiny shoes became covered in dust as he stumbled over deep tank tracks cemented in the hardened soil. The children ran up to him on stick legs. Nabil pulled out his wallet and started handing out dollar bills. A few people as emaciated as the children appeared out of nowhere and slowly approached Nabil, too weak to move any faster. During the war all the water mains had been destroyed. What little water could be found was used for drinking and cooking, not washing or bathing. The figures emerging through the swirling dust appeared to be part of the soil itself.

Nabil continued to hand out dollar bills. There was a stirring in the nearby ruins, and soon dozens of desperate people pounced on Nabil. They pulled at his pockets and suit jacket, grabbing and pushing until he was knocked to the ground. Somehow Nabil, completely disheveled and covered in dust, managed to make his way back to the Land Cruiser. We pulled him inside and slammed the door shut. The human skeletons vanished into the rubble. This is what the end of civilization looks like, I thought.

Nabil, bloodied and bruised, sat stunned, breathing heavily. His proud clothing now dirty and torn, his combed and oiled hair in disarray, his once shiny black shoes now scraped and gray with dust.

"We told you, and you didn't listen!" one of the men shouted at Nabil.

Another laughed.

"This is not funny!" Nabil said, shaking and upset.

I said nothing but thought, "Now he looks like he belongs here."

We continued through neighborhoods once full of people, flowers, and birds; neighborhoods where children flew kites from rooftops amid the aroma of grilling kebabs; neighborhoods with groves of pasha kona trees, their canopies of leaves so thick they blocked the sky; neighborhoods where the shouting of merchants and the laughter of children and the cries of babies filled the streets; neighborhoods once teeming with life. Now there were no children, no animals, no flowers, no trees, and no laughter—only destruction and the smell of death.

Karta-i-Char had been a clean, lush neighborhood whose houses had color and character, a neighborhood full of people I knew. It pained me to think that now it was nothing more than piles of destruction. As we approached my street, I was prepared for the worst. On a visit to Uncle Ali in Germany, I had seen a video of our compound taken by a cousin who had returned to Karta-i-Char years earlier. There was nothing left but ruins.

As we turned the corner, I braced myself.

Then I could not believe my eyes.

57

Kabul, Afghanistan, 2002

The Gate

My house was still there.

How could that be, I wondered? I had seen the video. Then I looked across the street. Everything looked so different with all the destruction—perhaps my cousin had gotten confused. He had taken a video of the other side of the street, which had been destroyed.

The outside wall of my compound was peppered with bullet holes and pockmarked from rocket blasts. But it was still standing. Everyone protested when I told them I was going inside.

"Nay, Bar," Haroun said. "It's too dangerous. You don't know who might be in there. They could have weapons. You would put us all in danger. First you must find out who is occupying your house."

We drove back to the guesthouse at sunset, the sky streaked red, something that had not changed—the beauty of twilight in Kabul. Soon darkness descended. There was no electricity. The city was a black ocean. The few people out in the streets moved quickly, as if being chased by wild dogs. By daylight you could see the scar of war on their starving, miserable faces, in their eyes full of terror. Evenings in Kabul had once been a time for taking strolls to enjoy the cool evening air. I thought of what had been lost, at what my city had become.

The next morning I found a driver who would take me to my house. I went alone. Armed men occupied every street corner in Karta-i-Char. Cars and bicycles pulled up, exchanged money for packages, then left quickly. My neighborhood had become a drug bazaar.

We pulled up to my house to find the outside door standing open.

"There are many people inside the yard," I said to the driver.

"There are many people in every house," he replied. "There's no place they won't live. They have nowhere else to go. They will fight you for your house. They will kill you for it. Forget about your house. Be happy it's still there. We must leave—it's not safe to stay here."

"Nay, wait for me. I won't be long." I leaped out as my driver howled in protest.

Just before I reached the door, it shut. I knocked loudly. I knocked again and again. Finally, it opened to reveal a small boy. He stepped aside as I entered my yard for the first time in over twenty years. I was home.

On the ground old men and dozens of young men holding AK-47s regarded me with curiosity. Baba and Babu, my uncles and cousins, were gone. The glass in the window frames was missing, the stucco riddled with craters and bullet holes.

I approached an elder. "I am the owner of this house. I need to talk to everyone who lives here."

"Not everyone is here," the elder replied. "Come back Friday."

As we were leaving, I gave the driver directions to the house of Hadji, an old family friend who lived nearby. "No one in Kabul still lives in his own home anymore," the driver said, disgusted at my ignorance. But he did as I asked.

Hadji's house looked much like mine—like all houses in Kabul still standing—disfigured by the war. Many people, including Uncle Ali, had completely bricked up their windows for protection from bullets and shrapnel. Hadji's windows had been bricked over, but a small opening had been left to let in light. I knocked on his door. No one answered. I turned to leave. The door opened a crack just enough for a pair of eyes to look out. "Baleh?" a voice said.

"Does Hadji still live here?" I asked.

The door opened wider, revealing an old woman, withered and bent. "What do you want?"

"I'm Baryalai Popal. I've come to see Hadji."

"I'm afraid he's not well."

"I'm sorry to hear that. He was very kind to me when I was young."

"Who is it?" a voice croaked from another room.

I recognized Hadji's voice. "Hadji, it's me, Bar Popal."

"Bar? Bring him to me."

Hadji lay in bed regarding me with rheumy eyes, his body sickly and thin. He looked ancient. "How you have changed!" he said. "But it's so good to see you. I was sorry to hear about your father's death. He was a great man."

"Tashakor, Hadji. How are you getting along?"

He lay quiet for a bit, then with a great effort he sat up, his white gebi in great folds over his thin frame. "You don't know the things I've witnessed while you were gone. The bombs and rockets fell like an unending rain, the explosions so loud I thought my head itself would explode. We hid in our houses day after day, waiting to die. When the fighting stopped, we went outside." He looked down for a moment before continuing. "You could not go for a walk without stepping on something terrible: a body or part of a body—sometimes only a head. We couldn't leave it like that . . . it was too awful . . . we had to clean it up. Then the fighting would begin again."

"Why didn't you leave?"

"There was no way to get out. The warlords divided the city into zones. You could not go from one zone to another without being stopped. They would kill you without a second thought. The Hazaras controlled Karta-i-Char. This was their chance to take revenge on the Pashtuns and Tajiks who had murdered them by the thousands. They were brutal. No one could stop them."

Just then a young man in a blue gebi and white turban entered. "My son Ratep," Hadji said. Ratep helped his father out of bed and led him to a seat at a small wooden table in another room beneath which Ratep had set a bucket of hot coals. As we sat there, Hadji and I wrapped ourselves in shawls against the cold. Ratep brought us bowls of tea. As he leaned over to set mine down, his turban unraveled. His ears were blackened holes. He blushed, quickly rewrapped his turban, and disappeared. I couldn't hide my shock.

Hadji looked at me. "My two sons used to bicycle to work in downtown Kabul. The city was divided by gates, and there was a curfew from dusk to dawn. One day my sons worked late. By the time they reached Karta-i-Char, it was dark, and Ratep rode his bicycle into a gate—a thin iron cable the fighters had stretched across the roadway. The guard demanded to know why my son had ridden into the gate. Ratep apologized, saying he did not see it in the dark. The guard told Ratep he would teach him a lesson he would not forget so that next time he would be more careful. The guard grabbed Ratep and sliced off both his ears, then placed the severed ears in my son's hands. He grabbed my other son and did the same. As they pedaled away as fast as they could, the guard yelled after them, 'Now you will respect our gates.'

"When my sons arrived home, the sides of their heads were swollen and bleeding terribly. I blackened a rag in the fire, then held it against the wounds to stop the bleeding. The next day a doctor gave them opium—it was all he could do. From that day they have worn turbans to hide the shame of having no ears."

We just sat for a few moments. "Your wife was always very kind to me," I said, breaking the silence.

"She was a very kind person," Hadji said. He fingered the edge of his shawl. "She died in the war." Suddenly his face brightened. "To hear your voice again, Bar, is a balm to me. It's so lonely here. So horrible. It's good to see a familiar face after so many years. To hear a familiar voice. Thank you for remembering me."

"It's good to see you as well," I replied. I waited a few moments before asking him who was living in my house.

"Many families live there. Sixty or seventy people. They are from the Panjshir Valley. Some fought with Massoud. They are very tough. Some are drug dealers."

"What can I do?"

"Nothing, I'm afraid. They'll never leave. How can they? They have no place to go. And Karta-i-Char is the best place in all of Kabul to sell drugs. Nay, Bar, you must forget this."

"But I cannot forget it. Do you know what my father said? 'A lie is the worst of crimes because it steals the truth.' If I let them stay in my house, I would be admitting it is their house, and that would be a lie. That I cannot do."

"What you say may be true, Bar, but fate is also the truth, and fate has taken your family's houses from you."

"Sometimes will is stronger than fate," I said.

"Now you sound like your father. If that is how you feel, you should wait and see what happens. Zahir Shah may return, and things may change. You must be patient. Please stay and take some food with us."

"Thank you, Hadji, but I must be going. It fills me with joy to have found you alive."

"I am happy to find you alive as well. But I would like to see you stay alive. Listen to me, Bar. Forget about your house."

I rushed outside, relieved to find my driver still there.

"I thought you might be dead," he said as I climbed into the car. "Is your friend still alive?"

"Baleh. But he had many sad stories to tell."

"Afghanistan is the land of sad stories."

58

Kabul, Afghanistan, 2002

Ghosts

On the day I was to return to my house, I decided to stop by Abbas's house first to see if it was still standing. As we drove down his street, I saw armed men in every front yard. When we arrived in front of Abbas's house, I was relieved to see it was still there. But unlike all the other houses on his street, it looked deserted. No armed men occupied its front yard. I called to an old man who was slowly making his way down the street. "Salaam! Does anyone live in that house?"

He looked at me for a moment as if surprised to hear a voice, then said, "Only ghosts."

"Only ghosts?" I asked him.

"You must not be from here."

"Nay, I am visiting."

"The Hazaras locked prisoners in the septic tank of that house. A few days later, when the Hazaras had not returned, we managed to open it. We found only one person still alive, and he did not live very long. Now no one will go near that house—not even the drug dealers—because of the ghosts."

I left for my house, taking another terrible memory with me.

When I entered my front yard, dozens of old men, young men, and children emerged from inside and from around the back of the house. All but the children carried weapons. One of the young men aimed his gun at me while he eyed me suspiciously.

I was an unwelcome stranger in my own home.

"I am Baryalai Popal," I told him. "This is my house."

Still pointing his gun at me, he laughed. "I have lived here for over five years, and you come here and tell me, 'This is my house.' Why should I believe you? You've been gone a very long time. Where have you been?"

"I had to leave when the Communists came. I returned as soon as I could."

"While you were safe, we were living in hell. Your house is the price you pay for abandoning your country."

"It was not just me. Many escaped to Pakistan or Iran. It's not my fault you had to live in hell."

"This place belongs to those who survived the horrors."

I approached an elder. "This is my home," I said, "the home of my father, Rahman Popal. Tell the people who live here to send someone to me who can speak for each group, each family."

When they had all gathered, I said, "I know your life here has been very difficult. You have suffered terribly from the war, and I do not wish you to suffer any more on my account. But this is the house of my family. Many of you are fathers who have sons, so you will understand. You can leave now, and I will pay you. If you need time, I will give it to you. If you refuse to leave, you give me no choice but to go to the government."

"How do we know you are the owner?" one of the young men asked.

"That's not your problem," I said. "You are not the owner. You will know I'm the owner when the government sends people to remove you. But I don't want it to come to that. It's only your problem if you don't leave."

"Your house is still here because of us," another young man said. "It's better for you that you wait and see what happens. You don't know if the new government will survive. Things might return to the way they were, and you will need us here to protect your house. Better you let us stay."

"Nay, I don't wish to wait. I want my house back now."

"Go back where you came from! There are powerful men behind us. Leave now, and don't come back," a young drug dealer shouted.

One of the elders accepted my offer of money, saying, "We are several families, twenty-two people."

"God bless you," I replied. "I will take your names and thumb-prints so there will be a record of who has been paid."

"Don't do it!" someone shouted at the elder. "If we stick together, we can stay."

"It's not right to take his house," someone shouted back. "If he's the rightful owner, he should have it."

Some of the elders said they needed a few months to find a place for their families to live. Several others said their families would leave immediately and refused to take any money.

Soon dozens of people carrying battered suitcases and bedsheets straining with belongings emerged from the house. The women, hidden beneath shawls, stayed close to the men. They tossed their possessions into cars and pickup trucks, crowded inside, and drove off.

Those who remained fingered their AK-47s, looking more determined than ever.

59

Jalalabad, Afghanistan, 2002

Hazrat Ali

"The UN is having a difficult time finding a large property in Jalal-abad to rent," a friend who worked for the United Nations in Kabul said at dinner. "We need a place where we can distribute food and provide other aid. Every place is too small or has been destroyed."

"I have a large house in Jalalabad," I said. "But I haven't seen it since I left."

"Let's take a look," he said. "If it needs restoration, the UN will pay for it."

A few days later, seven of us climbed into two Land Cruisers for the journey from Kabul to Jalalabad. Before the Russian invasion, the trip had been a two-hour ride down winding mountain road-ways. The highway was now shattered by mines in many places, and almost every bridge and tunnel had been dynamited, so we were often forced to detour off the highway. On every hairpin turn and switchback and in every unlit tunnel, we feared landmines or surprise attacks. For six hours we traveled on the bone-rattling highway and off it on hard-packed dirt roads.

Early the next morning, before the others had awakened, I took an auto rickshaw across what was left of the Behsood Bridge to Malem's house in Abdien. I had not trusted Malem at the time of my escape, but decades had passed, and I wondered if he had sur-vived the wars. I knocked on his door. An emaciated, sickly figure stood in the open doorway. "Malem?" I asked.

He was as shocked to see me as I him. "I thought I would never see your face again," Malem said. "I must let Nasir know you are here."

We sat on cushions on the floor. "After the mujahideen defeated the Communists," Malem said, "I was arrested and imprisoned for a year because I was a member of the Party. When the Tali-ban came, they moved me to a prison in Kandahar and tortured me. I spent another year in prison before they released me." He stopped abruptly, and we spoke no more.

When Nasir arrived, he looked almost as sad as Malem.

"How are you?" I asked.

"Not well, but then none of us are. I have a headache that won't go away."

"Have you seen a doctor?"

"There are no doctors anymore, Bar."

"It must have been terrible," I said.

"Baleh, it was. In the daytime, government troops occupied our area. But in the nighttime, those troops would leave, and the mujahideen would come. If the government troops thought we were supporting the mujahideen, they would imprison or kill us. And if the mujahideen thought we were supporting the government, they would kill us. Although we had almost nothing to feed ourselves, the mujahideen demanded food for fifty fighters each month. We had to find chickens, oranges, and bread any way we could to keep from being killed. Eventually, the food ran out. We fled to Jalalabad. One night, men broke into our house there, tied us up, and stole everything—even my wife's jewelry and the carpets on the floor. Then they came back and forced us out, and we returned to Abdien."

I returned to Jalalabad burdened by what my friends had suffered.

The next morning we drove to my Jalalabad house in the Land Cruiser. As we turned the corner of my street, I could see my house looming in the distance, and my heart raced. I would recover one of my family's houses and would have a very good tenant. Baba would have been proud of me.

As we approached, the driver suddenly slowed down. In the front yard hundreds of armed fighters stared menacingly at our Land Cruiser. "Let's go," my friend told the driver. "We don't want to be involved with warlords."

"Stop," I shouted. "This is my house!" But my words fell on deaf ears.

After a sleepless night in the UN guesthouse, I dressed in a gebi and pakol and drove to my house alone. "Salaam!" I called to the armed men camped in my front yard. They fingered their AK-47s and eyed me with curiosity. When no one replied, I approached my front door. "Who lives here?" I asked the armed guards standing there. They just stared at me, so I repeated my question. Still no one answered. I turned and shouted into the yard. "Can anyone tell me who lives here?" No one spoke.

"This house belongs to Hazrat Ali," a voice suddenly called out.

This was not good. Hazrat Ali was a warlord who had created a twenty thousand–man army with money from the CIA.

"My name is Baryalai Popal," I said. "This is my family's house."

"If this is your house, you must speak with Hazrat Ali," one of the fighters said.

"Is he here?" I asked.

"Nay."

"Where can I find him?"

"Better for you that you never find him!" someone yelled.

The others all laughed.

60

Kabul, Afghanistan, 2002

The Cemetery

After making the frightening journey back to Kabul, I sat dejected on the edge of my bed in Haroun's guesthouse. My family's house in Kabul was still occupied by drug dealers, our house in Jalalabad by a powerful warlord. Although Uncle Ali had fled his home in Kabul with almost nothing, he did take the deeds to my houses in Kabul and Jalalabad and a document that transferred ownership of my family's houses to me. No matter what it would take, no matter how long it would take, I would recover my family's houses.

My parents' final resting place was a cemetery at the base of a mountain a half-hour outside Kabul where two friends of the Prophet Muhammad were also buried, making it a place of pilgrimage for many Muslims each year.

Thousands of gravestones covered the mountainside. My family's plot had filled with ancestors, so Baba had bought a small plot for himself and his brothers in another section of the cemetery. Somewhere on this mountain Baba and Babu lay buried side by side.

For hours I trekked up and down the mountainside. What had once been a well-kept cemetery was now an abandoned and untended field of broken stones, shriveled plants, and dead trees. I could not find their graves among so many stones and began to grow tired. An old man who lived at the cemetery so he could be near the tombs of the Prophet's friends noticed me.

"Are you looking for someone?" he asked me.

"Baleh. I cannot find the graves of my father and mother."

"What is your father's name?"

"Abdul Rahman Popal."

"Come," he said.

We wandered through the cemetery until it seemed hopeless. Suddenly the old man stopped. "Here," he pointed.

A broken piece of gravestone lay at me feet. I stooped down, picked it up, and turned it over. The inscription was filled with dirt. I scraped at it with my fingernails until I could read the name: Abdul Rahman Popal.

Babu's broken gravestone lay beside it.

How miserable is war, I thought, when even the graves of the dead suffer.

61

Kabul, Afghanistan, 2002

Money

In the Presidential Palace, guards slept on mattresses stuffed not with horsehair but hundreds of millions of dollars in U.S. and British currency. The enormous sums of money pouring into Afghanistan were wasted or stolen by the few, while the Afghan people suffered terribly.

Money changed everything in Afghanistan, even buzkashi. What had always been a game played by the masses was now a toy for the newly rich. An Afghan's wealth used to be measured by how many horses he had, how many wives, how large a farm, how big a house. Now it was how much he paid for a buzkashi horse. The best buzkashi horses had been killed during the war. Tribes in the North had always bred large, strong horses for their buzkashi competitions. Afghanistan's new millionaires paid $50,000 for a northern buzkashi horse, when the average Afghan made $370 a year. Bigger, stronger chapandaz were needed to control these larger horses. The wealthy bought the best chapandaz.

Chapandaz used to compete for their families and tribes. Now they competed for wealthy owners who wanted to win to impress their friends. The circle of justice into which a chapandaz would drop the goat carcass had become a money pit. Our beloved national sport had lost its soul.

That summer of 2002, the year I first returned to Kabul, a loya jirga elected Hamid Karzai president of the Afghan Transitional Administration. Many of the delegates thought Zahir Shah was Afghanistan's rightful leader, but the United States wanted Karzai. After we returned from Wali's in Kandahar, Haroun and I had dinner with Hamid in the Presidential Palace.

"Few understand the difficulties we face, Baryalai," Hamid said to me in frustration. "When the Russians took over, there were buildings, ministries, departments, clerks—all the necessities of running a country. They had only to replace these people with Party members. After twenty years of war, I am expected to run a country in which all of the institutions have been destroyed—even the buildings. I must build the new Afghanistan from scratch. Getting a bridge built is difficult enough. To create an entire government from nothing is almost impossible. But we have no other choice. We must do the impossible, and it will be done."

Karzai's new government worried me. He wanted a diverse government representing Afghanistan's many ethnic groups. But he chose Afghans who had been living in Europe, Australia, and America for two decades who did not understand what the people needed. The Afghan people did not trust these outsiders who had returned from abroad. And he appointed former warlords as well—warlords who were corrupt and had killed many Afghans. There were choices to be made, but the United States and Karzai were making the wrong ones. Years later a friend spoke at Uncle Ali's funeral.

"Ali Ahmad Popal began work for the Afghan government as a teacher and served as ambassador to several countries. He served his country for sixty years. During all that time he lived in only one house, which was owned by his brother. Today politicians who have only worked a few years for the Afghan government and have accomplished nothing own dozens of houses in Dubai and other countries. Ali Popal poured his heart and soul into his country and left with nothing. Today politicians think only of themselves and take all of the wealth out of the country, leaving the people with nothing."

62

San Diego, California, July 4, 2002

Citizens

On my return trip to San Diego, the flight from Kabul to Dubai was full of young Afghan men. During the week they worked in Kabul, a city in ruins, where people moved about quickly, fear still in their eyes as if the war had never ended. On weekends they escaped to the paradise of Dubai. In the airport lounge awaiting my flight to London, a man sitting next to me introduced himself. "My name's Kamal," he said. "You have the look of someone who has been in Afghanistan recently."

"Baleh, that's true," I said. "Do I look that bad?" I smiled at my own joke.

"What brought you back?" Kamal asked. "Things are still very difficult there."

"I wanted to see my neighborhood again. I thought my family's house in Kabul had been destroyed but was surprised to find that it is still standing. But many families and drug dealers now occupy it, and they have refused to leave."

"What is your name?"

"Baryalai Popal."

"Rahman Popal's son?"

"Baleh."

Kamal reached into his pocket. "Here, take my card. I work in the military. Call me when you return to Kabul. I'll introduce you to Number 3—I'm sure he can help."

On the Fourth of July 2002 Afsana and I were sworn in as United States citizens. It had been a long journey, the final step a test on the U.S. Constitution, the flag, and the names of the states. Now our new home would take on a more profound meaning for us.

A black-robed judge stood before hundreds of applicants and their families who had gathered in Golden Hall in downtown San

Diego for the ceremony. He looked over the crowd full of so many different, anxious, excited faces and addressed us in a firm voice.

"All those who are to become new citizens, rise and raise your right hand and repeat after me," he said. Afsana and I stood, raised our right hands, and spoke his words.

"I hereby declare, on oath, that I absolutely and entirely renounce and abjure all allegiance and fidelity to any foreign prince, potentate, state, or sovereignty of whom or which I have heretofore been a subject or citizen; that I will support and defend the Constitution and laws of the United States of America against all enemies, foreign and domestic; that I will bear true faith and allegiance to the same; that I will bear arms on behalf of the United States when required by the law; that I will perform noncombatant service in the armed forces of the United States when required by the law; that I will perform work of national importance under civilian direction when required by the law; and that I take this obligation freely, without any mental reservation or purpose of evasion, so help me God."

When we finished, the judge said, "With your new status come new rights and responsibilities. But know this as well—you are now equal to every other citizen of the United States. You are now part of the American dream."

63

Kabul, Afghanistan, 2003

Number 3

When I returned to my house in Kabul in February 2003, many of those who had been occupying it had left. But many still remained. And the drug dealers with their Kalashnikovs had no intention of leaving. I went to see Kamal.

"It's good to see you again, Mr. Popal," Kamal said. "I'm sorry to hear about your house, but no matter, we can take care of that."

"That's good news," I said. "Tell me, how will you do this? At the airport you mentioned Number 3."

"Baleh. Number 3 was a general with the Northern Alliance. He's a Tajik from Panjshir Province." Kamal paused for a moment. "I hope these people are not from Panjshir."

"Baleh, I'm afraid they are," I replied.

"That's unfortunate. I'll speak with the general and arrange for you to meet him tomorrow morning."

When I arrived for my meeting at the Ministry of Defense the next day, the guard behind a glass wall regarded me with suspicion. When I told him who I was there to see, his demeanor changed immediately, and he picked up the phone and made a call before escorting me upstairs.

The reception area was full of people waiting to see the general, some in Western clothing, others in gebis and turbans, many others dressed in military uniforms. I squeezed beside a man on a couch and waited until my name was called.

To my great surprise, as soon as I sat down with Number 3, he handed me a bottle of pills. "A friend brought these back from America," he said. "Tell me, what are they for?"

I studied the label. "These are garlic pills. They are for indigestion and high blood pressure."

He laughed. "Garlic pills? How strange. Why wouldn't I just eat fresh garlic?"

"That would be very good for you," I said, "but not so good for the person sitting next to you." The general laughed, and I began to relax a bit.

"You've spent a lot of time in America," he said. "I was there once but only for a very short time and only to tour military installations. The American military people ran every day. I did not see any fat ones. Here we sit and talk and eat and grow fat. So I started jogging and eating less, and I feel better. As you see me now, I have a good figure, baleh?"

"Baleh, you are in very good shape."

"One of my officers told me someone is building a mosque in your country, but this can't be true."

"Baleh, it is. Anyone can build a mosque in America."

"But it is a Christian nation. We do not allow Christians to build churches here; why would they allow the building of mosques?"

"In America there is freedom of religion. You can practice whatever religion you like, and you can build a church or a mosque or a temple."

"That is difficult to believe. You are telling me that every Friday in America I can pray?"

"Baleh."

"And wear Afghan clothing?"

"If you want to."

"I can't believe that."

"It's true. I have become a U.S. citizen and have the same rights as any other citizen."

"But you were born in Afghanistan."

"It doesn't matter. Once you become a citizen, you have the same rights as everyone else. Becoming an American citizen was the happiest day of my life."

"You tell me one thing more unbelievable than the next. In the UAE or Saudi Arabia you can live and work for twenty-five years and still have no rights. How is it possible that in America you can become a citizen and have the same rights as someone born in America?"

"I don't know. That's just the way it is."

Question after question followed: "What are the women like?

Have you been to Disneyland? Are all the people in Hollywood crazy?" For three hours we talked only of America, and I could not change the subject. Before I was able to ask about my house, it was time for lunch.

We entered a large conference room next to the general's office where a table was spread with beef, rice, sauces, salads, and cans of Coke and bottles of water.

"I had heard the military has very good food now, and it's true," I said.

"Baleh," he replied. "Even in the field, our soldiers have fresh food brought to them by American helicopters."

When we returned to his office, the general began asking questions again. But then he stopped in midsentence. "I've been so busy talking. I haven't asked you why you're here."

"I want to get my family's house back, and I need your help."

"What's the problem?"

"My house is occupied by many families and drug dealers who refuse to leave. I was willing to pay them and give them time, but many did not accept."

"I hope they're not from Panjshir," he said. When I fidgeted in my seat, he smiled. Kamal must have told him. "We didn't defeat the Russians and the Taliban so we could steal each other's homes. I'll get your house back. How many people are there?"

"Forty or fifty, maybe more. The men have guns."

The general called in his assistant and explained the problem. "Take care of this and report back to me."

"How can I thank you?" I said.

"You can do me a favor."

"I will do anything you ask."

"Come see me after you have your house back. I want to hear everything about America. I want to know about the people, the families. Do the young people keep their parents in their homes when they grow old? What kind of work do they do? What kinds of cars do they drive? America fascinates me. I want to know all about it. And I want to know how long it will take me to learn English. I must leave you for a meeting now. My aide will take care of you."

"I'll send forty soldiers," the aide said. "Will that be enough?"

"Forty soldiers? Baleh, that would be very good," I replied.

"When do you want them?"

"How soon can you send them?" I asked.

"Tomorrow," the aide replied.

"Tomorrow? That would be wonderful."

"What time do you want them there?"

"Nine o'clock?"

"Good, I'll see to it that the soldiers are at your house at nine o'clock. Give my secretary the address, and I'll take care of the rest. Oh, and one more thing—you should not be there."

Back at Haroun's guesthouse that evening, I lay on my bed staring at the ceiling, thinking about the people I was about to evict, an uncomfortable feeling growing in the pit of my stomach. Some of the people might be from influential families. I didn't want to make enemies here. Making enemies is never good.

The next morning, I arrived at my house very early and spoke to the people there.

"I'd like to speak with you as a fellow Afghan," I said. "I don't want to cause you trouble. I don't want any violence. I just want to do what is right. I will pay you to leave so we will have a good relationship in the future."

"We've already given you our answer," one of the drug dealers said. "Why do you waste our time? You're lucky I don't shoot you right now. For the last time go and don't come back, or the next time someone will have to carry your body away."

"Soldiers will be here soon," I said, "and they will force you to leave. I don't want anyone to get hurt. There has been enough violence in our country already. Go while you still have time."

"Ha! We're not fools. You're bluffing. You are the one who better leave while you still have time!" The man lifted his gun and pretended to shoot me. The others laughed.

Suddenly a half-dozen military vehicles screeched to a halt in front of the house. Forty soldiers scrambled out and stood at attention. The commander stepped out. An elder came running up to him.

"In the name of God, don't let your soldiers enter! Our women are inside. We'll get our belongings and go."

"When?" the commander asked.

"Tomorrow."

I ran up to the elder and shouted, "Nay! Tomorrow isn't good enough! I gave you time. You will leave now!"

"Who are you?" the commander asked.

"I am Baryalai Popal, the owner."

"You're not supposed to be here."

"True. But as you see, I am. They must leave now."

The commander looked from me to the elder. "Go! Now!" he shouted to the old man.

Men carrying sacks on their backs and dragging sheets full of belongings poured out of the house and tossed their things into the beds of rusty pickup trucks parked on the lawn. They were followed by many women hidden under shawls and their many children. After the trucks were gone, only the young drug dealers remained.

"On orders of the general, you are to leave this property immediately," the commander announced. Everyone from Panjshir knew who the general was. To defy him would be unthinkable.

One of the drug dealers stepped forward, trying to smile.

"Mr. Popal didn't know that we were joking," he said. "We were going to leave all along. We don't want to stay. This is not our house. We told him that."

"Good. Then leave," the commander said.

Several more pickup trucks appeared, and the drug dealers left.

"Anything else?" the commander asked me.

"Nay, you've done more than I could have dreamed, and no one was hurt. I'm very grateful."

"Good. Don't forget to tell the general that when you see him."

The door to my house was open—as if it had been waiting for me all this time.

But in this happy moment a disquieting thought disturbed my mind: the rule of law had been enforced by the ones with more guns.

64

Kabul, Afghanistan, 2003

Rebuilding

It wasn't just the couch where we had spent so much time during the war that was missing. Everything had been destroyed or stolen: the furniture, the wiring, the pipes, the sinks and tubs, the cabinets, even the glass in the windows. The roof, walls, and front door were all that remained. But there was one thing that could not be destroyed: my memories. My house was now an empty, battered shell, but in my mind's eye it was full of people and voices. I could hear the cook yelling at Baba Naeem and Baba Naeem yelling back even louder. If I could bring back these memories, surely I could bring back the house itself.

I bought a padlock for the front door.

As I sat in the Kabul Bank waiting to talk to the loan officer about a loan to rebuild my house, I overheard him talking. "Send 100,000 to my account in Switzerland." He was stealing the money intended to rebuild our country. I was outraged and wanted no part of this corruption. I borrowed money from a private lender at a much higher interest rate.

With the money I received, I hired Pakistani workers who had come to Kabul in large numbers because there was much work to be done and much money to pay for it. They did good work but would often return to Pakistan after earning some money, so I constantly had to replace them. And there were other problems as well. After eating, they would toss their leftovers in my front yard.

"You're throwing your garbage in my garden," I said one day, pointing at the soggy tea bags, banana peels, crusts of bread, and clumps of other food. "Do you do this in your own yard?"

"Baleh, we do," one replied. "It's good for the grass."

Eight months later my house was finished. It had taken over twenty years to realize the dream of returning to my house and to feel the happiness of being home once again.

I should have been content, but as long as Hazrat Ali occupied my house in Jalalabad, it meant the warlords were still in control. I had recovered my house in Kabul because the government had more guns. Hazrat Ali had thousands of men with guns—far too many for even the government to take on. But if Afghanistan was to have a future, it was necessary to restore the order of the past. I would not rest until I recovered my house in Jalalabad. The United States was supposed to be helping Afghanistan, a country destroyed by war for which it was partly responsible. But whatever good was being accomplished in Afghanistan, whatever good faith was being won, was destroyed when the United States invaded Iraq in March 2003. The Afghan people viewed America as its savior. But the people of Afghanistan are Muslim. When the United States invaded Iraq, it lost all credibility in the Muslim world.

The United States thought that by driving the Taliban from Afghanistan, they had defeated them, but it failed to understand how the Taliban had infiltrated Afghan society. In the Afghan tradition there is a separation between the laws of the mosque and those of the tribe. Religious matters are dealt with by religious leaders. Social matters are dealt with by tribal elders. But the Taliban had assassinated tribal elders, even in mosques at wedding parties and at funerals. They educated the youth in the schools of the mosques and taught them that strict Islamic law controls not only religious issues but social issues as well. The Taliban destroyed respect for the tribal elders and undermined their authority. The Iraq invasion reenergized the Taliban and gave them new support among radical Muslims intent on retaking Afghanistan.

65

Kabul, Afghanistan, 2004

Orders

Every time I asked someone about recovering my house in Jalal-abad, I received a different answer: "You should go to the Ministry of Justice," one said. "The quickest way is through the Ministry of the Interior," said another. Yet another advised me to go to the top, to the office of the president. Confused, I asked a friend if any of these approaches would work.

"Nay, they will not," he replied without hesitation. "There is not yet any law or order here. To go against Hazrat Ali would be very dangerous. He's still a powerful warlord who controls that area. Things have not changed—the one with the most weapons still makes the law. Better to wait a few years until the government gets established."

But I could not wait. During the war many Afghans' homes were unlawfully taken over. To return property to its rightful owner, the new government created the Office of Disputes in Land Titles. A clerk at the Office of Disputes in Land Titles handed me a form.

"State what the problem is and why you're entitled to the property. The minister will interview you, and if he is convinced you have legal title, he will issue an order to the occupant to vacate your property."

After filling out the form, I handed it to the clerk. As he read it, his eyes widened.

"Why put yourself in such danger?" he asked. "Hazrat Ali is a very powerful man. Don't do this."

"Tashakor," I said, "but I want to file this."

"It's just a house."

"Nay, it is not just a house. It may seem like just a house to you, but it is much more than that. It is a test of our new Afghanistan. If you cannot return property to its rightful owner, what will that say about our country?"

The clerk reluctantly accepted it. "We will review your application. Come back in a week for an interview."

As I left the building, I heard Baba's voice. "Our country is like a baby taking its first steps, trying to find itself in its new world. You must take things one step at a time, Bari."

To my great surprise, when I returned the next week, the clerk handed me an order directing Hazrat Ali to vacate my house.

"You have your order, now go," he said.

"I thought there would be an interview with the minister," I replied.

"That won't be necessary."

"Nay, I want to see the minister," I protested.

"You can't."

"Why not?"

"He's very busy. He would get nothing done if he had to see everyone who asked for an order."

"But this is no ordinary situation," I protested. "It will not be easy to enforce. You cannot expect me to just hand Hazrat Ali this order."

The clerk returned to his desk.

"I have all day," I called over to him. "I will wait here for my interview with the minister."

After several hours of being stared at by me, the clerk disappeared into a rear office and then returned. "The minister will see you now," he said coldly.

The minister did not look pleased to see me as I explained that if I did not get help with Hazrat Ali, the Ministry's order would be useless. He tried to look patient. "This is just the first step," the minister said. "If it doesn't work, there are other channels. The minister of justice and the minister of the interior can also issue orders. You can get an order from the president. If all that fails, you can get an order from a judge."

This was not good news. I knew the minister of justice would do nothing, and Hazrat Ali was now chief of police in Jalalabad, a position that was part of the Ministry of the Interior. The interior minister would not issue an order to his own police chief—especially one who was a warlord.

"Come back if this fails," the minister said.

We both knew it would.

Because I could not go to the minister of justice or the minister of the interior, I had only one option left—the Office of the President. I asked a friend to arrange the meeting.

"I would be happy to," he said, "but we must respect the new government's hierarchy. First, you must go to Jalalabad and speak with the governor, Hadji Din Mohammad. Tell him you have an appointment with the president. You must give him the opportunity to solve the problem himself. If that fails, call me."

I agreed but knew it was a fool's errand. Hadji Din Mohammad was the brother of mujahideen commanders who had fought against the Russians alongside Hazrat Ali. After the Taliban were ousted, one of the brothers, together with Hazrat Ali, had formed a *shura*—a kind of informal government—to rule Jalalabad. When Hamid Karzai became president, he appointed the brother as one of his vice presidents. What chance was there that someone close to Hazrat Ali would enforce an order against him?

66

Jalalabad, Afghanistan, 2004

Din Mohammad

Din Mohammad sat at a desk in the garden of the King's Palace that served as the governor of Jalalabad's office. He was dressed in a white gebi, gray waskat, and gray and black turban tied in a large knot at the top. He greeted me warmly. When I explained why I was there, his expression changed. "What you ask is not a simple matter. I will need some time to look into it."

I knew Din Mohammad would do nothing, but out of respect for him, I stayed in Jalalabad for several weeks. Soon after arriving back in Kabul, I went to see President Karzai.

"The president is out of the country at the moment and won't return for some time. However, I've heard about your problem. The president has signed an order directing Hazrat Ali to vacate your house. Bring this to the governor. He will see that it's carried out."

As soon as I arrived in Jalalabad, I presented the president's order to Din Mohammad. He examined it for a while, then said, "Hazrat Ali is a difficult man to reach. I will inform him of this order, but I will need a few weeks."

"As long as you recognize that I am the owner, that is good enough for me. I will wait to hear from you."

I returned to Kabul and awaited his call.

Once again, however, I received no word from Din Mohammad, and once again I had to make the dangerous trip to Jalalabad to see him. I found Governor Mohammad at his desk in the palace garden.

"Is there a problem with my paperwork?" I asked him.

"Nay, your paperwork is in order," he said.

"Then why do I not have my house back?"

"Don't worry, Mr. Popal. We know what we're doing. What you want takes time."

I made several trips back and forth between Kabul and Jalalabad to check on the order, and each time Din Mohammad assured me all was well. After yet another useless trip, I finally realized that Hazrat Ali was playing me for a fool. He was trying to wait me out. Many people who had returned from the United States or Europe to recover their property had grown soft and impatient in the West. The warlords knew that these foreign owners wanted to leave Afghanistan again as quickly as possible. All the warlords had to do was delay and delay until the owners gave up—something I would never do.

There was only one other person in Jalalabad with the authority to enforce the presidential order against Hazrat Ali: the chief of police. Unfortunately, the chief of police was Hazrat Ali. When I explained the problem to my friend Yasir, he said, "I must warn you, Bar, you have taken on a very dangerous foe. I fear for your life if you pursue this."

"I'm afraid too," I said. "Is there any hope?"

Yasir thought for a moment. "Hazrat Ali is a stubborn man, but he's part of the new government now and has ambitions. It would not be good for him to become involved with you in a bad way. I think if you speak with him face to face, you may have a chance. But you should not see him alone—that would be too risky. I'm from Nuristan, like Hazrat Ali, and I fought with him in the war. We'll go together to see him first thing in the morning, before he is tired of seeing people."

I would have done anything to get back my house in Jalalabad, but confronting Hazrat Ali face to face was not one of the things I had considered.

67

Jalalabad, Afghanistan, 2004

Hazrat Ali

As we walked to police headquarters the following morning, Yasir said, "Hazrat Ali has many, many houses and plenty of money. He doesn't need your house. It's a matter of pride and his stubborn nature. He doesn't like anyone telling him what to do because he thinks it makes him look weak. You must convince him that you are Rahman Popal's son and find a way for him to save face. There's one thing you must be careful of. Ali will ask and answer his own questions. 'Do you have the title to the property?' he will ask, and before you have a chance to answer, he will say, 'Nay!' and tell you to go away. You must speak quickly and not give him a chance to cut you off. Only then will you have any chance against him. I will tell you what to say."

People prefer to be outdoors in Jalalabad's warm climate—even officials. We found Hazrat Ali dressed in a suit on the terrace in the back garden of the police station, where he had set up a desk and chair. Several men, some dressed in gebis, others in police uniforms, stood nearby as Hazrat Ali spoke in Nuristani to two elders. When he saw us, he dismissed the elders and motioned to us to come. Hazrat Ali looked at me with close-set dark eyes that sat beneath thick, arched eyebrows. "What is it you want?" he said impatiently.

"I am Baryalai Popal, Rahman Popal's only son. The house you claim in Jalalabad is mine."

"I have taken care of this house for seventeen years," he said, eyeing me with contempt, "and you come here and tell me after all this time that it's yours? How is this your house? Anyone can say, 'This is my house.' Why should I believe you?"

"Because I have the title."

"For twenty dollars anyone can buy a title in Kabul."

"Many have said I was crazy to come here, but I'm not crazy enough to bring you false documents. You know the title company cuts the title in half and keeps half for itself and gives the other half to the owner. Do you have the matching half? Nay! I do."

Hazrat Ali considered this. "If your title is as you say, I will call you, and you will have your house back. If not, I will be your worst nightmare."

He never called me about my house.

I went to the minister of land disputes and told him that Hazrat Ali had ignored all the government's orders.

"I spoke with the governor in Jalalabad," the minister said. "He told me Hazrat Ali was prepared to return your house, but you never came to get it."

"That's a lie!" Although I should not have shouted at a minister, I could not contain my anger. "Hazrat Ali is trying to save face by saying he offered to give me my house back, but he did not, and he has no intention of doing so."

"Apparently, Hazrat Ali's offer is still open," the minister said, remaining calm. "You must go speak with the new governor of Jalalabad, Gul Agha Sherzai, and claim your house."

68

Office of the Governor of Jalalabad, 2004

Gul Agha Sherzai

Less than an hour outside of Kabul on the way to Jalalabad, the taxi I was riding in with several others came to a halt. "What is it?" we all cried at once to the taxi driver. "Why are you stopping?"

"Police roadblock," he replied. A policeman explained that the road to Jalalabad was closed for construction and we would have to detour through the valley. This was not good. It was late afternoon, and by the time we reached the valley, it would be dark. We all feared the officer was setting us up to be robbed.

"That way would be very dangerous," our driver told the officer.

"It's your choice," he replied. "You can drive back to Kabul and try again tomorrow."

One moment we were all terrified; the next moment we were all complaining that we did not want to spend two hours on that terrible road just to get back to where we had started. We told the driver to drive on. "If that's what you want," he said, "we will sit and wait."

"Wait for what?" I asked.

"For other vehicles to arrive."

Soon eight cars were ready to make the journey into the valley below the highway. In Afghanistan, as on the wild African plains, there is safety in numbers. After the worst journey ever, I arrived in Jalalabad.

The next morning I went to the governor's office.

Everything about Governor Gul Agha Sherzai was thick: his eyebrows; his hair, which swooped in a semicircle over his forehead; his face, with its heavy, dark beard.

"I understand my house is ready for me," I told him.

"Not so quick, Mr. Popal," Sherzai replied coldly. "Tell me—why did you go above me and complain to the minister of land disputes? This is not America. You cannot just show up and demand to have someone like Hazrat Ali give up a house he occupies. You must take things slowly if you want to get your house back."

"I know this is not America. I live in America. In America, if a government official orders something to be done, it gets done. Here I have an order from the Office of the President, and nothing has been done. Why did you tell the minister of land disputes I should come to Jalalabad if I could not get my house?"

"You have put me in a very bad position, Mr. Popal. If I do not tell the people in high positions what they want to hear, I will lose my job. And if I try to enforce this order against Hazrat Ali, we could both be killed and you will have accomplished nothing."

"So then you lie to the government and to Hazrat Ali," I said, losing patience.

"Give me some time to get this done peacefully, Mr. Popal. I'm sorry, but that's the way it is."

"Don't feel sorry for me," I said. "It's only one house. Feel sorry for Afghanistan. The Taliban have been gone for years, and the government cannot return one house to its rightful owner. How can the Afghan people trust such a government? All you do is pass around orders. How can you expect to bring change to the country when you can't restore the ownership of one single house?"

"You cannot just come to Jalalabad and snatch your house back."

"Snatch it back? Nay, I am not snatching anything back. You said my house was ready. I have made a very difficult journey to get it back. Nay, I will not wait any longer. I want my house returned to me now."

"You don't listen. I told you—you cannot rush into these things. You need to take things slowly. I tell you this for your own good."

"Slowly! I have waited over twenty years to get my house back! Before the Russian invasion, government ministers would be insulted if their orders were ignored. They would see to it that their orders were carried out. Now government ministers have no power, and you have no power. Your only interest is in passing the problem on to someone else!"

Sherzai's face grew redder and redder. He called out to his aide, "Close the door, and let no one enter." Then he leaned toward me, looking as if he were about to explode. "Who do you think you are coming here from another country and giving me an order?"

"I'm not the one ordering you. The president of Afghanistan is ordering you."

"Hazrat Ali has twenty thousand soldiers. I have only ten men. Why should I get myself killed for your house?"

"If a person attacks someone, would you sit there and do nothing because it's too dangerous? Of course it's dangerous. If you didn't want a dangerous job, you shouldn't have taken it. Now I'll have to go to President Karzai and tell him you won't do your job."

I stood up to leave.

"Nay, wait, Mr. Popal," Sherzai said, sounding conciliatory for the first time. "Hazrat Ali is the most powerful man in Jalalabad, maybe in all Afghanistan. I am only saying that you can't go rushing in like this. You must begin like friends. Hazrat Ali's security head, Hadji Jawid, controls your house. Let me arrange a meeting with Hadji Jawid for you. That's what you want, right?"

"Nay, that's not what I want. I don't want to see Hazrat Ali. I don't want to see Hadji Jawid. But you people give me no choice."

69

Jalalabad, Afghanistan, 2004

Hadji Jawid

Hadji Jawid's older brother had fought with Hazrat Ali against the Russians. When a rival of Hazrat Ali pulled a gun on Hazrat Ali, Hadji Jawid's brother put himself between Hazrat Ali and the gunman and was fatally wounded. With his dying words he asked Hazrat Ali to look after his youngest brother. "Please take Jawid into your hands and protect him," he said.

As one who had made the pilgrimage to Mecca, Jawid had earned the title "Hadji." Hazrat Ali arranged the marriage between his sister and Hadji Jawid and appointed Hadji Jawid head of his security forces. He built the new couple a house in a public park near my house in Jalalabad. In Afghanistan a brother-in-law is a powerful member of a family. My only hope against Hadji Jawid was Afghanistan's new government.

At the beginning of April I went to meet Hadji Jawid in Hazrat Ali's compound, which was directly across the street from my house. Armed men in the front yard stared at me as I walked to the compound's doorway. Two gunmen stood in front of the door. In the garden beyond, I could see another twenty men armed with automatic rifles and machine guns. As I stood at the doorway, one of the guards began roughly patting down my gebi. "You think I'm crazy enough to bring a gun here?" I said.

"I think you're crazy to come here at all," he replied.

"I am Baryalai Popal. I own the house across the street. I am here to see Hadji Jawid."

"Hadji Jawid isn't here. Look for him at his house in the park across the street. If you are smart, you will return to Kabul right now and never again come closer to Jalalabad than the Darunta Tunnel."

I found Hadji Jawid sitting in his garden. Unlike Hazrat Ali, who always wore a suit, Hadji Jawid wore a white gebi and turban. He invited me to sit with him. A servant brought a tray of tea, dates, and nuts, but I wasn't hungry.

"What business brings you here?" Hadji Jawid said, fingering a honey-soaked date.

"I'm Baryalai Popal, the son of Rahman Popal. I am the owner of the house across the street. Hazrat Ali controls it. I want it returned to me."

Hadji Jawid stared at me. "Rahman's son was killed many years ago in a landmine explosion."

"Nay, that's not true. As I stand before you, I am Baryalai Popal."

"Where is your proof?"

I handed him my documents proving my title. He looked at them quickly. "I have documents too. Everyone in Afghanistan has documents. This proves nothing."

My anger rose in my throat. "You asked me for proof, and I have given it to you. Now you reject it. You are just playing with me."

Jawid held up his hand. "Let me ask you a few questions about your house," he said calmly. "If you are who you say you are, you should have no trouble answering them."

After I correctly answered his questions, Hadji Jawid said, "My gardener worked at the house when Rahman and his son were there. If he recognizes you, you can have your house back. If not, you are to leave and never return. Agreed?"

I knew the "gardener" would be one of his fighters or an elder allied with Hazrat Ali or in his debt. I had been set up, but to question the honesty of Hazrat Ali and Hadji Jawid would be the greatest of insults, and this I would not do.

"Why do you hesitate? If you are Baryalai Popal, you have nothing to fear."

"I have changed a lot in twenty years," I said, thinking quickly. "When my own cousin, who I had not seen in a very long time, saw me at a wedding recently, she did not recognize me."

"What you say may be true, but it's the only way. Meet me at the Security Office tomorrow morning, and we will settle this once and for all."

That night in my room in Jalalabad, I heard Baba's voice in my head. "Why put yourself in such danger for a house, Bari?" he said. "I have invested everything in you, not a house. A house is not an important thing compared to a son."

Maybe he was right. Anyone foolish enough to enter the headquarters of the secret police could expect only one of two things: imprisonment or death.

70

Security Headquarters, Jalalabad, Afghanistan, 2004

The Gardener

I could not go to Security Headquarters alone. I called my friend at the UN and asked if there was someone from the UN who could accompany me to the meeting at KHAD headquarters.

"Nay, it's far too dangerous," he said. "It's very foolish of you to go there, Bar. Don't do this." When I did not respond, he said, "You're going anyway, aren't you? Call me after the meeting. If I don't hear from you, I can at least let your family know what happened to you."

The walls of the waiting room in the Security Office were painted a sickly green. Men waited nervously on hard wooden chairs pushed up against the walls. In front of the door to Hadji Jawid's office hung a tribal rug the color of dried blood. Every time the rug was flung aside, I froze.

After a while, an elderly man accompanied by a guard emerged from behind the rug and paused before a man sitting in a chair against the wall opposite me. The old man squinted into the man's face and stared thoughtfully. "Nay," he said to the guard, then moved on to the next man, mumbled "nay," and continued until he reached me.

The old man's eyes were so clouded with age that I was surprised he had any vision at all. Suddenly he brightened and pointed a bony finger at me.

"I know him."

I sat up in my chair.

"This is Baryalai Popal, Rahman's son."

"How do you know me?" I asked, surprised.

"My sister was your housekeeper. I worked as a gardener at the Winter Palace. Your father hired me to take care of your garden. I often saw you and your father sitting together talking in the yard, and you would ask me questions about the flowers I grew. There's no doubt. You are Rahman's son."

The blood-colored rug was pushed aside, and Hadji Jawid's deputy appeared. "So you are Baryalai Popal," he said.

"Baleh, as I have said all along. Now will Hazrat Ali return my house?"

"Baleh, but first Hazrat Ali asks a favor of you. He is constructing a new house and needs your house until the work is completed."

"If Hazrat Ali needs time, he shall have it. As long as he acknowledges that I am the owner, I am satisfied."

"We will call you when his house is done. It should only take five or six months."

"That's very good to hear. Give Hazrat Ali my thanks."

I returned to Kabul. By the end of the summer I had still received no word about my house from Hadji Jawid. I called and called, but no one ever answered. I returned to the governor's office in Jalalabad.

"Hazrat Ali has acknowledged my ownership, and I have given him time to leave, but he has no intention of leaving," I told Governor Sherzai. "His armed men still occupy my front yard. I have many friends in high places. If you don't get my house back immediately, I will tell them what has happened, and you can explain to Hazrat Ali why the United States, the UN, and NATO are all upset with him."

Sherzai immediately picked up the phone and called Hadji Jawid. "I have Baryalai Popal here in my office. He says you agreed to give his house back but haven't done so." He listened for a while, then hung up.

"Hadji Jawid says he doesn't know what you're talking about. He never agreed to any such thing."

Now I was fuming. "Call him back and tell him what I said. Hazrat Ali is a senator now. He cannot afford this."

Sherzai sighed. He placed his hand on his head, then dialed again.

Thirty minutes later Hadji Jawid strode into the room, accompanied by five armed men.

"Hazrat Ali will return your house after you pay him the money he has spent for repairs," Hadji Jawid said.

Sherzai looked relieved. "What do you think?" he asked me. "You pay for the repairs, you get your house back. That should settle it."

"Baleh, I will pay Hazrat Ali for the repairs," I said.

"Good, then we have an agreement," Sherzai said, happy to have it resolved.

"But only if Hazrat Ali pays me rent all the years he has used it."

"We will pay nothing!" Hadji Jawid responded.

Sherzai looked distraught. "Both of you are making this very difficult. I've done all I can. You must resolve this yourselves or have the court resolve it."

"We will never go to court!" Hadji Jawid said.

Sherzai turned to me with a look of desperation. "For everyone's sake, Mr. Popal, please think about Hadji Jawid's offer. If Hazrat Ali is to return your house to you, he needs compensation."

I looked at them both, then walked out.

I drove back to Kabul and sought out a friend in the Senate. He agreed to call Hazrat Ali.

"Salaam, Hadji Sahib. There's someone sitting in my office who says he has some unfinished business with you. . . . Baleh, Bar Popal, Rahman's son. He wants to know why you haven't returned his house as you've agreed."

"This is an old story," Hazrat Ali said. "I would have returned his house months ago, but he never came for it."

"That's not what Mr. Popal says. He says you refuse to give it back."

"I'm a busy man. I don't have time for this foolishness."

"But if you don't resolve the situation," the senator said, "Mr. Popal will bring the problem to the Parliament."

"I will have Hadji Jawid speak with him."

"Hadji Jawid says you want Mr. Popal to pay for repairs, and Mr. Popal wants you to pay rent."

"I'll talk with Jawid and have him sit down with Mr. Popal and resolve this. Good-bye."

There was no new Afghanistan. I had lost my family's house to a warlord.

71

Abdien, Afghanistan, 2004

The Funeral

Before I returned to Kabul, I attended the funeral for Malem's cousin Sabur in Abdien. Hundreds attended the funeral for this beloved son of the village.

Sabur had left Abdien to attend medical school. He returned after the Taliban left to provide medical care for the people of his village, often without charge. His sudden, unexpected death was a sad loss for Malem, Abdien, and Afghanistan.

After the funeral service a small group gathered at Malem's house for food and drink and to remember our friend. Abdien was a small village. Although there were many here, everyone seemed to know each other, which was not surprising because so many were related to each other by blood or marriage. As I spoke with several friends and relatives, an elder approached me.

"Salaam, Mr. Popal. I hear you are having a problem with your house."

"Baleh, that's true," I said. "Hazrat Ali acknowledges my ownership, but he won't leave unless I pay for the repairs he made. He has refused to pay rent for all the years he has had it. The local authorities here and the new government can do nothing against Hazrat Ali. I'm afraid it's hopeless."

"What will you do now?" the elder asked.

"What more can I do?" I replied. "I have accepted the fact that my house is lost to me, like Afghanistan is lost to me now."

"Who would take a family's home away and refuse to return it to the rightful owner?" the elder said. "Men like Hazrat Ali have become a problem now. They do not care about the law or people's rights. It was never like this before. It's not good that men like Hazrat Ali have become so powerful that they can ignore the orders of the government."

"Baleh," I agreed. "Our new government has failed. It's an injustice for which there is no solution."

The elder looked lost in thought for a moment. Then, as if he had suddenly found what he was searching for, he looked at me.

"There is a way, Mr. Popal. You must call a jirga. Hazrat Ali is from Nuristan. For his side, you must seek out elders from his Pashai tribe. For your side, find elders from Abdien and Jalalabad. Both sides will have known your father. Even Hazrat Ali cannot ignore the call of the elders."

"But he is a powerful man now, and there is only me on my side. Won't he lose face?"

"Right is on your side," he said. "Don't worry—the elders will protect you. Let the jirga define the terms, not you. Hazrat Ali will have to listen, and he will not lose face obeying a decision of the elders."

Malem's family was from Nuristan like Hazrat Ali. Malem persuaded a dozen elders from Hazrat Ali's tribe to meet with me. I began the meeting with the elders by explaining that I did not want to make enemies.

"Can money settle it?" they asked me.

"Nay," I told them.

"How can you say 'Nay'?" one said. "I have lived a very long time, and there's nothing in this world on which you cannot put a price."

"You cannot put a price on my memories. Those are not for sale. All I want is my house."

They agreed to a jirga, and we shook hands.

72

Compound of Hazrat Ali, Afghanistan, 2004

Jirga

The jirga was held at Hazrat Ali's compound in the fall of 2004 on a rug-covered stone terrace. Dozens of men sat on thick cushions arranged in a large circle. Hadji Jawid was there to represent Hazrat Ali. Three armed men stood behind him. I shook hands with each of the elders and joined the others on the floor. One of the elders, who had been chosen to speak for the jirga, rose from his cushion.

"I know Mr. Popal's family," he began. "It is a good, honest family that has worked for the benefit of Afghanistan for many years. I also know Hadji Hazrat Sahib Ali, and you, Hadji Sahib Jawid. Many times the two of you have put your own lives in danger for Afghanistan's freedom. You are both deserving of great respect. A problem has arisen between you over Mr. Popal's house, and Mr. Popal has called us together to find a peaceful solution so both sides will live as friends, not enemies. When our business here is finished, Mr. Popal will respect Hadji Hazrat Sahib Ali and Hadji Sahib Jawid and their families. They will respect Mr. Popal and his family, and both sides will help each other in the future. The jirga wants this problem solved. Today we will come to a peaceful resolution. First, we will listen to you, Hadji Sahib Jawid, and hear your side. Then we will listen to you, Mr. Popal, and hear your side."

Hadji Jawid looked at the elders as he spoke. "For the past seventeen years we have protected Mr. Popal's house and repaired it at our own expense. We need to be compensated for this. That is all we have to say."

"Tashakor, Hadji Sahib Jawid," the elder said. "We have heard you. Now we will hear from Mr. Popal."

"I come here with great respect for all of you and for Hadji Hazrat Sahib Ali and Hadji Sahib Jawid. I want nothing more than to have this matter settled in a peaceful manner. I have been away from Afghanistan for many years. The house in Jalalabad was built by my father and contains many memories for me. I do this for my father and my family. Hadji Sahib Jawid has said that they have kept my house safe and in good repair. That may be true. But they have not paid any rent for the use of my house. Did I ask for rent for their use of my house for these past seventeen years? Nay, I did not. Now all I ask is that my house be returned to me as soon as possible so that I can live in it once again. Whatever you decide, I know it will be the right decision, and I will accept it. That is all I have to say."

"Tashakor, Mr. Popal. You have each spoken well. The jirga will retire to the house and discuss this matter. We will return when we have reached a decision."

Hadji Jawid, his bodyguards, and I stood as the elders left to make their decision. I glanced over at Hadji Jawid. He was not happy to be here. He did not look at me, and we did not speak. Not even his bodyguards would look at me.

A short time later the elders returned and sat down. As I joined the others seated on the floor, I could feel my heart beating heavily inside my chest.

"We have discussed your problem and reached a decision," the elder said. "Out of respect for Mr. Popal and what is right, Hadji Hazrat Sahib Ali is to return Mr. Popal's house. Mr. Popal, out of respect for Hadji Hazrat Sahib Ali and what is right, you shall give him whatever time he needs to move out. As for payment for the repairs, we know Hadji Hazrat Sahib Ali does not need money." The elder stopped here and smiled slightly, as did the others—everyone knew Hazrat Ali was one of the richest men in Afghanistan. "Even so," the elder continued, "Mr. Popal will pay whatever he requests. If he cannot afford it, the elders will pay for him." They all knew Hazrat Ali would not accept money from the elders. It was their way of allowing him to save face.

"This is the decision of the jirga," the elder concluded. " Hadji Sahib Jawid, do you accept on behalf of Hadji Hazrat Sahib Ali?"

"Hadji Hazrat Sahib Ali has many houses, and as you say, he does not need the money," Hadji Jawid replied. "All along his only interest has been to make certain that this man who sits before you and who claims to be the owner of the house is who he says he is. You, the tribal elders, say that he is. That is enough for him. We thank you and accept the decision of the jirga."

"Mr. Popal?"

"I am grateful to the jirga for resolving this, and I accept its decision."

"We thank you for allowing us to settle this matter peacefully," the elder said. "We will draw up a letter for both of you to sign. Mr. Popal, you agree that you will never again complain about this matter to anyone and you will not ask for rent. Hadji Sahib Jawid, on behalf of Hadji Hazrat Sahib Ali, you agree to return the house to Mr. Popal four months from today."

We nodded our assent.

"Shake hands as friends. Our tribal business here is ended."

73

Jalalabad, Afghanistan, 2005

The King's Arabians

Four months later, my taxi turned the corner of my street in Jalalabad. My yard was deserted. The front door knob turned easily in my hand. The door swung open.

I stepped inside.

Light reflected off newly painted walls onto bright stone floors. I walked from empty room to empty room overwhelmed by memories. In the room where Baba used to sit in a large armchair and tell me stories, I saw him sitting there once again.

"Baba," I said, "you taught me well. I have used a jirga to get your house back from a powerful warlord, from Hazrat Ali himself." Then I heard his voice as clearly as if he were sitting in that chair. "It pleases me to see that you did learn something that day at the Winter Palace," and I saw that rare smile, and that day came back to me.

The king had called my father to the Winter Palace because two tribes on the border were driving him crazy with their fighting. The king asked Baba to put a stop to it, but Baba told the king, "With all due respect, Your Excellency, I will not be good for this job because I don't know why the tribes are fighting."

"They are fighting because they are Pashtuns," Zahir Shah said. "They don't need a reason to fight. You are a Pashtun, Ustad, you go deal with them."

"That may be true," my father said, "but even I cannot control the Pashtuns in the border areas."

But Zahir Shah would not be put off. "You are the only one I can trust with this, Ustad," the king said. "I'm asking you to do this for me."

Baba arranged a meeting at the Winter Palace with some of the tribal elders from both sides. "You must come with me, Bari," he said to me. "You will learn a lot."

When we arrived, two elder Pashtun men from one tribe and

three from the other were already seated on the ground. Baba and I joined them.

"How are your families?" Baba asked. "How is the weather? How are your crops this year?"

What is Baba doing? I wondered. The king did not ask him here to make small talk. Baba continued in this way for a time, then said, "Tell me, how are things in the border area?"

One of the tribesmen became agitated. "They have killed several of our men. We want compensation."

The elders from the other tribe jumped in, saying that they had not started the fight. The elders began shouting back and forth as if they would never stop. Baba simply waited and waited until they grew tired of shouting.

"I will hear one side at a time," Baba said. "Choose someone to speak for you." As soon as the elder from the first tribe began talking, Baba inclined his head toward him and listened, listened as if the elder were the only other person in the world, as if each word the elder spoke might change the world or if a single word were lost the world would be lost as well.

Those on the other side could not hold their tongues.

"I don't care what you decide!" an elder cried out. "Even if it's the word of the king! There are more deaths on our side than on theirs, and we will fight them until it's settled."

The two sides once again began arguing fiercely, and we were back where we started. What could Baba do now? How could he get these tribesmen who would listen only to the sound of their own voices to listen to him, let alone agree on anything?

Suddenly Baba stood up. The tribesmen stopped arguing and looked at Baba.

"One cannot fight on an empty stomach," Baba said, "and I cannot discuss this on an empty stomach." He called to one of the servants, "Bring us food and drink." Then he sat down.

A huge spread of chicken, rice, naan, grapes, raisins, dates, and green tea was laid before the warring parties, cooling their passions.

"I had a horse once," Baba said, as the men ate. "It was the finest Arabian in all Afghanistan."

The elders' eyes widened. Mine did as well. My father had never once mentioned owning a horse, let alone the finest Arabian in all Afghanistan. I thought he didn't even like horses.

"He was a powerful Arabian with an easy gait. He ran with the speed of a swallow, sure-footed and tireless, carrying his tail high." The elders nodded their approval. Horses are the most important thing in the world to Afghan men, even more important than women—or revenge.

"Did you know the king of Saudi Arabia has given Zahir Shah five Arabian horses as gifts? Four are chestnut, with perfect white markings. One is as black as a moonless night."

Baba had everyone's complete attention—especially mine.

"These are the only horses I have ever seen that are finer than that Arabian of mine." Baba casually reached for some grapes and started eating them as if he'd just been talking about the weather.

Suddenly the garden erupted with talk of Arabian horses. The elder who had demanded the death of his rivals said, "Do you think the king would give us sperm from one of those horses?"

The elder from the other side quickly jumped in. "And us as well?"

Baba looked as if their questions had caught him completely by surprise. He stopped to consider them.

"If it will bring peace between you," he finally said, "I will speak to the king."

The elders all smiled.

Baba nodded quietly to a servant. The servant approached and set a tray down beside him.

"Ah, the sweets have arrived," Baba said.

When the last of the sweets had disappeared, Baba stood up, his large figure looming over the tribesmen.

"Let us pray together," he said.

We all closed our eyes and bowed our heads.

"O, Allah, the parties gathered here have given me the power to mediate the dispute that has driven them apart. Give me the power and wisdom to make a decision that both parties will accept. Allah, in the name of Afghanistan, Islam, and the king, guide us to a peaceful resolution."

As Baba and I walked home from the Winter Palace, I asked, "Why did you never tell me about your Arabian horse? You know I love horses."

"Some things, Bari, you must find out for yourself" is all he said, and I wondered if he ever really owned that horse at all.

74

Karta-i-Char, Kabul, Afghanistan 2008

Rasoul

"Bar!" an excited voice shouted over the phone.

"Shabir?" I exclaimed, surprised.

"Rasoul has run away to Kabul!" Shabir sounded frantic.

"Is your son so afraid of you that he had to run all the way to the other side of the world to get away from you?" I laughed.

"This is no joke, Bar!" Shabir said, annoyed. "He's supposed to be in Australia studying English. He's only eighteen and doesn't know how dangerous Kabul is. I'm afraid for him. You must find him, Bar, and send him back home to Japan."

"He's too much like his father," I said, "and will be difficult to persuade. But don't worry, Shabir. I'll find him and make sure he's safe."

"Tashakor, Bar. Please, find him quickly."

I called everyone I could think of who might know about a Japanese Afghan teenager who had recently arrived in Kabul but could find out nothing. I did not want to give Shabir this news and delayed calling him. Two days later I answered my phone. "Uncle Baryalai? It's Rasoul."

"Rasoul?" I said excitedly. "Your father has been trying to find you. He's very worried. Where are you?"

"I'm staying with a man I met on the plane. He thought I should call you and let you know I'm here."

I rushed over.

When the door opened, I found myself looking into the apprehensive almond eyes of a young man dressed in a gebi.

"You're a good-looking young man," I said. "I can see your father in you. It gives me great joy to finally meet you."

His apprehension quickly dissolved into the happiness that only family can bring, and he hugged me like he'd found home.

I called Shabir with the good news.

"Thank God," Shabir said, relief in his voice. "We've been so worried. Ever since he was a boy, he's been obsessed with Afghan-

istan. He doesn't know the culture. He doesn't know how dangerous the country is."

"Our children have minds of their own," I said. "Remember
that night in Paghman on the walk home from the party in the
garden when you were so happy? You said you'd found paradise
and never wanted to leave Afghanistan. You did leave. But now,
through your son, you have come home."

As for me, my heart is in two places now—California and Afghanistan. "You should sell those houses!" my family keeps telling me.
But I cannot. Why? Maybe it's because I'm stubborn. Maybe it's
because of the memories they hold for me.

Or maybe it's because I know that if I did, part of me would be
lost forever.

Bibliography

Adamec, Ludwig W. *Afghanistan, 1900–1923: A Diplomatic History*. Berkeley: University of California Press, 1967.

———. *Afghanistan's Foreign Affairs to the Mid-Twentieth Century: Relations with the USSR, Germany, and Britain*. Tucson: University of Arizona Press, 1974.

———. *Historical Dictionary of Afghanistan*. Lanham MD: Scarecrow, 2003.

Afghanistan: A Country Study. Baton Rouge LA: Claitor's Publication Division, 2001.

Coll, Steve. *Ghost Wars: The Secret History of the CIA, Afghanistan, and Bin Laden, from the Soviet Invasion to September 10, 2001*. New York: Penguin, 2005.

Edwards, David B. *Before Taliban: Genealogies of the Afghan Jihad*. Berkeley: University of California Press, 2002.

Ewans, Martin. *Afghanistan: A Short History of Its People and Politics*. New York: Harper Perennial, 2002.

Nojumi, Neamatollah. *The Rise of the Taliban in Afghanistan: Mass Mobilization, Civil War, and the Future of the Region*. New York: Palgrave, 2002.

Rashid, Ahmed. *Descent into Chaos: The U.S. and the Disaster in Pakistan, Afghanistan, and Central Asia*. New York: Penguin, 2009.

———. *Taliban: Militant Islam, Oil, and Fundamentalism in Central Asia*. New Haven: Yale University Press, 2000.

Shah, Ikbal Ali. *Afghanistan of the Afghans*. New Delhi: Bhavana Books & Prints, 2000.

Shalizi, Abdussattar. *Afghanistan: Ancient Land with Modern Ways*. Kabul: Ministry of Planning of the Royal Government of Afghanistan, 1960.

Tanner, Stephen. *Afghanistan: A Military History from Alexander the Great to the Fall of the Taliban*. New York: Da Capo, 2003.